AF574879

Italian and Italian American Studies

Stanislao G. Pugliese
Hofstra University
Series Editor

This publishing initiative seeks to bring the latest scholarship in Italian and Italian American history, literature, cinema, and cultural studies to a large audience of specialists, general readers, and students. I&IAS will feature works on modern Italy (Renaissance to the present) and Italian American culture and society by established scholars as well as new voices in the academy. This endeavor will help to shape the evolving fields of Italian and Italian American Studies by re-emphasizing the connection between the two. The following editorial board of esteemed senior scholars are advisors to the series editor.

Queer Italia: Same-Sex Desire in Italian Literature and Film
edited by Gary P. Cestaro
July 2004

Frank Sinatra: History, Identity, and Italian American Culture
edited by Stanislao G. Pugliese
October 2004

The Legacy of Primo Levi
edited by Stanislao G. Pugliese
December 2004

Italian Colonialism
edited by Ruth Ben-Ghiat and Mia Fuller
July 2005

Mussolini's Rome: Rebuilding the Eternal City
Borden W. Painter Jr.
July 2005

Representing Sacco and Vanzetti
edited by Jerome H. Delamater and Mary Anne Trasciatti
September 2005

Carlo Tresca: Portrait of a Rebel
Nunzio Pernicone
October 2005

Italy in the Age of Pinocchio: Children and Danger in the Liberal Era
Carl Ipsen
April 2006

The Empire of Stereotypes: Germaine de Staël and the Idea of Italy
Robert Casillo
May 2006

Race and the Nation in Liberal Italy, 1861-1911: Meridionalism, Empire, and Diaspora
Aliza S. Wong
October 2006

Women in Italy, 1946-1960: An Interdisciplinary Study
edited by Penelope Morris
October 2006

A New Guide to Italian Cinema
Carlo Celli and Marga Cottino-Jones
November 2006

Debating Divorce in Italy: Marriage and the Making of Modern Italians, 1860-1974
Mark Seymour
December 2006

Human Nature in Rural Tuscany: An Early Modern History
Gregory Hanlon
March 2007

The Missing Italian Nuremberg: Cultural Amnesia and Postwar Politics
Michele Battini
September 2007

Assassinations and Murder in Modern Italy: Transformations in Society and Culture
edited by Stephen Gundle and Lucia Rinaldi
October 2007

The Missing Italian Nuremberg
Cultural Amnesia and Postwar Politics

Michele Battini

Translated by Noor Giovanni Mazhar

Edited by Stanislao G. Pugliese

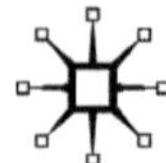

THE MISSING ITALIAN NUREMBERG

This book was made possible, in part, by the Dorothy and Elmer Kirsch Endowment Fund for the Hofstra Cultural Center.

First published in 2007 by
PALGRAVE MACMILLAN™
175 Fifth Avenue, New York, N.Y. 10010 and
Houndmills, Basingstoke, Hampshire, England RG21 6XS.
Companies and representatives throughout the world.

PALGRAVE MACMILLAN is the global academic imprint of the Palgrave Macmillan division of St. Martin's Press, LLC and of Palgrave Macmillan Ltd. Macmillan® is a registered trademark in the United States, United Kingdom and other countries. Palgrave is a registered trademark in the European Union and other countries.

ISBN-13: 978-1-4039-8478-4
ISBN-10: 1-4039-8478-6

Library of Congress Cataloging-in-Publication Data is available from the Library of Congress.

A catalogue record of the book is available from the British Library.

Design by Scribe Inc.

First edition: August 2007

10 9 8 7 6 5 4 3 2 1

Printed in the United States of America.

In memory of my mother and father.

Memory
is not a sin, while it is beneficial.
Afterwards it is
the lethargy of moles, the baseness
which grows mouldy on itself.

Eugenio Montale
"Voce giunta con le folaghe"
in *La bufera e altro*

Contents

Acknowledgments

Claudio Pavone has, for a long time, been an essential reference point in my research on the Italian crisis of 1943–47, from the Resistance war to the origins of the Republic, and it is to him that I am indebted for the foundations of my work and a constant lesson in achieving the proper balance. Adriano Sofri is an interlocutor of my reflection, since the now-distant time of enthusiasm. In recent years, the disgraceful judicial episode, of which he is a victim, has brought him back to my city. The dialogue with him has value for me that he cannot imagine.

Finally, I have a long-standing debt of gratitude to Alessandra Peretti.

Chronology

1922, October 28	The March on Rome by the Fascist action squads. Under threat of a coup d'état, King Victor Emanuel III charges Benito Mussolini, the Duce (leader) of Fascism, to form a government.
1922, December	Formation of the Grand Council and of the Fascist Militia: the Fascist action squads become a state police force.
1923, July 23	Subjected to violence and intimidation, the Italian Parliament approves an electoral law—the Acerbo Law—which guarantees a two-thirds majority in Parliament (the Chamber of Deputies) to the party that obtains a 25 percent plurality of the vote.
1924, April	Employing violence, the Fascists win the political elections and gain, thanks to the Acerbo Law, two-thirds of the Chamber of Deputies. Giacomo Matteotti, a deputy and Secretary of the Social Democrats, denounces the violence and is killed by the Fascists on June 10, 1924.
1925–26	Some laws abolish political and press freedoms. A police state officially comes into being and proceeds to become a totalitarian dictatorship. The Fascist Party becomes the only party permitted by law.
1927	The Work Charter (Carta del Lavoro) is issued, thus laying the foundations of the corporatist regime. At the same time, the system of totalitarian propaganda comes into existence.
1929	On February 11, the Lateran Accords (an agreement between Italy and the Holy See) is signed, signaling the reconciliation between the Fascist State and the Vatican.
1934	The "Corporations" of arts and crafts are set up.
1935–36	The Italian Fascist regime attacks Ethiopia, allies itself with the German National Socialist regime (the

Rome-Berlin Axis), and supports the rebellion of the Spanish military against the Popular Front Republican Government, which had won the political elections.

1937 The Fascist regime has the Rosselli brothers—opponents of the regime, in exile in France—killed. Antonio Gramsci, another opponent of the regime, dies in prison.

1938 The Fascist regime issues laws for the persecution of the Jews.

1939 In March, Germany occupies Czechoslovakia and, in September, Poland; World War II begins.

1940 On June 10, Italy enters the war on the side of Germany against France and the United Kingdom. Italy invades France and Greece.

1941 April: Italy and Germany attack Yugoslavia. April: Italian troops are defeated in Ethiopia (the end of the Empire), but they participate in the Nazi invasion of the Soviet Union. December: Germany and Italy declare war on the United States.

1942 English troops defeat the Italian Army at El Alamein, in Africa. The very heavy Allied bombing of many Italian cities produces tens of thousands of victims.

1943 In May, Italy's war in Africa ends. In March, there are the first strikes by Northern industrial workers. In June, English and American troops land on the island of Pantelleria and in July in Sicily. On July 25, the Fascist Grand Council votes against Benito Mussolini, and King Victor Emanuel III has him arrested. A military government under Marshal Pietro Badoglio comes into being. Peace negotiations with the English and the Americans begin, without the Nazi allies being informed. Officially, Italy continues fighting on Hitler's side. On September 8, the Armistice between Italy and the Allies is announced. The German Army occupies Italy. The King and Badoglio flee to the south and take refuge in the zones freed by the English and the Americans. The Italian Army is left without orders from the King. The Germans capture hundreds of thousands of Italian soldiers. Many resist and thousands are wiped out; the entire organization of the Italian Army collapses. Mussolini is freed by the

Nazis. On September 12, a new Fascist State comes into existence, the Repubblica Sociale Italiana (the Italian Social Republic), whose sovereignty is limited to northern Italy. Northern and central Italy are, in reality, governed by the German Army. Naples, the main city in the south, is liberated by the Anglo-Americans after a popular uprising. Italy is divided in two and in the center-north the armed and political Resistance of the anti-Fascists is born: the CLN, Comitato di Liberazione Nazionale (the Committee of National Liberation) is established. In October, the Italian monarchical government enters the war against Germany at the side of the Allies.

1944 The Allies return the zones south of Naples and Foggia to Italian administration. The Congress of Anti-Fascist Parties, which is held in Bari, asks for a constituent assembly after the end of the war.

In March, the Soviet Union recognizes the Badoglio government, and the Italian Communist Party agrees to cooperate with it (the so-called svolta di Salerno). Rome is still occupied by the Nazis, but the inspirational reference point for Italian public opinion in central Italy and the capital is the Pope and the Vatican. In March, after a partisan attack in Rome, hundreds of anti-Fascists and some dozens of Jews from the capital are massacred at the Ardeatine Caves. In June, the city of Rome is liberated. The German Army retreats through Umbria, the Marches and Tuscany. The armed Resistance attacks the retreating German Army, and the civilian population does not collaborate with the Nazis; in some cases it openly defies their orders. For these reasons, the German High Command unleashes reprisals against the civilian population and, in many cases, a war of repression, which produces thousands of victims, above all in Tuscany and the north. There are new workers' strikes in the north against the Italian Social Republic. After the liberation of Rome, a new government of anti-Fascist parties, led by Ivanoe Bonomi, comes into being. The Allies begin many legal investigations regarding the massacres of civilians carried out by the occupying German troops. In August, there is an uprising in Florence. Tuscany is liberated, and the front comes to a halt along the line of the Apennine mountains, from the Tyrrhenian Sea to the Adriatic. During the winter and spring of 1944–45, the North remains under the occupation of the Nazis, who heavily exploit the industrial and agricultural economy. There is agreement between the CLN in the North and the Allied General Maitland Wilson regarding the creation of a Supreme Partisan Command.

1945 In winter, the Resistance movement encounters grave difficulties. General Luigi Cadorna is appointed commander of the CVL, Corpo dei Volontari della Libertà (the Liberation Volunteer Corps), and is helped by the deputy commanders Ferruccio Parri (a democrat and leader of the Action Party), and Luigi Longo (a Communist). In April, when the Allies arrive, the cities of northern Italy have already been liberated by the Partisan Brigades of the Liberation Volunteer Corps. In June, a new government is formed, headed by one of the leaders of the Partisan insurrection, Ferruccio Parri. The latter is succeeded by the Catholic Christian Democrat, Alcide De Gasperi, in December 1945.

1946 On May 9, King Victor Emanuel III abdicates in favor of his son, Umberto. On June 2, the result of the popular referendum means the abrogation of the monarchy: Italy is a Republic. On the same day, the first free political elections are held and are won by the Christian Democrats (but the alliance between the Socialists and the Communists is, nevertheless, very strong). In the course of time, the composition of the parties will vary, but the overall picture of Italian politics will remain the same from 1946 to 1994. The national government begins dealing with war damage, unemployment, and the purging of Fascists from public administration. Only a few trials of German and Italian war criminals are held between 1946 and 1948.

To Prosecute and Portray the Enemy

An Introduction to the American Edition

At the time of this writing—after the trial for crimes committed during the invasion of Kuwait in 1991, the massacre of Shiite civilians at Dujail, and other crimes—further legal proceedings against Saddam Hussein and other leading figures of the Iraqi Baathist regime have begun in Baghdad. Saddam Hussein, Ali Hassan al-Majiid, Sabel Abdul al Duir, Hussein al-Tikriti, and other Baath leaders are on trial for their crimes against humanity committed during the Anfal Offensive in 1984 and 1988. The Kurdish city of Halabja and over 4,000 Kurdish villages in the North of Iraq were, at that time, subjected to chemical warfare, the men were deported and killed, the women were raped, and the crops destroyed. The British expert David McDowall has estimated 150,000 dead. The Anfal Operation was only a part of the genocide of the Kurds, which had already begun in the 1960s and 1970s, during the reign of the Shah of Persia, and was further extended to include Yezidi, Assyro-Chaldean, and Turkoman civilians. Kenneth Roth, the executive director of Human Rights Watch, has stated that the war crimes, the crimes against humanity, and the genocide committed by Saddam Hussein are fully documented. As early as January 2004, Roth recommended the setting up of a mixed ad hoc tribunal, made up of local (Iraqi) and international judges. Human Rights Watch has also recommended that Saddam Hussein, Yassin Ramadan, Mohammed al-Ali, and the others should be granted POW (Prisoner of War) status in accordance with the 1949 Geneva Convention.

However, Saddam has been tried, convicted, and sentenced by a national court of law, composed solely of Iraqi judges. This decision, the behavior of the tribunal, and his execution have occasioned much controversy. Alan Dershowitz, Professor of Law at Harvard University, has stated: "This is no longer the era of Nuremberg. . . . The historical conditions have changed and a comparison between Iraq and the Third Reich is inconceivable." Paul Berman, on the contrary, has likened the present juridical situation to that of the trial in Jerusalem in 1960 of the *Obersturmbannfuhrer* Adolf Eichmann, one of the major Nazi perpetrators of the deportation of European Jews to the death camps during World War II. But the recourse to an international ad hoc tribunal, along the lines of that of Nuremberg, has been rejected by some observers who see it as the paradigm of "the justice of the victors." The national Iraqi court of law that tried Saddam and the others in accordance with national law was regarded by other observers as being subordinate to the Iraqi government and, consequently, to the United States of America.

The debate is still raging. It revolves around the legitimacy of the tribunal, its laws, and the nature of the sentences, but it is essentially political. It revives a question that had already emerged in 1945: how should the crimes of a totalitarian regime be judged and punished? Paul Joseph Jean Cardinal Poupard, an important French religious figure, has asked, in the name of the Vatican, that the death penalty not be carried out in Iraq. Many European jurists also maintain that capital punishment, decreed in that country after the fall of Saddam Hussein, should be suspended. This means that the most important question concerns the present situation regarding legitimacy and the law. The question is this: does international law regulate and exercise authority over political power, or, on the contrary, is Thomas Hobbes, yet again, right that *auctoritas facit legem* (politics governs the law)?

The continuous references on the part of political analysts and jurists to the Nuremberg trials of the leading Nazis and, therefore, to the international law resulting from World War II lead me to reformulate the question in another way: are we still immersed in the cultural, legal and political context that developed at the end of World War II? How much does the memory of that war, constructed at the time on the basis of the international trials of Nuremberg and Tokyo, still count? What sort of balance is possible between the moral necessity to restore the rights damaged by a totalitarian and mass authoritarian system and the equally unavoidable imperative not to lacerate social cohesion through measures of purgation that would inevitably involve too vast a portion of the population?

It is difficult to offer satisfactory responses to these questions, which remain extraordinarily relevant after the conclusion of the military operation dubbed "Enduring Freedom" in the spring of 2003. World opinion today is pondering the same question that the Allies asked themselves after the collapse of the Axis in 1945: what should be done with the leaders of a totalitarian regime?

Antonio Cassese, who for years served as president of the International Criminal Court charged with prosecuting war criminals from the former

Yugoslavia, has on several occasions argued that the alternative of trials conducted under the authority of international courts of law offers at least three advantages: above all, it safeguards the legal principle that prescribes "impartial justice" as the preliminary condition for returning a guilty verdict; it initiates for the populations a path of "democratic pedagogy" founded on the proven demonstration of crimes perpetrated by the dictatorship; and, finally, it establishes an inventory of crimes and consigns them to historical memory.

The trials cannot be entrusted to institutions that are emanations of the victorious powers, however. Such institutions, it is argued, would administer the "justice of the victors," as was the case at Nuremberg and Tokyo after World War II. Although these trials undoubtedly had merits in their exercising of judgment over war criminals, they also sparked highly polemical and partially legitimate reactions in the public opinion of the countries that were subject to their decisions. (Cassese instead upholds the new International Criminal Court established in 1998 as a positive example of authentic justice.)

If the United States were to agree to such a decision, and if the United Nations assumed responsibility for its implementation, the Baathist regime's opposition to the Court would be circumvented and U.S. objections, motivated by the fear that the Court and the UN act under the impulse of "ideological prejudices" towards the ruling class and the military leadership of the United States, could be overcome. In fact, for some time now the American leaders have demonstrated a sort of schizophrenic pathology in their inclination for political and military interventionism, based on their role as the "world's policeman" and protector of human rights—in addition to national interests—together with a sort of ethical regression that leads them to refuse any type of court that would defend international law. They seem to be experiencing a paradoxical heterogenesis of goals: it was, after all, the U.S. President Franklin D. Roosevelt whose doctrine of the "Four Freedoms" in 1941 led to the proclamation of the Charter of the UN in 1945 and the Universal Declaration of Human Rights in 1948. In accordance with the Statute of the International Criminal Court (July 1, 2002), this new international justice could represent an extraordinary phenomenon and mark the end of an era that began during World War II by proposing a judicial response to the perpetration of crimes against humanity that is not limited to an exclusively repressive reaction. The new system would instead aim to establish a peaceful, impartial, and democratic process for assessing the truth, not only to punish the guilty but also to placate the victims' desire for revenge.

In reality, some new forms of international justice are already at work, even if they are acting on different levels: their current levels are in fact represented by the International Criminal Court and the International Tribunals, created ad hoc for crimes committed in the former Yugoslavia between 1991 and 1994 and in Rwanda in 1994; by the "mixed" tribunals composed of magistrates of the country where the crimes occurred and international judges (such as in Sierra Leone, East Timor, Kosovo, and Cambodia); and, finally, by the initiatives of judges who, in putting to good use particularly enlightened national legislation, have undertaken legal actions against foreigners for crimes committed abroad (as have certain Spanish and Belgian judges). This new international justice can draw on the anti-nationalistic principle of the universality of jurisdiction, even though it still suffers from the lack of an international judiciary police that would serve as the executive arm and military force. This limit continues to relegate international tribunals to a position of dependence on the decisions of individual nations or the Atlantic Alliance instead of the cooperation of the UN Council.

So innovative procedures and institutions have gradually begun, even if timidly, to surmount the ambiguities and contradictions of the international justice administered after World War II. The "justice of the victors" of 1946, 1947, and 1948 had, in fact, also violated the principle of non-retroactivity of the law and suffered from ambiguities that perhaps were largely inevitable and objective. For example, it allowed the Soviets to be among the judges and simultaneously to attribute to others the massacres of Polish officers at Katyn, and it permitted the Americans to claim impunity for Hiroshima and Nagasaki.

Until the collapse of the Soviet Union and the system of the "People's democracy" States in Eastern Europe between 1989 and 1991, the contradictions of the justice of Nuremberg remained alive and impeded the formation of an authentic international law. The cause of this long period of stalemate largely goes back to the primacy of national sovereignty and deference to national governments. Thus, from 1946 to 1991, crimes against humanity remained on the margins of international law and international relations, which were regulated by the strategic and diplomatic confrontation of NATO and the Warsaw Pact. After 1989, the Soviet decline and the resulting tendency towards global unification offered the premises to revive the importance of the protection of human rights and humanitarian interference—the political premises, obviously, but not the certainty.

But the question regarding the possible balance between the need to redress damages of crimes against humanity, together with the imperative not to forget and the necessity to move beyond the past and safeguard the cohesion of society, contains many other questions. For example, regarding fratricidal struggles, is it preferable that they be remembered or forgotten? Which is the best way to preserve memory?

In fact, the politics of forgetfulness had many supporters after the end of World War II: governments and French public opinion canceled the memory of Vichy, at least until the 1980s; Kurt Waldheim's Austria did the same for the consensus about the Anschluss imposed by Nazi Germany in 1938; and, after 1975, Spain cancelled the question of responsibility for Franco's regime. After World War II and an initial radical and massive purging, even West Germany combined amnesties with amnesia. The silence of President Konrad Adenauer must be considered in part a reaction to what was perceived as "the justice of the victors," but it was loudly criticized by the 1968 student and intellectual rebellion that suddenly claimed the imperative of memory.

In Central Eastern Europe the question was raised later, in particular after the 1989 revolutions. It was greatly complicated by the disintegration of old State structures and modifications of territorial dimensions: only five countries of Eastern Europe—Poland, Hungary, Rumania, Bulgaria and Albania—still had the same borders as during Communism when they began to reckon with their Communist past. Thus the majority of the countries—Russia, Belarus, Latvia, Estonia, the Ukraine, Georgia, Croatia, Slovenia, Serbia, the Czech Republic, and Slovakia (the successor States of the Soviet Union, Yugoslavia, and Czechoslovakia) had no difficulty in refusing to be considered inheritors of, and responsible for, that past. Lithuania represented an extreme case, because it considered itself a country subject to a foreign occupation and domination that usurped its identity. The awareness that there was large-scale complicity with Stalinist-type authoritarian systems in Communist political regimes led the Czechoslovakian president Václav Havel to declare in 1991 that a clear watershed between the victims and the persecutors was in fact impossible to determine. (In this Havel was preceded by an Italian Communist: in 1946 the Secretary of the Italian Communist Party, Palmiro Togliatti, responded to the vehemence of the Deputy High Commissioner for Purges—his party colleague Mauro Scoccimarro, who demanded extensive and massive repressive actions—by stating that "there is no one in Italy who did not make a mess of things in the years of the Fascist regime"). Urged in part by the European Council's protests, Havel refused to countersign a purge measure passed in 1991 by the Czechoslovakian Parliament: the so-called law of "lustration" (from the Bohemian word *lustrace*, which means transparency) would have banned from State employment entire categories of people such as party officials, members of the people's militia, agents of services, and their collaborators, even "unwitting" ones. The abolition in 1993 of the impunity for crimes not prosecuted during the Communist period led, in the end, to the trial of three high officials of the Czechoslovakian Communist party who were accused of having favored the invasion of the Warsaw Pact troops in August 1968.

In reunited Germany after 1990, hundreds of trials against leaders of the Stasi, the political police of the DDR (the German Democratic Republic), were conducted on the legal basis of East German criminal categories, so as to avoid the errors of the Allies at Nuremberg—such as the violation of the principle of non-retroactivity of the law and the exercise of justice according to laws that differed from those of the country of the accused. In the post-1989 judicial inquiries regarding responsibility for the repression of the 1956 national insurrection in Hungary, the juridical categories classified by the Charter of the Nuremberg trial were applied instead: conspiracy to commit war of aggression, war crimes, and crimes against humanity. But the country in which it turned out to be most difficult to reconcile the assessment of the truth with the defense of social cohesion was Poland, however. This country passed easily from the politics of forgetfulness to *noc tezek*, "that night of the dossiers": in December 1995, a poisonous game of revelations, accusations, and counter-accusations began between the Minister of the Interior and the Prime Minister and led to the resignation of the latter, who was accused of continued "collaborationism" with the Soviet secret service.

Because the examples drawn from the transition in Eastern Europe are contradictory, it has become commonplace to mention South Africa, even though the South African solution of a "Truth and Reconciliation Commission," in which the confession of crimes committed to protect the apartheid regime becomes an object of exchange for a definitive armistice, does not seem at all a balanced model of justice and memory.

So we do not really know if we are really emerging from the juridical horizon imposed at the end of World War II, as well as from its categories.

***

I do not believe that it is yet possible to arrive at a single, overall conclusion about the historical episode of justice regarding the European Nazi and Fascist war criminals in the years 1945–49, but the comparative study of the different national situations permits the identification of some common factors in European countries. The legal machinery wheeled into place in Europe was highly complex. The general epithet "war crime trials" could obscure the variety of proceedings in nations that had been allied to, occupied by, and in conflict with Nazi Germany and Fascist Italy. We must first of all consider that the highest number of trials, legal and semi-legal, in Europe between 1944 and 1948–49 were conducted against those whom the new postwar Western democracies and the East European People's Democracies defined as the German "war criminals" and the "collaborators," or the compatriot "traitors." Apart from the trials, in each country a mechanism of purging was established with the aim of removing all traces of Nazism and Fascism from the State and the economy. Such a mechanism should be considered and analysed by the historian as distinct and separate (even if this was not always the case in practice) from the trials aiming at prosecuting the clearly illegal acts committed by fellow countrymen and foreigners in order to realize the political and military objectives of the Axis.

These trials are at the center of my study. Over fifty high-ranking officers of the Wehrmacht, the SS, and the various German police forces in Italy from 1943 to 1945 were identified as being responsible for the machinery of reprisals against the Partisans and for the terrorist policy against the civilian population. In order to prosecute them, the Allied authorities set up a single, large-scale trial that in some British documents was defined as the "Italian Nuremberg." This terminology needs explaining.

From a legal point of view, the high-ranking officers commanding the Nazi occupation system in Italy were, as far as the Allies were concerned, "minor war criminals," referring to the rank of the criminal, rather than to the magnitude of the crime. Those regarded as "major war criminals" were, in fact, the highest-ranking figures of the Third Reich and its organizations, who appeared before the International Military Tribunal (IMT), the judicial creation resulting from the agreement between the Allies. (This tribunal presided over what is erroneously referred to as the Nuremberg Trial, but which instead consisted of twelve trials in addition to that of 1946; all were held in Nuremberg within the framework of the American occupation machinery and under the authority of the Office of the Chief of Counsel for War Crimes). The trials (of the military, the industrialists, and other representatives of the Nazi élites) continued until 1949. From a conceptual and juridical point of view, all of the thirteen "Nuremberg trials" stemmed from the plan to prosecute the leaders and the organizations of the Nazi regime involved in the global criminal policies of the Third Reich, regardless of "geographical location." The twelve that came after the International Military Tribunal were, however, conducted only by the American authorities. The four Allied powers, the Soviet Union, the United States of America, the United Kingdom, and France, in their respective occupied zones of Germany held a series of trials of minor perpetrators that would have served as a guide for those that the German national institutions should have subsequently conducted. (Such trials would not generally have had recourse to the broad charges used at Nuremberg, though there were exceptions, as in the case of the industrialist Hermann Röchling, who was tried by the French for "crimes against peace.")[1] Many of the trials held by national tribunals (like those in Poland of the men in charge of some of the camps) also had an international resonance.

It was above all the United States and the United Kingdom, who were deeply involved in a large number of investigations not related to any infringement of their national interest, who sought to hold a series of trials genuinely inspired by international law. These two countries also concerned themselves with a very large number of trials of minor Nazi war criminals in Germany, Austria, and Italy. It is, however, important to compare the English and American judicial and sentencing policies pursued in Germany and Italy and correlate them with the overall framework established by the precedent of the IMT and of the subsequent Nuremberg trials.

There was, therefore, on the one hand a judicial legislation that was formalized in stages leading to the final draft of the IMT's programmatic document, the so-called Nuremberg Charter;[2] on the other hand—this is crucial to understanding the course of the devising and the collapse of the "Italian Nuremberg"—there was the decision of the Allied governments and consequently of the British government to prosecute, under its own authority, those responsible for Nazi war crimes committed in Germany and Europe against the Allies and, starting in October 1943, against the Italian civilian population (that is, the population of a former enemy country that subsequently fought on the side of the Allies).

The legislation applied in the zones under British control and in Italy was termed the "Royal Warrant," while the cases were prepared and conducted under the authority of the Department of the Judge Advocate General of the Army (JAGO), who was answerable to the War Office. (It should, however, be remembered that the policy of the British trial program was the responsibility of the Foreign Office.) Both in Germany and in Italy the English trials began in the autumn of 1945.[3] The Americans also began a program of trials for war crimes,[4] which very soon revealed itself to be more effective than the English one, at least in Germany. In fact, when the trial conducted by the International Military Tribunal concluded, there emerged the first differences of opinion among the British authorities: the British Chief Prosecutor, Baron Hartley Shawcross, gave assurances that the British would participate in the other international trials, especially those of the German military and some groups of industrialists and entrepreneurs, but the Foreign Office made clear its lack of enthusiasm, fearing that the second trial could become a platform for anti-capitalist Soviet propaganda and could weaken the process of the reconstruction of German economic self-sufficiency. This was the situation that resulted in the twelve Nuremberg trials being held under the authority of the American occupation. On the other hand, among the Americans themselves, the conviction that the new trials of the war criminals should be conducted by the single occupying power was gaining ground. In August 1946 agreement on this point was reached between the British Foreign Secretary, Bevin, and the American Secretary of State, James Byrnes.[5] But the agreement was used by the British not only to avoid new international trials, but also to suspend their own proceedings (which were paralleling those of the Americans) and eventually to transfer to the authorities of the United States those defendants also involved in trials in the American Zone. The majority of the Germans prosecuted by the Americans in the twelve Nuremberg trials had been transferred from the English Zone. Dissociating themselves from the new proceedings set up under the authority of International Law, the British conducted all their legal actions within the framework of the Royal Warrant. This was the case for the few trials that were held in Italy in place of a single general trial of the leading figures of the Nazi occupation system.

More and more frequently, the members of Nazi organizations came to be referred to ordinary German courts, which could pass maximum ten-year sentences, while thousands of them, considered "relatively harmless," were released without trial. While the parameters of the Royal Warrant became more and more rigid (every trial was supposed to end by September l, 1948), many de-Nazification measures tended to wane. Nor did the Americans, though more decisive in the purging trials, succeed in going beyond a certain point and demonstrating that the élites—the industrialists, the entrepreneurs, the bankers, the government officials, and the other executives and managers—had really been involved in the Nazi conspiracy and Hitler's aim of world conquest through the planning of the war. Nor was it possible to apply the conspiratorial paradigm to the heads of the *Einsatzgruppen*. Conspiracy was "demonstrated" only in three of the twelve trials held by the Americans at Nuremberg, those of the SS chain of command.[6] Nevertheless, it was the American authorities—the Office of the Chief Counsel for War—who succeeded in putting in the dock the representatives of the big industrial groups: Farber and Krupp and the Dresdner Bank. The British displayed less and less enthusiasm both for these initiatives and for collaboration with the French and the Soviets; this revealed their many concerns about the effects of the trials on German public opinion against the backdrop of increasing tension between the Anglo-Americans and the Soviet Union. In the political climate of the cold war, it was becoming more and more complicated, for example, to approve the extradition to Poland and the Soviet Union of the high-ranking officers of the Wehrmacht, Runstedt and Manstein. (The latter was tried by the Allies.) In the British Parliament, Winston Churchill; George Bell, Bishop of Chichester; the Socialist Richard Stokes; Reginald Paget; and Lord Maurice Hankey declared their opposition to the continuation of the trials. Because of the deliberate confusion that had arisen between the trials conducted in accordance with both the British code of the Royal Warrant (against criminals guilty of common war crimes and of civilian massacres) and trials conducted in accordance with the International Law, an unrelenting press campaign was conducted against political justice. The authors—Hankey, Paget, Montgomery Belgion, F. J. P. Veale—insisted on a select part of the truth, that the Allies had also committed war crimes, but they did not mention the extreme and systematic nature of the criminal Nazi conduct of total war and the war of extermination of the European Jews. They tried to demonstrate the inconsistency of the general hypothesis that had underpinned the legal proceedings of Nuremberg.[7]

The totally American hypothesis of a conspiratorial plot against peace was vigorously attacked, and the Nazi plan of exterminating the Jews was itself, in the context of the total war in Eastern Europe, disputed. The articles contained elements of anti-Semitism, as well as a marked anti-Communist tendency.

As will be seen, these same politicians and authors also took part in the campaigns in favor of the leading German military figures, defending not only Manstein but also Field Marshal Albert Kesselring, Commander-in-Chief of the Italian forces in Italy.

* * *

The evolution of the judicial situation and the trials, as well as the political context, evidently contributed to the inexorable eclipsing of the dominant theory behind the American-led prosecution in the International Military Tribunal in Nuremberg, which Bradley Smith termed the conspiracy-criminal organization plan. This theory was an idea of Colonel Murray C. Bernays, who linked the brutalities and the genocide committed by the Nazis with the plan for continental and world domination. But Robert N. Jackson, a Supreme Court Justice appointed to lead the American prosecution in Nuremberg, also spoke of "the existence of a general conspiracy to which the Nazi Party, the Gestapo, and other organizations were parties. The object of the conspiracy was to obtain, by illegal means, by violation of treaties, and by wholesale brutality, the control of Europe and of the world. When this plan should be proved, the second phase would be entered upon which would consist in the identification of individuals who were parties to this general conspiracy."[8]

The power of the Nazi Führer was not only considered the formulation center, but also the expression and the purpose of the force of the National Socialist regime, its military strength, and its economic imperialism. Thus the highest ranks of the institutional, political, military, financial, and industrial structures could be included in the planning machinery so that the individuals in these organizational structures could necessarily be regarded as defendants in the Nuremberg trial.

It certainly cannot be claimed that the hypothesis of the conspiracy for the conquest of world power was satisfactorily "proved" during the International Military Tribunal's proceedings—assuming, without any anachronistic irony, that judicial powers of such a nature can be proved in a court of law. But neither can the question be put aside with undue haste, since it has continued to emerge forcefully in the realm of historiographic interpretations of Nazi foreign policy, themselves also polarized around two concepts: a policy directed by a plan and an intention, both clearly formulated, or, on the contrary, a policy produced by circumstantial pressures and those of the economic structure of the Third Reich?

Hugh Trevor-Roper was among the first to identify *Mein Kampf* of 1924 and *Zweite Buch* of 1921 as the two Hitlerian texts that would tend to demonstrate the immutable consistency of the Nazi plan regarding the conquest of *Lebensraum*. Andreas Hillgruber, instead, stated that the expansionary objectives were directed at Eastern Europe, the Middle East, and the other British colonial territories. Günter Moltmann also set against that background the prospect of a clash with the United States, and he advanced the hypothesis of a planned assault to gain world dominance. In any case, above and beyond the differences between the historians who have stressed the continental objectives of the Nazi plan of conquest (Trevor-Roper, Jackel, Kuhn) and those who have hypothesized a global dimension (Hillgruber, Moltmann, Hildebrand, Dülffer, Hauner, Thies), they all highlight the international nature of the Nazi policy of aggression. Those who are opposed to such a thesis—Hans Mommsen, Martin Broszat, Tim Mason and others—believe that the outbreak of the war in 1939 was never planned; Hitler was subject to the pressures from the Wehrmacht and industry (but this state of affairs would not prevent the conception of a plan), and the foreign policy and the war were, above all, the outward projection of the country's internal social problems. Certainly Nazism tried to pursue a course of action free from the constraints of international law, the League of Nations, and treaties, but its foreign policy, up to the watershed of 1939, was, on the whole, a combination of decisions taken in particular circumstances and, at the same time, the calculated result of a longstanding plan, in its turn made up of relatively circumscribed objectives and ideologically-dictated global aims (economic self-sufficiency, a return to an agricultural community, the creation of the "master race"). *Lebensraum* itself was a concrete aim but also a metaphor. (Before 1939 the Nazis had no clear plan regarding Poland, and yet—because of its geographical position—it was necessarily of central importance in the planned attack on the Soviet Union.) At the same time, from the mid-1930s, to the ideologically conditioned, anti-Soviet (and anti-French) line was added the anti-English one, upheld above all by von Ribbentrop, inspired more by pragmatic power politics.

But the sudden anti-Soviet and anti-Polish turnabout of 1934–35 and the launching of the Nazi policy of *Lebensraum* presupposed a link with the revisionist Right, hostile to the Versailles Peace Treaty, and, furthermore, also to the German High Command's military objectives in the Western European campaigns during the Great War. In post-1933 German foreign policy and in the discussions about the Nazi strategic choices in the course of World War II, there is an evident continuity, which constitutes, at least in part, the basis of the wide range of common interests (at least until 1938) between the conservative élites and the Nazi leaders, rooted in the pursuit of the traditional approach of German power politics in Eastern Europe.[9]

The question of the conspiracy spread, at Nuremberg, from the implementation of the "crime against peace" to the scale of the genocide of the Jews, descending subsequently into the sphere of historiographic controversies, in the fundamental contributions of Raul Hilberg, Philippe Burrin, Martin Broszat, Kurt Pätzold, Erika Schwarz, Christopher Browning. Today we know that it was precisely the implementation of the war and, in particular, the attack on the Soviet Union, which enabled, between the summer of 1941 and the first months of 1942, the anti-Jewish Nazi policies, begun in 1933, to reach their peak through a progressive radicalization and the definition of three objectives: to assign the "Jewish problem" to the Reich's General Security Headquarters (Heydrich, on behalf of Goering and Himmler), to coordinate all the Reich's institutions, to realize the final aim of the elimination of the eleven million European Jews. In January 1942, at the Wansee Conference, the only decisions to be reached concerned the technical and organizational aspects of a solution resulting from an accumulation of conditions and intentions.

The Hitlerian plan had, from the beginning, envisioned the destruction of Judaism, but there was no implicit "teleology" in the extermination of the European Jews. The decision regarding the final solution took shape "in bits and pieces," in line with the typical procedures of the "organized disorder" that, for Franz Neumann, constitutes the structure of the Nazi system. As far as the Shoah is concerned, the procedures were more decisive than the instructions: the "how" more than the "why." But the circle of those who were jointly responsible included, from the beginning, not only those who formulated the "plan" in the top Nazi echelons, but also the keenly active agents and the various organizations of the army, the bureaucracy and industry. An interpretation of the Shoah that includes the "conspiracy," the functions and the structural conditions does not exclude either the responsibility for the policy (Hannah Arendt has written that the Holocaust cannot be understood without taking into account the totalitarian connection between ideology and terror) or Hitler's intentions (documented by Fest, Toland and Haffner), but it enables one to understand that the absence of an official order does not in any way support the thesis of the Holocaust deniers.

Today, the opportunity to utilize and synthesize these new sources of knowledge, which come from historical interpretations—both intentionalist and structuralist—of Nazi foreign policy, total war and the massacre of the Jews (which was for the Nazis, from a military perspective, a counterproductive operation), permits us to shed new light also on the theory of the Nazi conspiracy formulated by American jurists and judges, between 1944 and 1946, in order to prepare the proceedings for the International Military Tribunal.

One cannot help being struck by the fact that the theory of the conspiracy and of the Nazi plan for world dominance could represent the overturning of the Nazi theory about the Jewish conspiracy to control the world and European economies (which was also a root cause of Germany's defeat in 1918). The paradigm of the theses of Rosenberg, Goebbels, and Streicher was notoriously based on the *Protocols of the Elders of Zion*, which was published in Russia for the first time in 1903 but became known throughout the world only after the October Revolution, an event that a large part of the reactionary press had presented as the result of a Jewish conspiracy. The German translation had, in fact, appeared in 1919. Despite the fact that an Italian philologist has recently tried to demonstrate that it originated in Russia, in 1903, it is very probable that the origins of the Protocols can, instead, be traced back to the period of the Dreyfus Affair and that it has to be seen in the context of French anti-Semitism. Those who compiled the text most probably derived their material from French sources, utilizing the "previous mould" of the Jewish plot.[10]

But the absurdity of the anti-Semitic, and subsequently Nazi, theory of history, based on the paradigm of a Jewish conspiracy, does not automatically invalidate, on the grounds of absurdity, every explicative thesis, judicial or historiographic, based on the conspiracy. Carlo Ginzburg, in a book dealing with the stereotype of the witches' Sabbath in medieval and modern Europe, has, in fact, demonstrated that, often, false conspiracies conceal real conspiracies, but of an opposite nature.[11] Taking into account the "conspiratorial obsession"—spread by nineteenth-century European literature and traceable to the French Revolution's theory of a Jewish-Masonic conspiracy—and a "healthy scepticism" in relation to the possibility of explaining World War II by means of the official version upheld at Nuremberg, it is possible to propose a new conception of the plan. In this case, the Nazi plan of overturning the European equilibrium would have been an intervention of deliberate "coordinated" actions, but also influenced by the evolution of the historical context, aiming at directing, in a predetermined course, conflicts and tensions already extant. Rather than supposing the existence of a single coordinating center, conspiracy and plot can, essentially, be understood in this way.

The same connotation of "plan" can prove to be interesting if used to interpret the mechanisms of the anti-Partisan reprisals and of the armed repression of the civilian population in some parts of Europe occupied by the Nazis and in Italy, between 1943 and 1945.

***

The time for rethinking the whole history of twentieth-century Italy (and Europe) is clearly upon us: that history can no longer be divided into chronological blocks: for instance, pre-1914 (the liberal age), 1918–45 (the age of tyrants) and post-1945 (the age of the democratic and welfare state). In 1945, with the collapse of Fascism, the democratic vote that ended the Monarchy, and the emergence of republican institutions, this accustomed and convenient way of writing contemporary European and Italian history changed completely. In fact, in the case of Italy, and other countries, the conflicts of World War II were themselves echoes and transpositions of disputes whose roots lay in the post–World War I crisis and even in the imperfect and conflicting forms in which States had been created in the nineteenth century. Moreover, from 1945 to 1968, not only the history, but even the memory of the first half of the twentieth century was blurred, or forgotten. In 1968, the younger generation in Italy, Germany and France began to ask what Fascism had really been and what had happened during and after the war. The Resistance, as the moral and political cement of postwar democracies, was questioned, and collaboration and alliance with Nazi Germany were finally remembered. The related question of justice was another reason for reviewing memory and rewriting history: jurists and historians began to discuss the nature of the way in which trials had been conducted and punishments for wartime crimes had been meted out after 1945; furthermore, since 1989, the debate concerning crimes committed under Stalinist auspices re-opened the question of postwar and post-totalitarian retribution, and its contribution to collective amnesia.

All this concerns, first of all, the consequences of the International Military Tribunal at Nuremberg, the most famous of the postwar judiciary proceedings, where the definition of war crimes was extended, the crime of planning, preparation and waging of a war of aggression was established, and a new crime was given a name: crimes against humanity[12] (the International Military Tribunal at Nuremberg claimed the right to try criminal behaviour on the basis of laws and principles that did not exist at the time the crime was committed).

From a certain point of view, judging the Nazi leaders seemed to exculpate the German nation, while taking the issue of trials and punishments out of German hands. In the other countries formerly allied with Germany, an order for trials and punishments was included among the clauses of the surrender terms. Postwar Europe was, in fact, dominated by Popular Front Governments, made up of progressive Catholics, bourgeois democratic socialists, and Communists representative of the wartime patriotic Resistance, and the courts were often under the control of jurists delegated by governments. After a few months, this type of People's Court was divested of power and in Italy, France and Austria the courts became more and more traditional in their outlook. Many judges had in fact faithfully served the prewar or even Fascist regimes. (In Eastern Europe, on the contrary, the courts continued their revolutionary behavior, but under Soviet supervision).

"From the end of World War II until the revolutions of 1989," Tony Judt has written, "the frontiers of Europe and, with them, the forms of identity associated with the term 'European' were shaped by two dominant concerns: the pattern of division drafted at Yalta and frozen into place during the cold war and the desire, common to both sides of the divide, to forget the recent past."[13] So postwar justice contributed to the distortion and sublimation of the memory of the wartime experience and built up a false identity: in the climate of the Liberation, everyone sought to identify with the victors and to distance themselves from those who had been the enemy.

Thus it was necessary to forget that most of occupied Europe had collaborated with the Nazi forces, or accepted with equanimity their presence and activities. Norway, France, the Baltic States, Ukraine, Hungary, Slovakia, Croatia and Flemish-speaking Belgium had taken advantage of the benevolent German occupation or had been governed by active partners in ideological collaboration. From 1945 to 1948—the first years of postwar reconstruction—Europe's memory was moulded and an official version of wartime history was established, founded on the principle that responsibility for the war and its crimes lay only with Nazi Germany and that Austria, Hungary, Slovakia, Croatia, the Baltic States and others were the victims (Austria was the first in 1938) of Nazi aggression.

The attribution of war responsibility solely to Nazi Germany was used to justify the expulsions of German minorities from Poland, the USSR, Czechoslovakia, Yugoslavia, Romania and Hungary: it was like a sort of response to the violence visited on these lands by Nazi German war criminals.

Judt continues:

> Next, there was the issue of denazification. Within a short time after the Liberation, it became clear that Germany (and Austria) could not be returned to civil administration and local self-government, even under Allied supervision, if the purging of responsible Nazis was not undertaken in a sustained and consistent manner. Moreover, the local Social Democratic and Christian Democratic Parties in both countries could not be expected to ignore the votes of the former Nazis, once these were allowed to re-enter public life; thus the 1948 amnesty in Austria, which returned full civil rights to some 500,000 former registered Nazis, inevitably resulted in a sort of instant amnesia, whereby all sides agreed that these men and women were henceforward no different from the rest. Even the remaining 'more incriminated' Nazis (some 42,000 of them) were nearly all amnestied within the following seven years, as the Western Allies sought to minimize the risk of alienating Austrians and Germans from the Western Bloc through any excessive emphasis on their past and its price. In a process that would have been unthinkable in 1945, the identification and punishment of active Nazis in German-speaking Europe had effectively ended in 1948 and was a forgotten issue by the early fifties.[14]

The other side of the question was the clash between guilt and innocence. The first was absolutely tied to the Germans and the second to the others. The myth of national Resistance legitimized this divide in every country and government leaders in France, Italy, Belgium and the Communist-dominated National Front governments in Eastern Europe told their citizens that their sufferings were attributable to a small number of collaborators and to the Nazi occupation. Both Left and Right had an interest in forgetting their recent prewar past and their responsibilities in making Fascism's victory easier. That is the reason why, in the two parts of Europe, justice, with regard to war criminals and collaborators in the post-Liberation era, was aborted. It seemed impossible to charge and purge tens of thousands of people for activities legalized by governments in power, as in Vichy France (and, in fact, a large quota of the summary executions were carried out in that country before the beginning of the war for Liberation in June 1944, that is to say before formal judgement). So postwar justice was, first of all, a sort of political and symbolic legitimization of the new States that had arisen from the Liberation, but an inadequate one from the juridical point of view.

***

In order to test this hypothesis, I must follow in this essay an oblique course that goes back at least to the moment of political and judicial reckoning with the Italian Fascist and nationalist regime. To this end I will use the expression "Italian Nuremberg" not to define the trials—never activated by the Allies—of those responsible for the Italian occupation of Greece and the Balkans, but in order to indicate the lack of a global procedure against those responsible for the system of Nazi occupation in Italy starting in September 1943. The reckoning unfolded on two distinct levels: the punishment of criminals (a criminal matter) and the purges (an administrative problem). The existing historiographical situation of the purge is not fully satisfying, however, since for many years the critical literature merely rested on judgements formulated at the time of the post-war polemics. On the tenth anniversary of the April 25, 1945, insurrection, the jurist Achille Battaglia wrote:

> All things considered, none of these norms, with the exception of those on collaborationism, were effectively applied. The early condemnation sentences were annulled by the Court of Cassation, even when the law had expressly aimed to remove them from its jurisdiction. The amnesties and pardons of 1946 and 1948 and the criteria adopted by the magistracy in their application, subtracted vigor from the sentences as well. Patrimonies were not confiscated. The crimes of the action squads, painstakingly unearthed from oblivion, were not punished. The purges of the bureaucracy failed dreadfully. Significant political responsibilities of fascism were transferred to a criminal level and then punished through the formality of legal trials: the absurdity of this pretense was realized too late. The true cadres of state command, that is, the upper levels of bureaucracy, remained unchanged, and they would not agree to a trial of the past in which they would be directly attacked. Thus there was an uncertain liberty and a false justice.[15]

The law regarding the purging of collaborators, however, was applied by underestimating or silencing the anti-Fascist value of the Resistance, connecting punishable behaviour exclusively to the category defined under the military penal code of war. The paradigm of the purges as a "joke" (Alessandro Galante Garrone's expression) has long been repeated by historians from Zara Algardi to Marcello Flores, from Lamberto Mercuri to Mimmo Franzinelli and Roy Domenico, in this way reviving the corollary of the continuity of the State.[16]

With the work of Hans Woller, a researcher at the Institut für ZeitGeschichte of Munich, and that of the Italian magistrate Romano Canosa, we saw a certain inversion of this trend.[17] We now know that a first phase of the Italian purging was quite radical, above all in central and peripheral public administrative and political circles, on the basis of the Bonomi government's decree of July 27, 1944. In addition to confirming the High Commissariat instituted by Marshal Pietro Badoglio in order to counter Allied suspicions, the decree established the High Court of Justice and the extraordinary Courts of Assizes. The purging of the bureaucracy and of local institutions thus had—at least until July 1945—a broad scope, above all because of the largely "inclusive" criteria that were adopted; they permitted the examination, if only summarily, of hundreds of thousands of cases, the initiation of more than 35,000 measures and the conclusion of more than half of these, resulting in 7,312 sanctions and 2,553 expulsions.

A moderate turn took place a few months later, in November 1945, with the enactment of the Nenni law (Pietro Nenni was the leader of Italian Socialists). Paradoxically, Nenni was accused by the moderates of "reopening the question of purges instead of closing it," while in reality he had intended with his legislation to conclude the phase of incriminations and trials, suspend the work of the CLN, stop the purges in industrial companies and the financial system, all with the goal of avoiding lethal counter-attacks on economic reconstruction and of delegating many trials to the Ministries. It is therefore Nenni's action of 1945, and not De Gasperi's hostility or the amnesty of the Minister of Justice, the Communist leader Palmiro Togliatti, in 1946 that we must consider in order to comprehend the beginning of the crisis of the purges (even if it is true that some technical imperfections in the amnesty text of June 26, 1946, allowed the ordinary magistracy and the Cassation to interpret the document broadly, so as to include the high political and military positions of the State).[18] However, at least until the end of 1945, the purging was real. It is important to remember as well the dimension of the purges, rather outrageously defined by Togliatti as "plebeian," that were carried out by the partisans and the radicalized sectors of the popular classes in the weeks following the insurrection in the North. At the end of July 1945 thousands were expelled from factories and offices, 9,364 fascists were killed without trial, and 30,000 trials were held in the extraordinary Courts of Assizes, resulting in many death sentences. Between May and July of 1945, the desire for justice was pure and profound; even if there was an attempt to confer a mantle of legality, this desire often tore at that mantle, thus acquiring vitality but harming the law and individuals. The difficulties of including justice within juridical regulations perhaps gave the impression of revenge. The end of the punishment of crimes and of purges around 1946 was sanctioned by a diagnosis of "complete recovery" from Fascism that proved lethal for the assessment of the ruling classes' historical responsibilities for the accession and consolidation of the regime. That decision also compromised the start of the proceedings on crimes against humanity perpetrated by the Italian military during the war in Greece, Yugoslavia and Albania. In the meantime, in the areas governed directly by the Allied Military Government of Occupied Territory, the purges and criminal punishment carried out through the emissaries of the combined General Staff and the Allied Control Commission would seem to have been more incisive, both in the South and in Rome, where the staff of Colonel Charles Poletti was working. Hans Woller claims that even in the North "the majority of the purging action unfolded on the basis of the allied ordinances."

The image of the Allied government forces as more decisively engaged than the Italian Government in the purging of fascists and the punishment of war crimes is apparently confirmed by the documentation on the inquiries and investigations of British military judges conserved in the archives of the Public Record Office. The International Commission for Penal Reconstruction, founded in Cambridge in 1941 on the initiative of jurist Hans Lauterpacht, had promoted the idea of the constitution of the UN War Crimes Commission founded in London in 1943. In Italy the UN Commission was more or less an emanation of the General Headquarters of the Allied Forces of the Mediterranean, which entrusted to the British in particular the creation of an organizational structure to carry out investigations (the Special Investigation Branch); it was absorbed into the South Europe War Crime Group in 1948.

Even with its logistical and organizational limitations, the work of the British War Crime Section was extremely serious. The documentation of the War Office Section of the Public Record Office remains today an excellent base for reconstructing the history of war crimes perpetrated by German troops against the Italian civilian population compared to the well-known and grave lacunae of the Wehrmacht documentation preserved in the Bundes Archiv Militär Archiv in Freiburg. Italy collaborated in the investigations and forwarded the results of the inquiries carried out by organizations such as the CLNAI (National Northern Italian Liberation Committee) through the government's Central Commission for War Crimes, presided over by the Undersecretary of State, Aldobrando Medici-Tornaquinci.

This system of orders behind the centralized strategy of the repression of partisan warfare and, above all, of the passive resistance of civilian populations and their activities in support of the partisans, shows that while the Nazi occupation was a disorganized structure with more than one power center, its repressive strategy was instead planned coordinated and centralized by the Wehrmacht, according to the agreement reached between Kesselring and Wolff, General of the SS, at the end of March 1944. The system of orders planned by the South-West Oberkommando, chaired by the Field Marshal and carried out by the leaders of the 10th and 14th Armies, assumed the adoption of anti-guerrilla warfare procedures that had already been put into effect previously in Central Eastern Europe, based on an order from Hitler of October 18, 1942. With an order in December 1942, Keitel, the Supreme Commander of the Wehrmacht, later extended it to the Balkans and Greece. The conviction that the Germans had prepared in advance an authentic "machinery of reprisals" persuaded the Allied investigating committees to hold two grand trials against the Nazi leaders in Italy: one, for the Fosse Ardeatine massacre, against the Field Marshal and his immediate subordinates, General von Mackensen, Commander of the 14th Army, and General Mältzer, Commander of Rome; and a second trial against the entire military leadership, dozens of senior officers of the Wehrmacht, SS, Sichereits-Dienst and Sichereits Polizei considered responsible for the "machinery of reprisals." Because of the dimension and prominence the great Italian trial was to have assumed, the Allies compared it to the 13 trials held in Nuremberg against the major "categories" of Nazi criminals and the political, diplomatic, economic and organizational leaders of the terror of the Third Reich. The possibility of an "Italian Nuremberg" remained open from August 1945 until April 1946, but from that date on, three arguments began to develop that eventually persuaded the English to renounce the trial.

The first was the preoccupation—clearly formulated in a letter by the Commander of the Allied General Headquarters in Italy—that a trial could complicate the state of Anglo-American relations by radicalizing anti-Fascist public opinion in a moment of political uncertainty. The first free administrative elections, held in the spring of 1946, had delivered favorable results for the Socialists and Communists. All the big cities in the north and in Tuscany, as well as the regions of Piedmont, Lombardy,

Emilia-Romagna, Umbria, the Marches, Calabria, Sicily and Tuscany had voted in socialist and communist majorities. The quotas these two parties arrived at in the June political elections (40 per cent) and the defeat of the monarchy option in the institutional referendum confirmed the fears regarding a radical political shift in Italy.

The second reason lay in the profound differences between the United States and the Soviet Union over the supreme judiciary authority that should be responsible for judging war criminals. The United States favored an international authority, while the Soviets insisted that the criminals be tried in the countries in which the crimes were committed and by local judicial authorities.

Third, but no less important, was the contentious divergence among the Allies, the Italian government and the Yugoslav government (supported by the Czechoslovakians) regarding who should judge Italian soldiers accused of war crimes in the Balkans. General Mario Roatta's escape in March 1944 had cast well-founded suspicion on the General Staff of the Italian Army's intentions to evade the inquiries, and the Italian government, which had claimed the right to try Nazi war criminals based on its role as co-belligerent country, soon realized that excessive insistence would only legitimize the Yugoslav request to try Italian military responsible for war crimes. It was better to rely on the Allies and, in the meantime, shelve the requests of countries that were victim to Italian occupation.

The cancellation of the "Italian Nuremberg" produced grave consequences, first on judiciary grounds and later regarding the assessment of historical truth. The "evident proofs of a policy of reprisal conducted without respect for the distinction between the guilty and the innocent" and the proofs of a system of terror were found in dozens of files organized for some minor trials held in order to ascertain the responsibility of individual senior officers. Yet even the admissions of such men as General Lemelsen and the military judge Keller, who were among those responsible for the system of occupation, were neglected, and the President Judge of the High Military Court (Judge Advocate General) Sir Henry Foster MacGeagh's decision to hold the entire group of commanders responsible for the policy of massacres was abandoned. Only a few trials were held, including those of von Mackensen and Mältzer at the end of 1946 and that of Field Marshal Kesselring starting in February 1947. The same Italian government later conformed to this line of conduct and, after holding a few trials against some mid-ranking officers (Kappler, Reder, Strauch and others), it allowed hundreds of cases to be transferred to the Military General Attorney and, on the indication of the relevant ministers, buried for decades in a closet: a most Italian solution that favored the normalization of relations between the Italian Republic and the Federal Republic of Germany and in compensation allowed the prosecution of the Italian war criminals guilty of the massacres in Albania, Yugoslavia and Greece to be forgotten.

In the years immediately following, the awareness of the fragility of the juridical bases of the Allied-administered justice weakened all immediate attempts to reconsider the guilty sentences and capital punishments handed down to the few German senior officers who had been tried. So as to avoid new accusations regarding the violation of the principle of non-retroactivity of the law, in the trials held in Italy the British applied not the Nuremberg Charter but rather the Allied laws of war, which they considered more consistent with the international conventions of The Hague, as stipulated in 1899 and in 1907, and of Geneva in 1929. The position of the British judges on the policy of reprisals developed from the presupposition that a reprisal was only considered legitimate against those responsible for attacks on occupation forces, or as a possible retaliation—through expropriation and bombing of the territories of origin of guerrilla formations. However, the massacre of civilians, the indiscriminate shooting of hostages and the extermination of entire communities, such as had occurred in Italy, could not be considered legitimate. The British military judges nevertheless found themselves faced with a double contradiction: on the one hand, the German military codes, unlike the British ones, defined as legal even the most extreme form of retaliation; and, on the other, the Allied policy had encouraged and armed the partisan war that, in many of its forms, did not fit into the criteria of legality defined by the war law. In both aspects, even the justice of the Allied Military Tribunals in Italy was accused of being a "justice of the victors."

The stakes were evidently political, and not by chance, the conflict that developed within the English ruling class was completely political: on one side was the Military High Court of Sir Forster Mc Geag, who was determined to confirm the condemnations, and on the other the military leaders—General Harding and Field Marshal Alexander—together with authoritative exponents of the House of Lords and the former Prime Minister Winston Churchill, who were firmly intent on re-evaluating the trials and sentences. The outcome of the matter is well known.

The crimes committed against Italian civilian populations could also have been judged in light of the definition of "war crimes" codified in 1919 by the Commission of Responsibilities of Versailles, as well as on the basis of the Nuremberg Charter. The uncertainties first of the military magistracy and then of the English political leaders were, however, primarily the result of the difficulty in evaluating the contribution of the Wermacht to the structure of the Nazi system of occupation. The Allies considered the German army immune to the processes of Nazification and totalitarian integration, as emerged clearly in one of the 13 Nuremberg trials, specifically that regarding the army and the cases of von Brautchisch and Manstein; (but the primary contradiction went back to the framework of the first Nuremberg trial, in which war crimes and crimes against humanity were reduced to mere corollaries of the war of aggression and of the Nazi conspiracy against peace). As Hans Lauterpacht wrote, the question of whether the punishment of war crimes and crimes against humanity committed by the enemy was desirable, advantageous, and feasible could not be answered through the law, but only through a political decision: *auctoritas facit legems*. That process inevitably resulted in the systematic violation of legal principles, from the non-retroactivity of the law to the neutrality of the judge. The punishment of such crimes, although contradictory in its concrete application, nevertheless reinforced international law despite that fact that the *ratio politica* of the Allies, whose aim was to identify and punish those responsible for the outbreak of World War II and to act as a political deterrent against possible future wars, had forced the law.

While they violated the principle of non-retroactivity of the law and other values, the Nuremberg trials and, to a lesser extent, the military trials against German war criminals in Italy, affirmed a new principle: no horror—even if not codified by law—can remain unpunished. The merit of those trials was therefore to offer a definition of crimes against humanity, even if, by applying an artificial and false moral selectivity, they erred in attributing the responsibility of the crimes only to the Germans. From the judiciary procedures issued indirectly a deformation of historical memory that was founded on the separation of Germany's responsibilities from those of other European nations and, therefore, on the forgetting of the faults of the Allied armies and the responsibilities of he European ruling classes for Nazism's rise to power and their collaboration with Hitler's New European Order.

***

The consequences of the administration of justice after World War II lasted until the middle of the twentieth century. The most important jurists of the era, such as Kelsen, Lauterpacht and Lemkin, decided to concentrate on the juridical definition of the conditions to "dispense with war" and to construct peace through law: thus, the origin of World War II was attributed to the Hitlerian conspiracy and to the failure to prevent—though the

International Conventions and the Foundation of the League of Nations—conflicts that had been put in motion after World War I.

In the following years, the principle "no more war" gained supremacy over the prosecution of crimes against humanity because of the very formulation of the trials against responsible Axis figures, both in Nuremberg and in Tokyo. During the lengthy postwar period, the divergence of opinion between those supporting the principle of "no more war" and that of "no more Auschwitz," or between the construction of peace through the law and the protection of human rights, deepened, partly as a consequence of the contraposition of the United States and the Soviet Union.[19] The Soviet Union's hypocritical defense of the values of national sovereignty, non-interference and as the victim country par excellence of Nazi aggression in the postwar imagination—one thinks of the invasions of Hungary in 1956 and Czechoslovakia in 1968—contrasted with the American defense of Western values, often confuted, however, by forceful interventions and in support of dictatorships in the name of countering all sorts of "threat" represented by national liberation movements in the colonies or former European colonies. The identification of the United States as "policemen" by much of international public opinion has resulted in the suspicion of no legal interference even in interventions aimed to counter actual violations of human rights legitimately in every part of the world.

This stalemate provoked a long hibernation in International Law. For decades it was incapable of furnishing the tools with which to protect the values it affirmed in theory, and in the long run it impeded humanitarian interventions in order to prevent new genocides. In Cambodia, as in Rwanda and in Yugoslavia, it did not want to know, did not want to reflect, did not want to act.

Perhaps today something is changing. The new supranational justice can succeed in preparing the adequate means with which to intervene in order to reconstruct the divergence of opinion opened at the end of World War II.[20]

Prologue

Trials and Lessons of History

This book narrates the story of a major trial—of a "maxi-trial" in the political parlance of late twentieth-century Italy—of the entire military command of the Nazi power structure in Italy, operating from 1943 to 1945. It was a trial carefully prepared by the Allies on the juridical and technical model of the Nuremberg Trials, but a trial that never took place.

Here, an attempt is made to explain why and how it came to be replaced by a few contradictory trials of very minor significance, resulting in an enormous historical misrepresentation of the Nazi occupation of Italy and reducing this issue itself to the scale of individual responsibilities.

In order to explain that "unrealized event," I considered it necessary to go back to the outcome of the Nuremberg Trials of the highest authorities of the Third Reich, to Allied policy toward Italy in 1946 and 1947—when the country's political situation appeared extraordinarily uncertain—to the clash between the Allies and Italian governments regarding the peace treaty, safeguarding national territory and Italy's international status, which constituted the background for the dispute over who had the authority to try the Nazi defendants, as well as the Italian military personnel guilty of war crimes perpetrated in the territories occupied by the Axis powers until 1943. This was a tangle of issues, which Italian governments tackled with the tactic of playing on two fronts (or of the two roles in a play): employing a grueling delaying maneuver to avoid handing over to the Allies—or, even worse, to the Yugoslav authorities—the Italian military officials accused of crimes committed in the Balkans and, on the other side, the under-the-counter appeals to the Italian General Military Tribunal. The Allies' aim was to bury the legal proceedings against the members of the Nazi troops that would have provoked reactions in German public opinion, putting at risk the process of reintegrating West Germany into the European community.

This book does not seek, belatedly, to denounce political opportunism or inadequate justice: whoever undertakes historical research would be wrong if they intended to rectify the shortcomings of the courts, but they would be making a much more serious mistake if they presumed to make up for inadequate justice with a justicialist historiography. It is not a question either of conforming with the judgments of that time or of protesting against the trials that were never held, but of contextualizing the course of justice and politics in postwar history. In this way, one would not only throw light on the nature of the Nazi occupation and the Fascist Republican collaboration,[1] but they would also understand the nature of postwar justice. The latter was politically conditioned by the aim of constructing a public memory of the war and the recent past, which would be useful in the context of what appeared to be the new and uncertain identities of Italy and Europe. The whole matter was, furthermore, extraordinarily complicated by the lacunae and the uncertainties of international law regarding reprisals against the civilian population, war crimes, and crimes against humanity. In addition to the contradictions that had accumulated at Nuremberg—including ethical and juridical innovations and violations of legal foundations (starting with the principle of the nonretroactivity of the law)—there were also those produced by the ordinary and military justice of the different European countries, in relation to the occupiers and their collaborators. This showed itself to be incapable of resolving problems such as the role of the military in the implementation of terror and the acceptance of the totalitarian systems by the masses.

Those trials were the foundations of a gigantic operation, deconstructing the memory of a recent past, which included the responsibility of the ruling classes in the failure of the parliamentary democracies, the agreement with the new authoritarian solutions, and the subordination of equilibrium to the Nazi reorganization of Europe—the crimes perpetrated by the "just." Thus, a selective and partial public memory was developed, based on exclusively attributing the crimes against humanity to the German nation, identified with the National Socialist system. The arbitrary separation between "us" and "them," in Europe and in Italy, turned out to be conveniently complementary to the process of the democratization, without the de-Nazification, of Germany. Thus, since 1945, the Allies and Europe offered an entire set of official memories distorted for propaganda purposes. Judiciary oblivion was a crucial aspect of this.

It is not by chance that I dedicate a chapter to the recollection of Vichy in post-1945 French political, cultural, and juridical history. After a brief season of purging, the French Republic was, in fact, built on the conscious substitution of the memory of Vichy collaboration with the Gaullist myth of an undivided France, united in the most strenuous Resistance. This experience can be taken as a paradigm for those of many Western democracies built on oblivion—the Italy of Alcide De Gasperi, the Austria rehabilitated by Kurt Waldheim, and the Germany of Konrad Adenauer and his heirs—all tenaciously determined to forget.

But it was precisely in Germany that the upheaval of 1968 also had decisive repercussions in the realm of memory and brought back to public consciousness the moral imperative of remembering in the admonitory form of the Hebrew precept: "Remembrance is the secret of redemption." Later, the country would benefit a great deal from this exercise, when it found itself having to face, after the "trauma" of the end of National Socialism, that of the fall of a statist and oppressive communism. The question of the transition from a dictatorship to a hoped-for democratic stability is always linked to the way of guaranteeing justice in the face of human rights violations, tackling and, at the same time, understanding the past that has produced them.

The problem of finding a solution for providing justice, and at the same time understanding and surmounting a difficult past, is certainly not restricted to Germany, but, over the last decades, has concerned a number of States: Chile, Argentina, El Salvador, post-Franco Spain, Greece after the colonels, Cambodia, Ethiopia and, more recently, all the post-Communist States of Central and Eastern Europe. In most of these countries, the cause of oblivion has had excellent supporters—in Spain, after 1975, people spoke of a voluntary collective amnesia.

After the Polish Revolution of 1989, the line followed by Prime Minister Tadeusz Mazowiecki was, for example, "to draw a clear line between us and the past"[2] without trials and recriminations. Perhaps in the Polish transition, as in the post-1945 German one, the pressing need for economic recovery played a decisive role. In the case of Vaclav Havel in Czechoslovakia, the policy of rejecting recriminations and retaliation corresponded more with a deep conviction that has not, however, been shared by other post-Communist governments, such as the Conservative government of József Antall in Hungary. Havel has declared on several occasions that justice, punishing the guilty, and a judgment on the past—instead of reinforcing the new and fragile democracy—would have subjected it to the risk of tearing asunder the social fabric, a risk that is not comparable with the loss of eye-witness accounts or the unrealized ascertaining of the historical and criminal responsibilities.

Many of the post-Communist countries of Central and Eastern Europe have thus chosen to jettison the past. This had already been done in post-1945 Western Europe, running the risk of producing a chronic pathological condition such as the one in France, which has been defined as the "Vichy syndrome," the fever which gripped France on several occasions (the last being the case of the revelations about François Mitterand's past lapses). The pathological condition to forget risked unilateral distortions, such as those produced by the hardened generation of 1968 in Germany, which succeeded in rebelling against the inability of their fathers to deal with Nazism, but at the same time closed its eyes to the regime of the German Democratic Republic. In recent years, the situation has become even more complicated because only some of the countries of Central and Eastern Europe—Poland, Hungary, Rumania, Bulgaria, and Albania—have had to deal with understanding the past within the frontiers of the old States, while in the former Soviet Union, Yugoslavia, and Czechoslovakia the old supranational structures have broken down into new and smaller States.

Generally, in post-Communist Central Europe, the practice of prosecuting those responsible for oppressive policies or crimes against humanity has, in the end, proved to be of doubtful value. In fact, in these countries, in contrast to the Chilean or Argentinian dictatorships, the major or minor levers of the regime had been in the hands of a large number of people and a substantial part of society had, thus, found itself entangled in the network of daily conformism and compromises. It is not by chance that Vaclav Havel has always pointed out the impossibility of making a clear distinction between the oppressed and the oppressors, showing himself to be extremely hostile to countersigning the 1991 law that excluded entire categories. In Poland, great reservations were expressed about the action brought against General Jaruzelski for his part in the armed suppression of the Baltic workers' protest demonstrations between 1970 and 1971.

On the whole, the judicial proceedings in the countries of Central-Eastern Europe have proved to be fragmentary, episodic and ineffective. Nor can it be maintained that even the most systematic action by German justice, after the 1990 unification, has served to reinforce legality. The German judiciary succeeded in not repeating what the press had defined as "the Nuremberg style," namely, the legal prosecution of crimes not considered as such by the regime of that period, violating the principle of the nonretroactivity of the law. Despite this, its actions cannot be said to have been free from arbitrary selectivity and brutal political exploitation in applying the old laws of the German Democratic Republic to the crimes committed by its government officials. The only country that has tried to classify the actions of the Communist period—starting from the crimes committed during the 1956 Revolution—within the juridical categories laid down by the Nuremberg Trials is Hungary.

Analogous considerations could be made about the purges in Czechoslovakia or the ferocious recurring episodes of the defamatory political use of the documents of the past in the political struggle in Poland. If the issue that arose in 1945 remains, therefore, unquestionably of current interest, satisfactory solutions still appear to be distant.

One of the few positive examples was, perhaps, the Truth Commission adopted in South Africa. Some judicial solutions can be identified in constructing a system of regulations of international law regarding crimes against humanity, as well as in the creation of supranational institutions, such as the Tribunal at The Hague for Bosnia and Rwanda and the permanent International Court of Justice. But in practical terms, their application will probably not succeed in avoiding the problems already produced in the legal proceedings brought against Nazi criminals.

The patient search for historical truth—a truth that is always human and therefore susceptible to modification—remains an important way of understanding and surmounting the past. But studying the legacy and the consequences of any form of authoritarian or totalitarian power is also one of the best ways to demonstrate how difficult it is to reach historical truth. If the documents of a State founded on lies of propaganda remain unreliable, the historian must also continue to mistrust retrospective accounts and trial records themselves.

Chapter 1

The Deconstruction of Memory

In the winter of 1995–96, I was busy looking at the files of the British State Archives in the Public Record Office in London, consulting the documents of the investigative section of the army. Between 1944 and 1945, the Special Investigation Branch had inquired into hundreds of bloody episodes that had involved the defenseless civilian population during the Italian campaign. At the suggestion of Giuseppe de Felice, Gino Nunes, who was then President of the Province of Pisa, had entrusted me—I was, at that time, working at the Scuola Normale Superiore—and a colleague of mine at the University of Pisa, Paolo Pezzino, with the task of searching for evidence of massacres of civilians that had occurred in the province of Pisa and the region of Tuscany in the spring and summer of 1944. This was the period of the most dramatic phase of the war and the Resistance in our region. The only traces of those massacres were little more than local memories. Our research encompassed the British, American, German, and Italian archives.

At an earlier date, Roberto Battaglia had pointed out the particularly bloody nature of the German retreat from Rome and Florence, and we followed in his footsteps. While the Resistance in the North was developing, that of Central-Southern Italy was deeply involved in countering the German retreat from Rome, which was moving very quickly towards the Tuscan-Emilian Apennines. Kesselring had opportunely decided to effect a great backward leap of 400–500 kilometers in order to absorb the blow received in the Battle of Rome. Battaglia describes Kesselring as carrying out an

> aggressive retreat [. . .] characterized [. . .] by a series of rearguard actions which, inch by inch, opposed the Allied vanguard up to the definitive withdrawal on the Gothic Line [. . .]. A horrifying trail of massacres split the peninsula transversely and revealed the transition from the first phase of the retreat to the second. From East to West: at Gubbio [. . .]; at Cortona. At

> Civitella Val di Chiana [. . .]; at Castelnuovo Val di Cecina [. . .]. Thus, in order to follow the successive phases of the German retreat, one merely has to retrace the path of the scenes of the martyrdom of Tuscany, devastated by Kesselring's army: every massacre a pre-arranged stage. Along the Arezzo-Florence line of retreat, from South to North, San Giovanni Valdarno [. . .] and then up near Florence [. . .] at Marradi; Figline di Prato [. . .]. There was not a single zone of Tuscany, having a road of some importance, where the Nazi fury did not rage, increasing in intensity as it pushed northwards until it reached its highest point in the Province of Pistoia [. . .] near Padule di Fucecchio. The Nazi army carried out, to the letter [. . .] the orders [. . .] of Marshal Kesselring. [. . .] It transpired, in fact, from his memoirs [. . .] how "the war against the [partisan] bands had to be considered, tactically, on the same plane as the war at the front."[1]

It was not easy for someone like me, whose family was directly affected by the Tuscan tragedy, to read those documents. Fortunately, the book that emerged from the research provoked discussions both within and outside the academic world. Consequently, the so-called war against civilians also acquired a certain dignity as a historiographic subject, so much so that it was at the center of attention of an important international conference.[2]

I have on several occasions been assailed by doubt as to whether I was posing the right question when examining archive material. The British documents, together with those found in the Italian, German and American archives, certainly provided the answers to the queries about the genesis of the individual massacres, but as far as I was concerned, this documentation only acquired full meaning when it was considered as a whole. Very often, in fact, the inquiries into various episodes were full of references to other episodes, and the duplicates of some documents were to be found in files dealing with different cases. The investigators had continually linked the various episodes, not only because those responsible had been the same—whether the army units or the officers in command—but also because the dynamics of these episodes had appeared extraordinarily similar. As I compared documents and cases, it was not difficult to conclude that in reality all the files had been part of a single general investigation, which had originally been concerned with the military apparatus that the German occupation system had organized to fight the Partisan movement and the recalcitrance of the civilian population. The investigators themselves had termed that apparatus "the machinery of reprisals."

Between April and August of 1946, English investigators who wanted to assess the criminal nature of the mechanism of terror, had thought it necessary to organize a single major trial of the principal perpetrators, several dozen high-ranking officers and commanders of the armed forces, and the police. They had even considered utilizing the personnel and structures of the International Military Tribunal of Nuremberg for that trial. Without furnishing any explanation, however, in the course of a few months the English investigators had abandoned the idea of an Italian Nuremberg. The files were, therefore, only the residual pieces of the general inquiry: they had been separated from the original body of evidence for use in other trials of minor significance that had only been organized after the possibility of holding the major trial had been abandoned. It was not easy to track down the evidence of that phantom trial, as its documents had been separated in different preliminary investigations. In fact, there remained only a few indications of the juridical and political debate that had led to the abandoning of the major trial.

In these pages I have tried to reconstruct that scenario, reassembling the elements of the preliminary investigations of the trial that was never held, in order to follow up the consequences of that unrealized act of justice on the law and on the public memory. Since the postwar period, this unrealized judicial act has, in fact, had serious repercussions in terms of the repression and the selective and partial reconstruction of the recent past.

However, repression and selectivity have not disappeared even in subsequent decades. The trial of Erich Priebke began in Rome on May 7, 1996. Among the first decisions made by the military court there was an extremely serious one that completely nullified from the outset the possibility that the trial could shed any light on the tragedy of the Ardeatine Caves.[3] As a matter of fact, the court decided to forego listening to a witness, Colonel Dietrich Beelitz, who, in the spring of 1944, had held the difficult post of Marshal Kesselring's operational chief of staff.[4] If, in 1946, the inquiry into the mechanism of terror had been brought to a conclusion and those responsible had been put on trial, the key testimony of the witness Beelitz would have emerged fifty years earlier. The Italian military judges of 1996 could not have ignored the significance of the mechanism of terror that was put into effect by the whole army and not just by the specialized SS troops.

The first Priebke trial also turned out to be disastrous in other ways. Paradoxically, the Nazi officer came to be considered, by a section of public opinion, as a victim of the survivors of 1944 and of those who had witnessed the Holocaust: the explosion of anger on the part of the Jews of Rome in the course of the first hearings provoked reactions of alarm and irritation, and it was met by total intolerance; it was, in fact, seen as a fanatic insistence that the massacre of the European Jews was somehow unique, ignoring the other genocides of the twentieth century. Thus, the Priebke trial and the reactions public opinion that accompanied it succeeded in overturning the sentiment that had existed in 1944 that sympathized with the victims and excoriated their tormentors; this showed how there was by now, even in Italy, a fragile, distorted, unresolved relationship between society and its past, its memories and its history.[5]

Not only was Priebke's acquittal in itself sufficient to disqualify the military judges, but it also demonstrated that the Italian public believed him to be a victim. Priebke's crime against humanity even came to be reduced to a matter of opinion, revealing a situation tantamount to a moral and cultural emergency. Anti-Fascism was sinking, while there re-emerged an old tendency to reject all the historiography of the last half century and to accuse it of being ideological and unjust, written only for the benefit of the victors.

While I was writing a book on the war against civilians in Italy in 1944,[6] the symptoms of the Italian disease were multiplying. The pathology of recollection and of the faculty of distinguishing between war crimes and crimes against humanity were becoming intertwined with a cultural relativism, certainly not exclusively Italian, but here aggravated by the ambiguous combination of a tendency to return towards Republican Fascism and the lack of critical judgment regarding the totalitarian communist systems of Eastern Europe (and their link with the history of the parties of the Italian working-class movement). The mental confusion was certainly the result of silence, censorship, contradictions, and extraordinary indifference, but it could not be separated from other involutional phenomena, widespread throughout Europe in the 1990s. On the other hand, it was becoming unavoidable to consider the whole century of the Fosse Ardeatine and the *foibe*, by reassembling the fragments, without ending up comparing the numbers of victims, in a new, meaningless ideological war transposed to a historiographic or academic plane. I began to think that it was, at this point, absolutely necessary to go back to the immediate postwar period, which had witnessed the establishment of the terms within which, for fifty years, the war had been seen, and to the postwar presentation of history based on the "Nuremberg consensus," namely, the trial sentences characterized by a very strong emphasis on both education and memory, but which remained, as such, without adequate critical historiographic consideration.

The post-1945 trials—among those conducted by the British authorities in Italy, the most important being the trial of Marshal Kesselring—had, in fact, been justified by a two-fold aim: punishment of the leading political and military figures of the Axis and the "democratic re-education" of the nations governed by totalitarian regimes. The way these trials were conducted transformed the second "pedagogical" function into a standardization of the institutions in line with the Western democracies, without, however, purging the culture, the public spirit, and the collective morality of these societies of Nazism and Fascism. Grandiose public spectacles, the great trials of the "war criminals" ended in a glorification of the victors and a demonization of the vanquished, without the ruling classes of the Allied nations showing themselves capable of considering the relationship between totalitarianism and European history. The political rules, the juridical categories, and the judicial procedures have created an infinite number of events that can be traced back to the war in terms of an extremely simplified viewpoint that was itself incapable of explaining what the totalitarian system had been. The political-legal aims, laid down *a priori* by the Allied countries in preparing the cases for trial, starting with the Nuremberg International Military Tribunal, had a profound effect on the public presentation of National Socialist criminality. Only some of the characteristics of totalitarianism and its violent actions were taken into consideration, distorting the perception of the Jewish genocide itself. The trials were a decisive aspect of the Allied occupation policy in the Axis countries and thus became essential instruments in the breaking down and recomposition of historical reality.

This book is an attempt to consider the trials—both those that were held and those that were not—as the results of the deconstruction of memory. My hypothesis is that the judicial re-presentation of the war offered by the trials of the second half of the 1940s—the trials, conducted by the Allies, of the leading political and military figures of the Axis, as well as the purging trials in individual countries—has provided, for a long time, the categories of a selective memory. This has hindered an understanding of some deep-seated causes of the destruction of Europe between 1939 and 1945. It is as if the recent past has obscured the distant past.

Marc Bloch, in his incomparable account of the fall of France in 1940, wrote, "It is not long ago when the victims of war in the plundered countryside, reduced to hunger, or along the streets of the pillaged cities, were more numerous than among the ranks of the combatants. But who remembered it? [. . .] For the average man, the recent past is a convenient shield."[7]

The massacres of the civilian populations perpetrated during World War II were not, however, a return to the killings that accompanied the religious wars of the 1500s. The former can only be understood within the context of what we have defined as the "war against civilians," the destructive techniques of modern warfare and the brutality that characterizes it. A system of orders prepared by the Wehrmacht Headquarters, accepted by the commanders of the SS and of the minor army units, had taken up the action plans already tried out in other martyred areas of Europe and was the organizational basis of the "war against civilians." The punitive mechanism, into which the German military, the SS and the police forces had been integrated, had the effect of partially correcting the disorder produced by the multifaceted and polycratic structure of the occupation system.

The trial documents remain important sources for reconstructing the sequential order of those events and their most distant causes. In particular, the preliminary inquiries carried out by the British investigative authorities and the interrogations of the accused Nazi officers are decisive for reconstructing that "mechanism of terror," as it was then termed by the Special Investigation Branch.

It is necessary to examine these sources with great care. In fact, in the documents of the Public Record Office one can identify a plurality of narrative levels: the reconstruction of the facts according to a circumstantial paradigm; the investigators' regulatory framework; and the juridical principles that direct trials. This means that the significance of those sources is not exclusively confined to the trial proceedings. They presuppose, initially, a prehistory and, subsequently, a clash of power, a struggle regarding the carrying out or the modification of the sentences. That struggle leads one back to the multilayered political parlance and cultural codes deeply embedded in European consciousness.

In particular, the history of the trials held in Italy of some important German officers, starting with the Supreme Commander of the South-West Sector of the Wehrmacht, Marshal Kesselring, presupposes a long preliminary series of clashes of power about the juridical bases of the trials themselves, what type of trials would be held, and who would have the authority to hold them.

It was the status as a cobelligerent country on the side of the Allies, attained by Italy on October 13, 1943, that enabled the UN War Crimes Commission—already charged with investigating the war crimes perpetrated by the troops of the Third Reich against the Allied military, prisoners, and the civilian populations of the occupied countries—to extend its area of competence to include Italy. However, Italy could not participate directly in the proceedings because of the role it had played within the Axis up to September 8, 1943, which made it a State subject to investigation for the war crimes committed by its troops in the countries it had occupied together with Germany. The UN War Crimes Commission therefore assigned the Italian case to a subcommission, the War Crime Commission for Italy, retaining for itself the main responsibility for the setting up of the International Military Tribunal, which would have conducted the "Italian Nuremberg" Trials, with an aim defined at that time in a phrase that appears to me to be extremely significant, especially in the context of this work: "not only in the interests of justice, but more generally in the interests of security." The distinction between the two principles, security and justice, constitutes a decisive element for interpreting the judicial and political nature of the trials of the leading figures of the Third Reich within the framework of the European situation, as well as the trials held in Italy itself. From May 1945, the UN Commission collaborated with the Italian government's War Crimes Central Commission, presided over by Undersecretary Aldobrando Medici-Tornaquinci. Notwithstanding the contrary view of the Minister for Occupied Italy, Mauro Scoccimarro, that collaboration was reduced by the Allies solely to the investigative sphere. The holding of the trials was instead the exclusive reserve of the English military courts of justice, "for reasons of justice and expediency."

This idea of expediency is also very significant. It was, however, a subsequent decision that constituted the turning point. As late as May 1946, the British authorities felt they could prosecute the "German commanders responsible for the policy of reprisals and its planning" in a single trial. A few months later, the idea of holding only separate trials prevailed. What had brought about this change of policy? What was it that nullified what the English themselves were beginning to call the "Italian Nuremberg"?

There were probably three decisive causal factors: First, there had not been an unconditional surrender. Second, there was a power struggle between the Italian Ambassador in London, Count Nicolò Carandini, and the Judge Advocate General (the Presiding Judge of the Supreme Military Tribunal), Sir Henry Foster MacGeagh, about the handing over to the Allies of the Italian generals held to be responsible for the war crimes perpetrated by the Italian Army in the Balkans. Third, the British feared that a single trial could easily become a political issue ("a matter of policy," as the investigators wrote). As we will see from the sources, such concerns were heightened in the period from April to June 1946—namely, from the time of the spring administrative elections (the first free elections since the Fascist abolition of the office of elected mayor) to the general election and the constitutional referendum of June 2, 1946—which saw a sequence of political battles that brought to light the strength of the left-wing parties and of the antimonarchist feeling in the country. The defeat of the monarchist option in the constitutional referendum would have reinforced British concerns. By not holding a single major trial of the mechanism of terror and those responsible for it, the investigators, however, lost the opportunity to focus on one of the main causes of the massacre of civilians, defined by Colonel V. A. Isham as "the policy of collective reprisals conducted without regard to the distinction between the guilty and the innocent."

With the abandoning of the major trial, the issue shifted from the objective and functional terrain of the "terrorist mechanism" to the ascertaining of Kesselring's cultural predisposition, subjective intentions, and objective responsibilities. It could almost be maintained that the clash between the intentionalist and functionalist schools fought out among the judges preceded that among the historians. (If, at that time, the term "maxi-trial" did not in fact exist, it cannot nevertheless be denied that in effect the choice of a single major trial implied an interpretative hypothesis analogous to that which underpinned the 1987 maxi-trial of the Mafia, namely, the existence of a unified command).[8]

But after all, the Italians also proceeded very half-heartedly. In 1945 they brought to trial the former Minister of the Interior of the RSI (*Repubblica Sociale Italiana*, the Italian Social Republic), Guido Buffarini Guidi, and the ex-Prefect of Milan, Oscar Uccelli; in 1946 Pietro Koch, the head of a band of torturers, General Biagioni of the GNR (*Guardia Nazionale Repubblicana*, the Republican National Guard), and Carlo Basile, the head of the Province of Genoa; in 1947 Prince Junio Valerio Borghese; and in 1950 the Minister of Defense of the RSI, Rodolfo Graziani.

The 1947 trial of Mackensen and Mältzer, commanders of the XIV German Army and of the Rome Military Headquarters, respectively, highlighted the accountability of Kesselring, who had acted "as if the existence of the Partisan movement were the fault of the civilian population." For the episode of the Ardeatine Caves, the judges of the Mackensen-Mältzer trial, believing Kappler's evidence, laid the foundations for the conviction of the two defendants and, above all, of Kesselring himself. In Rome there was a clash between popular protests demanding severe sentences and Vatican pressure for the commuting of the death sentences of the two commanders. The trial of Field Marshal Kesselring, which began in Venice on February 10, 1947, raised the same issues. The English counterespionage officer, Scotland, and the witness Beelitz (a colonel assigned to the operational General Staff) confirmed that the agreement of May 1, 1944, between the Field Marshal and the SS Supreme Commander, Wolff, had conferred on Kesselring the highest authority for the anti-Partisan war. It was proved that he had been responsible for issuing the directives that had led to the implementation of the procedures, defined by the prosecution as "beyond any norm of the rules of war." It was concluded that the massacres had been the result of those procedures, and not of the actions of army units out of control, which would have acted—as the defendant claimed—autonomously because of the chaotic relationships between the Supreme Command and the front. On the contrary, the texts of the Field Marshal's orders contained substantial proof of his identification of the Partisan Movement with the civilian population.

It is not enough, however, to ask oneself why the course of the Kesselring trial followed such a procedure; one should, above all, ask why it was virtually the only trial held in Italy by the Allies. How does one explain why so few trials of German military officials accused of war crimes were held? Here a number of causes come into play, including the British authorities' judicial and political stance and the Italian authorities' double-dealing. The Italian government tried to make use of the outcome of this episode in order to avoid having legal proceedings brought against the Italian military commanders accused of war crimes and to modify the clauses of the peace treaty.

While the Chief Military Prosecutor had passed on his own charges to the UN War Crimes Commission on the basis of the evidence collected by the Commission presided over by Medici-Tornaquinci, which claimed the right to try its former Nazi allies, the government was instead trying to find ways of avoiding handing over the generals responsible for the Balkan massacres, most importantly Mario Roatta and Mario Robotti. Nevertheless, the English authorities' uncertainties in Italy also favored this delaying action, based upon Italy's claiming the right to be responsible itself for trying national war criminals by virtue of its new international status. This trial of strength resulted in the burying of hundreds of proceedings, already initiated, against Nazi war criminals by military prosecutors and passed on to the Chief Military Prosecutor.

The separation between Kesselring's trial, which was assigned to the Allies, and those of lower-ranking officers responsible for specific local episodes, which was assigned to the Italian judiciary, also favored the delay. As is known, the centralization of the data at the Office of the Chief Prosecutor of the Supreme Military Italian Tribunal favored the definitive confiscation of all the proceedings by the Chief Appeal Court Prosecutor Borsari, who was protected by the Foreign Minister Carlo Sforza from 1947 to 1952 and by the Defense Minister Randolfo Pacciardi from 1948 to 1953. After 1954, Borsari's successors, the Chief Appeal Court Prosecutors Mirabella and Santacroce, definitively shelved the bulk of the documents, leaving only those lacking any indication of the names of the perpetrators and therefore harmless. Finally, in 1956, Foreign Minister Gaetano Martino and Defense Minister Emilio Taviani determined to leave the question of the Nazi war criminals definitively in abeyance in order to favor the normalization of relations between Rome and Bonn. However, this was only one aspect of the "minor politics" that Italy was preparing to put into practice in the postwar period. The "major politics" being played out elsewhere in Europe concerned the balance between the various national States in the context of Germany's reconstruction and military and industrial destiny.

The Allies' judicial policy would not have been free of consequences. The defendants themselves were aware of this. It was not by chance that in the course of the trials, their defense deliberately stressed the differences between the German rules of war and those of the Allied countries, as well as the lacunae in international law. The Geneva Convention of 1929 and the preceding ones of The Hague of 1899 and 1907, had, in fact, codified reprisals, taken to mean the killing of hostages, as well as partisan guerrilla fighters, as illegal. Other forms of retaliation, from putting a price on someone's head to bombing raids, provided they were proportionate to the injury sustained, were, however, permissible. In the German codes—the Fleischmann, the List, and the Waltzoog (the last-named having been drawn up in 1941)—the "lacunae" in international law had been extended, amplifying the notion of "permitted reprisals" to include the detention and execution by firing squad of hostages in the event of attacks against the occupying forces. However, the British code—in accordance with which Kesselring was tried—categorically prohibited the killing of civilians and the indiscriminate punishment of entire communities, but remained ambiguous regarding the legality of partisan guerrilla warfare. Finally, there remained the open question as to whether the text of article 50 of the fourth Convention, attached to the second International Hague Peace Conference of 1907, permitted the conception of the war against civilians as practiced by Kesselring.

The purpose of Kesselring's trial, as in all the preceding ones, starting with those at Nuremberg, was, in fact, twofold: to understand the specific nature of Nazi criminality and to permit Germany to be part of the international community. The events of the war came to be interpreted through juridical categories in line with the political aim of democratization without de-Nazification, while the rules and the procedures were concerned with redefining and adapting, to this end, the trial material itself. The trials of the "minor war criminals" held in the various occupied zones—among which should be included that of Kesselring—also necessarily depended upon the system of principles, rules and juridical categories laid down by the Charter of the International Military Tribunal (IMT). As is known, the purpose of the latter had been above all to demonstrate the existence of a Nazi conspiracy to dominate Europe by means of a war practiced with methods contrary to the law. This "intentionalist" approach—in a way intrinsic to criminal law itself—had had as its main consequence the necessity of giving priority to indicting those in charge of the Nazi apparatus, introducing crimes against humanity only as a corollary of the crime against peace (though doing so through the violation of the principle of the non-retroactivity of the law: *nullum crimen sine lege*). Today historians know that the causal mechanism that led to the genocide of the Jews should be identified less with the effect of the Wannsee protocol than with the impasse in the German invasion of the Soviet Union and the consequences it provoked in the territories of the Polish governorate.[9] But in 1946 all this remained of necessity beyond the field of view because of the analytical model adopted in the Nuremberg Charter. The responsibility of the army in the massacres of the civilian populations, starting with those carried out in the course of "Operation Barbarossa," would also thus have been difficult to understand and judge.

This was the case at Nuremberg with regard to Alfred Jodl and Wilhelm Keitel, Chief of Staff of the German Armed Forces and Chief of the Army High Command, respectively. Analogously, in subsequent years, when the other twelve trials, consequent upon the IMT, came to be held, it was not possible to pass sentence on the Chief of the German Army Supreme Command from 1938 to 1941, Walther von Brauchitsch, nor on the conqueror of Poland, Gerd von Rundstedt. The so-called "brain of the Wehrmacht," General Erich von Manstein, also managed to slip free in the end. The British judicial program itself, even though less tied to the intentionalist-conspiratorial pattern devised by the Secretary of the American Department of War, Henry L. Stimson, displayed difficulties in taking into consideration the Wehrmacht's responsibility in the war of extermination. In other words, Kesselring's trial has to be viewed in the context of the lack of understanding of the mechanism of terror that in Italy had integrated the Wehrmacht, the SS, and the police forces. Leniency was not only the result of English concern about the Italian situation, the new wave of anti-Bolshevism, or the reduction of judicial policy to a dependent variable of occupation policy. The pressure exerted by Winston Churchill—as well as by Consverative Peers in the House of Lords, joined by the Archbishop of Chichester, General Harold Alexander, and T. S. Eliot—to save Manstein and commute Kesselring's sentence can be traced back to a mindset incapable of understanding the specific nature of Nazi criminality. The attitude towards the Wehrmacht in general, and Kesselring in particular, virtually reveals the psychological necessity of the British elite to distinguish between the German Army and the Nazi apparatus of the Third Reich. It is, I think, an example of the desperate attempt to keep alive a cultural code common to the victors and the vanquished—of the way in which British Conservatism and Prussianism belonged to the same European tradition—when Liberal, Christian Europe had collapsed beneath the ruins of a new Thirty Years' War.

Chapter 2

Why the Maxi-Trial for War Criminals Was Never Held

The historical situation in Italy between 1943 and 1945—to a certain extent, even up to the attainment of the Republic on June 2, 1946—remains one of the most complex in the European context, during World War II and the transition to the postwar order.

The fall of the regime in July, 1943, owing to the fact that the ruling class and the house of Savoy—and, subsequently, the Catholic Church—distanced themselves from Mussolini; the proclamation of the Armistice, with the ensuing declaration of war against Germany, enabled Italy to make a sudden leap into the camp of those who, until then, had been the enemies of the Axis. But this triggered tragic consequences within the country and notable political repercussions among the Allies of the anti-Fascist coalition. The transition from the Axis alliance to cobelligerence with the Anglo-Americans in fact nullified the hypothesis, prevalent among the Allies up to that time, of applying to Italy the terms of unconditional surrender (which were to be imposed on Germany). It disrupted the diplomatic understanding previously reached by the Anglo-Americans and the Soviets regarding the configuration Europe would have assumed after its liberation from the new Hitlerian order, starting with the question of Polish frontiers.[1] The disastrous conduct of the government, King Victor Emanuel III, and Badoglio after the public proclamation of the Armistice on September 8, 1943, led to the break-up of the Italian State and the division of the country. Concurrently, no anti-Fascist political force—not even those closest to the influential centers of power of the Vatican and the Court, such as the Catholics and the Liberals—succeeded in having a political say.

The "Black September" of 1943 can be considered the inevitable result of the inconsistencies in the conduct of the Court and the Badoglio Government. The Allies were forced to proclaim the Armistice publicly to reveal Italy's intentions, even though they were unable to carry out a military landing north of the capital that would perhaps have determined a different outcome for Rome and the war in Italy. They succeeded, after a difficult landing at Salerno, in pushing towards what the Germans called the "Gustav Line" and which, from the Garigliano north of Naples, reached the Adriatic south of Pescara. Here the military situation was to remain static until May 1944.

Below that line, the occupying regime of the Anglo-Americans established itself and, at least officially, the sovereignty of the Italian Monarchy (the so-called "Kingdom of the South") was established. At the same time, in the North of the country a system of German occupation installed itself and, up to the Apennine chain, the Italian Social Republic (RSI) exercised limited sovereignty. Italy, as Federico Chabod wrote, was divided into three zones, under different political regimes: the South, occupied by the Allies, with a restricted portion of its territory officially under royal sovereignty; the center, under German military control (at least until the summer of 1944), but in which the Fascist Republic made its presence felt to a certain extent; and the North, governed by the RSI, dominated economically and militarily by the Germans and the scene of the struggle against both by the forces of the Resistance.[2]

The decision of the Allied High Command to consider Italy as a decidedly less important front compared to that opened in France in June 1944 and that of Central-Eastern Europe brought about the enervating protraction of military operations, material destruction and the suffering of the civilian population. The various "Italies" thus lived and suffered very different political and wartime experiences.[3]

It was Benedetto Croce who spoke of an Italy cut in two. In his diary he recorded his doubts about the historical meaning of a war being fought on national territory between two foreign armies—a situation, however, already experienced by Italy in past centuries—while a civil war between Italians was being waged.[4]

September 8, 1943, opened an institutional vacuum into which plummeted many conflicting political factions; every Italian was now forced—an unusual occurrence in a nation's history—to choose which faction he would follow.[5] A new civil war between the opposing concepts of what the nation stood for aggravated and deepened a rift in the national community that can be traced back to a much more distant past. Weighing heavily on this tragedy were the means and the time span of the establishment of the unified State—namely, the Risorgimento—and, above all, the rifts that had occurred in subsequent decades between the State and the lower classes, which had split into the masses faithful to the Catholic Church and the

Socialist workers and peasants. The Fascist regime, after the end of the civil war of 1919–22, had severed the link between the nation and freedom—which had been developing during the Risorgimento—provoking a moral trauma whose after-effects exploded in 1936 in Spain, when the Italians, sent by the Fascist regime to support the generals' *pronunciamiento* against Spanish democracy, found themselves fighting against other Italians who had rushed to defend the Republic.[6]

In the Italy of 1943, defeated, divided, controlled by three governments and subject to two occupations, the Resistance, a political and military movement, still fragile and internally divided, did not even dare to think of being able to rebuild the national unity that had, in any case, been so tenuous at the time of the birth of the unified State and that the Fascist regime had definitively swept away.

In the course of that year, in the part of the country already freed from the Nazi occupation and subject to Allied military government, there not only began to emerge a confrontation between the Badoglio government and the CLN (*Comitato di Liberazione Nazionale*, the Committee of National Liberation), there was also the first serious strategic divergence within the CLN. The moderates opposed the democrats on the question of the abdication of King Victor Emanuel III and the convocation of a constituent assembly. This contrast, which was provisionally resolved only thanks to the recognition of the Badoglio government by the Soviet Union and the consequent decision[7] by Palmiro Togliatti, the Communist Party Secretary, to cooperate with the monarchy, made the South the part of the country in which an attempt was made to preserve the continuity of the institutions and machinery of the monarchical State in the post-Fascist State.

As is known, the evolution of events in Central Italy was radically different. In Rome, where the Resistance and the CLN were unable to carry out their role fully, the collapse of the State after September 8 accentuated the function of protecting the population and complementing the State's institutions exercised by the Catholic Church. Nevertheless, central Italy witnessed a great development in the political autonomy of the Resistance movement, starting from the experience of Florence, the first city to be liberated by a Partisan uprising and governed by a free administration nominated by the CLN.

Finally, the political and social experience north of the Gothic Line was different in a region in which, from October 1943, there developed a "duality of power" between the institutions of the Fascist Social Republic and the organizations of the Committee of National Liberation of Northern Italy (recognized by the Bonomi government and the Allied General Maitland Wilson in December 1944[8]). The problem of waging war against the Partisans and the civilian population opposed to the German occupation has, therefore, to be considered within the context of delimited and defined geopolitical parameters: Northern Italy and Tuscany in 1944–45, the period in which the RSI exercised a limited sovereignty only in the regions north of the Tuscan-Emilian Apennines.

The establishment of a National Fascist government had been advocated since September 9, 1943, by the Foreign Minister of the Third Reich. Initially, Von Ribbentrop backed figures who were by then marginal and discredited—Alessandro Pavolini, Renato Ricci, Giovanni Preziosi, and Vittorio Mussolini himself—maintaining that even a minimal presence of the Italian State would have guaranteed a political façade for the German occupation. The birth itself of the RSI, on September 18, 1943, in a resounding imbalance of Fascist and Nazi forces, can be considered an almost wholly German decision.[9] From the beginning its autonomy proved to be greatly conditioned by the preponderance of German strategic interests and their need to control the exploitation of Northern Italy's economic apparatus to set up the transfer of machinery and industrial technology to Germany, as well as to organize the deportation of the national workforce to the Reich.[10] For this reason, Mussolini's strategy of rebuilding the Fascist State through the refounding of the party and an autonomous army had, in the end, to recognize its failure.[11] In fact, the Social Republic exercised limited sovereignty, suffered the humiliation of having its interdepartmental communications controlled by the Nazis and their refusal to repatriate the six hundred thousand military personnel of the Royal Italian Army interned by the Germans after September 8. For his part, Mussolini was continually forced to defer the Republic's constitutive act, the convocation of the Constituent Assembly. The strategic contrast between Hitler and Mussolini emerged heightened and conditioned: suffice it here to refer to some of the more striking instances, such as the outcome of the Conference of Klessheim in April 1944 or the decisions regarding the withdrawal from Rome to Florence in the summer of that same year. The policy of reprisals against the Partisans and the civilian population was itself at the heart of the contrasts.

It should, however, be remembered that the real causes of the neo-Fascist State's crisis of political autonomy stemmed from the fundamental divergence between the strategic interests of the Republic of Salò, which was almost completely dependent upon German military and economic support, and those of Germany, which aimed instead at reducing the neo-Fascist government to the level of a satellite and exploiting Italian territory economically and militarily, expecting the new apparatus merely to give the occupation a political façade.[12] The struggle between the new

Republican leaders for the control of the many rival militias and police forces available to the government of Salò led to the creation of numerous small armies of a private nature that tended to obey only their own local leaders and have a tenuous relationship with the central authority of government. The political and military chaos into which the Fascist Republican system plummeted nullified its claim that it was "alleviating" the German occupation.[13]

As Claudio Pavone has noted, of the two indivisible faces of modern totalitarianism, Leviathan or Behemoth (the hierarchical order imposed on the whole of society or the chaos that can arise from the fragmentation of unregulated powers due to the absence of norms), the RSI mainly manifested the second. This did not prevent the occupying system from enacting a policy of terrorism, in which the institutions and the men of the RSI were totally involved.[14] On the other hand, the RSI's own armed forces, under the command of General Rodolfo Graziani and incorporated with the German forces under the name of the Army of Liguria, were hardly deployed in the front line. However, once placed under the supreme authority of Kesselring, they were almost exclusively employed in anti-Partisan actions, while Ricci's Republican National Guard always received scant autonomy from the commanding authority of the police forces and the SS. This humiliating condition has its roots in the Germans' lack of confidence in the reliability of their ally's military system. This attitude can be traced back to the last months of 1942, when Himmler had foreseen the collapse of the Italian Armed Forces and had already suggested a series of countermeasures, including the assumption by the Germans of direct responsibility for the defense of Italian territory.[15]

The German occupation system in Italy—as we know thanks to Enzo Collotti and Lutz Klinkhammer—had a complicated history. The disordered procedures could be traced back to the duality between the institutions, bureaucracies, and ministries of the German State on the one hand and the political bodies of the Nazi system on the other. The delegates of the Sauckel and Todt organizations, those charged with economic planning, as well as the police and the SS, for example, had been coupled with the structures of the German State and often deprived them of their functions.[16] The war and the requirements of the wartime economy called, furthermore, for a greater integration of the two levels of the dual State and, therefore, of the institutions of the occupying structure, while the system seemed to be governed by a dynamics that continued to undermine its internal order.

The way in which the German occupying system came to be set up is of particular interest to us because it had, as we will see, important consequences for the planning of the anti-Partisan war and the reprisals against civilians by the Nazi military authorities.

An early order of the Führer, issued on September 10, 1943, in fact directed that Italy should have its own autonomous government, to which Otto Rahn, the plenipotentiary of the Reich's Foreign Minister, von Ribbentrop, would have been assigned to represent German interests.[17] Rahn would have exercised his own direct sovereignty over the occupied territories of Northern Italy through the National Socialist organizations, such as Sauckel and Todt, and the apparatus of the police and the SS. Field Marshal Kesselring would instead have represented the supreme military authority south of the Apennine chain while Field Marshal Erwin Rommel would have commanded the group of the B Army in the Po Valley (even if, in fact, Kesselring also had a say in the northern regions, through Quartermaster General Wagner and the territorial military headquarters, which constituted the only structures of territorial government). The Field Marshal was, subsequently, favored with a role of primary responsibility by a second order of the Führer—issued on September 14, 1943, and contradicting the previous one[18]—in accordance with which the political functions and the administrative coordination of occupied Italy would have passed to the military administration under the command of the South-West sector of the Wehrmacht through the formation of military structures analogous with those envisaged by the order of September 10.

Thus the Wehrmacht assumed full responsibility for the operational zone situated south of the Apennine chain from Versilia to the Adriatic, as well as all the coastal areas and those directly annexed by the Reich, such as the Alpenvorland Tiroles and the Adriatische Küstenland, while the remaining territory, of which the Po Valley was the most important, remained officially under Rahn, who acted with the assistance of the Head of the Sichereitsdienst and the Ordnungspolizei (the Security Department and the Security Police), General Harster, and of the Head of the SS, General Wolff (who from May 1944 would also have assumed the command of the SD and the OP). Beginning on May 1, 1944, a new pact—the agreement signed by Kesselring and Wolff—granted Kesselring the responsibility for the anti-Partisan war in the operational zones while Wolff, following the directives issued by the Wehrmacht Headquarters, was to command the major anti-Partisan actions in the North. This began with the actions conducted in August and September 1944 in the Tuscan-Emilian Apennines.[19] Kesselring's own memoirs—whose title in German is very significant: *Soldat bis zum Letzten Tag*[20]—document how the Field Marshal had from the beginning sought to control the war against the Partisan bands, trying to wrest it from the SS and the police. In accordance with the premise that Partisan guerrilla warfare and the control of the population (which he identified with the former) were tasks to be tackled within the sphere of essentially military operations, he had reduced the Resistance—all the Resistance, even the unarmed one of the civilian population—merely to a military affair. His orders, as will be seen, were fully consistent with this strategic design and led to the beginning of a war without quarter that involved the civilian population to a great extent.[21]

The history of the organization and actions of the Resistance is obviously beyond the scope of this book, but it would be worth noting briefly that its organization and political orientation were also anything but homogeneous. It was limited to certain regions of the country. Even though some recent studies have stressed the spontaneous uprising of September 1943, for example, it is common knowledge that, from a political and military point of view, the people of the South did not experience the phenomenon of the Partisan movement.[22]

The fundamental event that characterized Italian history in 1943–45, therefore, remains the profound difference between the political experience of the South and that of Central-Northern Italy. There was also a big difference between the situation in Rome—where the clandestine military organization of the Badoglio government was dramatically overtaken in March 1944 by the CLN and continued to be dominated by the authority of the Church and the Vatican—and that of Tuscany, which instead lived through the experience of the armed struggle. Furthermore, there was the complex structure of the Resistance in Northern Italy, with its marked political pluralism, an extremely varied social composition, and a very pronounced internal tension between the revolutionary component, which aimed at a complete break with the Fascist regime and the monarchic State, and the moderates, who accepted the prospect of the restoration of the structure of the old liberal State.[23]

The military organization of the Resistance, swelled by the massive influx of draft dodgers that occurred after the Republic of Salò's call-up in the autumn and winter of 1943–44 and the spring of 1944, succeeded, nevertheless, in achieving some important results. These included the autonomy of military action and overcoming the difficulties posed by the extremely rapid maneuvers of an enemy who exploited a road and communications infrastructure that was still largely intact. However, the Resistance did not, nor would it have been able to, win a direct military confrontation with the occupying forces, as this was beyond the capabilities of its weapons.[24] The Partisan war, inevitably, turned out to be only an "auxiliary" war in military terms, but it achieved a decisive result on the political plane, attaining the autonomy of the Partisan movement. It acted as a training ground for direct democracy and self-government and thereby legitimized the aspirations of the Italian nation to define the nature of its own political community in the postwar period.[25]

Many of the observations about the diversity of the collective and individual experiences of the Italian population from 1943 to 1945 can also be repeated and confirmed regarding the relationship of armed combatants and unarmed civilians with the exercise of violence.[26]

No observation about violence can be simplistically reduced to the level of a quantitative comparison between the loss of human life in the various European countries. There is, in fact, no point in comparing the much greater losses sustained by the Eastern European nations with the more modest ones in an Italian context (200,000 dead between June 10, 1940, and September 8, 1943, to which should be added the tens of thousands of victims of the civil war, including Partisans, Republican Fascists, and civilians wiped out in reprisals). Arid statistical comparisons risk sidestepping the problem that at the time confronted all those who had lived through the collapse of the State in September 1943: defining one's own identity and, consequently, the possible "option of killing" in the name of opposing concepts of one's country. But the two extremes of the spectrum were represented by, on the one hand, the rejection of violence, regardless of the circumstances that could have justified it and, on the other hand, the acknowledgement of the acceptability of violence legitimized by a historical situation that was considered morally intolerable.[27] The former option risks not distinguishing between the different forms of violence and war. The reconstruction of the second option, however, permits us at least to interpret the ways in which the choice of violence came to manifest itself in the course of the civil war; above all, it permits us to understand the differences between the type of violence exercised by the Resistance fighters and that exercised by the occupying forces and their collaborators.[28] As E. P. Thompson has written, "neither terrorism nor counterterrorism can exhaust their significance in the light of a heavily quantitative examination, since quantities should be seen in a global context, and this also includes the symbolic context that ascribes different values to the different forms of violence."[29]

In 1943 the exercise of violence constituted the outlet for an accumulation of meanings that could be traced back in time, at least to the new significance that the Great War had conferred on mass destruction and war organized on an industrial scale, to which was added the new dimension of total war reached in World War II. Added to this was the end of the State monopoly on violence through the possibility of "settling accounts" with the Fascist regime by armed Partisan action. And yet the reopening of accounts left unsettled since the end of the civil war of 1919–22 certainly could not take on the significance of an absolution for whatever choices were to be made by the Partisan movement. However, violence remained a particularly ambiguous and insidious problem. That "demoniacal" characteristic of which Giaime Pintor wrote, in fact, also touched some of the attitudes of the Partisans, brought on by the terrible inurement to violence produced by continuously being confronted by the spectacle of death.[30] But the range of reactions remained highly diversified. In the world of the symbolic representations of the anti-Fascists, one can find the attitude of the relativization of individual death vis-à-vis a collective tragedy, as well as the assertion of the concept of a just war. A militant thinker like Andrea Caffi instead arrived at a total rejection of ascribing any moral or transcendent value to violence,[31] while the cult of death, which characterized the declarations from Fascism and Nazism,[32] remained alien to the viewpoint of the Resistance.

But in considering the question that interests us here—the military and political mentality with which the upper echelons of the German system of occupation in Italy, (the commanders of the major units, the officers, the military elements of the Wehrmacht, and the various police forces of the SS) dealt with the anti-Fascist war and the measures against the civilian population—one must go back to the cultural structures that permitted the choice of the repressive measures and the selection of the appropriate personnel to apply terrorist practices.[33]

More than in other parts of Western Europe, the Nazi occupation in Italy came, therefore, to be characterized by a succession of episodes of violence throughout its duration. Nevertheless, it certainly cannot be maintained that the massacres of civilians were due to a sort of racial or political prejudice towards the Italians on the part of the upper echelons of the German Army, nor that they can solely be explained by the Wehrmacht's reaction to the betrayal of September 8, 1943 (even if this was a fundamental component of the motive for some of the slaughters, massacres and reprisals in the first weeks following the Armistice). The reasons for the massacres should rather, in my view, be traced to a strategic decision, namely that of the Ober Kommando Wehrmacht (OKW, the Wehrmacht Supreme Command) to defend Italian territory, inch by inch, after the Allied landing in the Gulf of Salerno. Consequently, fighting any civilians, which could in any way constitute a hindrance or an obstacle to army operations, became a military matter to be tackled with the same combat rules as on the front line.[34]

The entire Italian territory, as the German forces were being pushed northwards by the Allied advance and the front line was moving up the peninsula, was involved in the theater of war. The psychological condition of the German troops during the retreat, harried and harassed by guerrilla warfare, certainly favored the propagation of acts of uncontrolled violence. The latter, however, came on top of the effects produced by the political-military line adopted by the Army Command and the mechanism of terror set in motion to realize it. The decisive element that contributed to the escalation of the measures against the civilian population was, therefore, certainly the gradual emergence of Partisan activity during the spring and summer of 1944. The consequent decision to define and prosecute the war against the Partisans and the civilian population as a real "combat front" revealed Kesselring's perception that the civilian population was also responsible for the Partisans' network of connivance (even if this did not correspond at all with the actual situation). This could not but effect a sense of insecurity of the retreating German units.

The Italian population was, in fact, treated with ruthless violence that was legitimized and prescribed by the repressive measures themselves, which were established by orders: beginning in September 1943 it was very clear that the German occupation would not only have constituted a legitimate reaction to the population's possible armed uprising but would have established rules of conduct ordered by the military upper echelons in order to forestall the explosion of potential hostility. It was, thus, a form of vigilance that was "programmed" as the daily demonstration of the occupying force's superiority and as preventative intimidation.

The first measure adopted by the Germans was, in fact, the disarming, capture, and mass deportation of their potentially most dangerous opponents, Italian soldiers. Whoever tried to resist was ruthlessly eliminated in accordance with the orders issued by Keitel, the Supreme Commander of the Army, which authorized the widespread use of violence throughout the Aegean. In fact, on September 12, 1943, Keitel had one of Hitler's orders carried out: the execution by firing squad of all the Italian officers who had consigned their arms to the Greek rebels or who had made common cause with them, as well as the deportation of the soldiers found to be in the same circumstances. In Italy, a few days later, on September 17, 1943, an order was issued for the mass evacuation of the male population from southern areas, while any form of passive resistance on the part of the military and civilians was crushed by the use of terror. In the following months, the Nazi commanders would, however, have understood that in order to combat the embryonic Partisan movement simple police operations were not sufficient. For example, on February 24, 1944, General Kübler issued a drastic order for the Adriatic coast, which had been taken from the RSI's sovereignty, putting into force the orders Hitler had issued on October 18, 1942, relating to the conduct of the war against the Partisan bands in Eastern Europe.[35] Those orders had the aim of smashing both the cover that the population was offering the Partisans and the behavior that was considered collaboration with the Resistance, regardless of the help and support actually given.

Today it is possible to show the existence of a very close link between the anti-Partisan military strategy and the systematic policy of plunder, killing, and terrorism that was enacted to terrorize the civilian population and deprive the Partisan Resistance of the human environment in which it could develop and so constitute a danger behind the front line. It is no coincidence, in fact, that a substantial number of the massacres perpetrated in Italy occurred in the operational zones of the Wehrmacht and in the areas with the greatest concentration of troops.[36] Nevertheless, there are still those who try to make morphological distinctions between the different forms of violence: the reprisals for acts of war carried out by the Partisans, as in the case of the massacre of the Ardeatine Caves or of Via Ghega in Trieste, which involved both civilians and hostages; the massacres of civilians in retaliation or for revenge, though not directly connected with Partisan activity (as at Barletta or the Fosse del Frigido); the slaughters during the rounding up of captured Partisans and prisoners (Benedicta and Montegrappa) or civilians (Vallucciole); and finally the terrorist massacres carried out in the areas having a high concentration of Partisans or at least of great strategic interest, with the goal of breaking the ties between the Resistance and the population, though without a direct link with specific actions of war (Padule di Fucecchio).[37]

What is certain is that the geographical distribution of terror did not spare any Italian region. From Naples to the Volturno, from Abruzzi to the Valle del Sangro, along the Gustav Line there were many massacres—above all in the Terra del Lavoro—which were probably perpetrated to repress a widespread popular rebelliousness and counter the unwillingness to do forced labor. Behind the Gustav Line, between the Lower Valley of the Tiber and the Province of Ascoli Piceno, in a zone enclosed by Latium, Umbria, the Marches, and Abruzzi, there occurred, instead, the first anti-Partisan reprisals (above all around Rieti and the Gran Sasso and in Tuscia). But the largest and most important area in which a total "war against civilians" was put into effect was that behind the Gothic Line: the Province of Arezzo, the Arno Valley, Versilia (between the River Serchio and the River Magra), the Tuscan-Emilian Apennines, where 30 percent of the Italian civilian victims fell (while numerous massacres also took place in the regions directly annexed by the Reich on the Eastern border).

There is, therefore, a geography of the massacres, but there is also their history. In the period of adjustment of the German occupation system, there were, in fact, numerous episodes of retaliation against soldiers of the Italian Army and the civilian population connected with the passing of the front in the Southern regions. The late spring of 1944 was, however, marked by the birth of the real Resistance and the consequent Nazi military reaction, with roundups and reprisals through North and Central Italy. The most sanguinary phase proved to be from May to October 1944, the period in which the Wehrmacht passed from roundups and isolated reprisals to the thorough planning of the repression of Partisan guerrilla warfare and the war against the population, made possible by the new operational directives worked out by Kesselring, which came into effect beginning in June 17, 1944, probably based on a *Bandenbefehl*[38] organized by Keitel in December 1942. This phase above all poses for the historian the problem of interpreting the German mechanism of terror in its relationship to the RSI's autonomous repressive initiatives, and it charcterizes the ordinary army's policy of occupation. As early as 1945, that period was placed at the center of the Allied Investigative authorities' inquiries, and in 1946–47 the authorities offered evidence to establish the main indictment against the so-called "minor war criminals" accused of the crimes committed in the Italian theater of operations.

As Gerhard Schreiber has written, as early as 1941–42 the Italian allies had assumed for the Germans the role of "scapegoat" and had fallen in the Germans' estimation "to the level of a nation without any political importance and belonging to an inferior race."[39] Following the defeats sustained by Italian troops in different theaters, German regard for their ally had plummeted, and Italy began to be suspected of having entered the conflict without proper preparation simply to participate in the share-out of the fruits of victory. From the notes dictated by Hitler to Bormann in the last months of the war, it emerges, however, that it had been the Führer himself, in his own strategy, who had contemplated having Italy enter the war beginning in 1939[40] and that it was only in 1942 and because of Albania that he had begun to ascribe to his partner Mussolini the blame for the delay in initiating "Operation Barbarossa" (the invasion of the Soviet Union) and hence for the failure of the campaign in Eastern Europe. It was obviously a view totally without foundation, but one that nevertheless continued to fuel the feeling of deep contempt on the part of the German High Command for the Army and the personnel of the Italian State.[41] In this context, one can quote the comments made by some members of the General Staff, Jodl, Keitel, Raeden and Lötz, which were colored by distinctly racist assessments of the Italian people and that confirm how, starting from the winter of 1942–43, there had developed, between Rome and Berlin "a by-now unbridgeable psychological, political and moral gap."[42]

The German commanders in Italy also came to be involved in this crisis of confidence. After September 8, 1943, Kesselring, who had been appointed Senior Commander of the Southern Armies and was responsible for the military operations below the line separating his forces from Heeresgruppe B, had a violent reaction at the news of the Armistice. He immediately issued two orders (completely contrary to the rules of war) that envisaged the execution by firing squad of the Italian commanders and officers whose troops had not surrendered their weapons or who had offered resistance to the German initiative. From that moment on, the German commanders deliberately ignored the obligation of loyalty that bound the Italian military to their sovereign—which, naturally, remained in force even after the declaration of the Armistice—and considered the Italian military's opposition to disarming as an act of hostility. In the following days, the directives issued by Keitel's Supreme Command, with the aim of limiting the indiscriminate executions by firing squad and the slaughters, prescribed this penalty only for the officers who had "made common cause with the rebels," but these new orders were never applied and so did not prevent the massacres in the Aegean, Corsica, Albania, and Slovenia. "Not even during the war of annihilation against the Soviet Union did the Nazi regime resort to similar reprisals. In fact, neither the officers nor the troops of the Red Army, who, in obeying orders, offered resistance, were ever threatened with retaliatory measures."[43]

As Schreiber suggests, the case of the mass execution of Italian officers and soldiers recalls, if anything, that envisaged by the decree of June 6, 1941, against the political commissars of the Red Army. The massacres of the Italian troops constituted the immediate precedent for the "war on civilians." The death of about ten thousand defenseless victims killed between 1944 and 1945 in the course of anti-Partisan reprisals (or more often unconnected with anti-Partisan actions), as well as the elimination of tens of thousands of Resistance fighters, can, however, be traced back to different causes. Trial sources, in particular the interrogations of Kesselring and his successor Heinrich Vietinghoff, crosschecked with the documents of the Wehrmacht and the Anglo-American forces, in fact demonstrate that the orders issued for the anti-Partisan war in Italy were based on the general directives of the army for the military action against the civilian population already adopted in Eastern Europe. In fact, in November 1942, a combat directive had been issued to declare war against the rebel bands in the East, (*Kampfenweisung für die Bandenbekämpfung in Osten*); in December of the same year it was followed by an order for the war against the bands in Eastern Europe (*Bandenbekämpfung*).[44] In these documents, the criterion for defining affiliation to the bands had been formulated in terms so vague that, in effect, they made possible an indiscriminate war against civilians. In the period following September 8, 1943, some orders were issued for the Italian theater of war, whose texts directly reproduce or indirectly take up the directives of November and December formulated for the Eastern Front. The commanders in Italy thus prescribed mass terror procedures that favored the indiscriminate use of repressive measures.

The evidence of a thorough "programming" of the campaigns of terror is massive. See, for example, order no. 9, issued on February 24, 1944, by General Ludwig Kübler, the military commander of the Adriatic coast operational zone. It is full of instructions for the troops on the need to adopt "a conduct towards the rebels" of "unprecedented ruthlessness," and, furthermore, the text contains guarantees of abundant assurances on the protection that the upper military echelons would have provided for the officers who had adopted "every measure corresponding with this principle."[45] Equally explicit were the orders issued by Kesselring that beginning April 6—and especially after June 17, 1944—intensified the general strategy of the direct war against the Italian civilian population, aiming in particular at blocking the possible links between the civilian population and the rebel bands. The threshold of moral restraint towards the civilian population collapsed completely. At the end of June, Kesselring and the Supreme Commander of the SS and the police, SS-Obergruppenführer and General of the Waffen SS, Karl F. O. Wolff, defined in a formal document their respective roles: the supreme direction of the fight against the Partisan bands throughout Italian territory would have been under the charge of Kesselring, who would also have "operational responsibility" in the army's zone of operations south of the Green (or Gothic) Line and along the coasts, while outside these parameters the operational command would have come under the authority of Wolff.[46] The line that Kesselring began to follow in relation to the civilian population at the end of spring 1944 is well illustrated by an additional document that was attached to the records during the trial brought against him by the English authorities between February and May 1947:

> Every village in which bandits have been found or there have been reports of attacks on German or Italian soldiers in order to damage or destroy war materials, will be completely razed to the ground. Furthermore, all the male inhabitants, aged 18 or over, of the place will be executed by firing squad. The women and the girls will be interned in labor camps.[47]

Also guided by the same line of conduct were the directives and orders issued by the army corps and divisional commanders, such as General Lemelsen (July 3, 1944), General Dorstler (July 5, 1944) and von Hoffmann, the commander of the First Parachute Army Corps. It is particularly interesting to compare the letter of May 10; Kesselring's order of June 17, 1944; the subsequent one of June 20 (relating to "anti-Partisan measures"); and the text transmitted to his own troops by von Hoffmann on July 20, 1944. The letter of May 10 and the order of June 17, 1944, carried the same directive:

> The war against the Partisans must be waged with all the means at our disposal and with the greatest severity. I will protect those commanders who could go too far in their methods of fighting the Partisans. In this case, the old adage sounds appropriate: it is better to err in the choice of a method, but follow orders, rather be negligent or not follow them at all.

The communication of June 20, addressed to the commanders of the X and XIV Armies, the SS, and the Navy stated,

> In my appeal to the Italians I have announced that severe measures would be taken against the Partisans. This statement must not represent an empty threat. It is the precise duty of all the troops and the police under my command to adopt the severest measures. Every act of violence committed by the Partisans must be punished immediately. Reports must provide detailed information about the countermeasures undertaken. Where there is a considerable presence of Partisan bands, a certain percentage of the male population will have to be arrested and, in the event of acts of violence occurring, these men will be executed by firing squad. The population must be informed of this. If the sound of shots is heard coming from a village, then it will be burnt down and those responsible, as well as the leaders of the bands, will be hanged in the public square. Neighbouring villages must be held responsible for sabotage to cables or damage to tyres. The most effective countermeasure is the use of local patrols. The members of the Fascist Party must not be included in the reprisal measures, suspects must be handed over to the Prefects and the reports on their cases must be sent to me. Outside the villages, soldiers must protect themselves with firearms. The commander of each military district will decide if and in which city it will be necessary to transport arms. Any kind of pillage or plunder is prohibited and will be severely punished. The countermeasures must be harsh, but just. The dignity of the German soldier demands it.[48]

In von Hoffmann's text, one finds the same tactical guidelines and above all a complete re-tracing of the direction regarding the preventative roundups of hostages to be executed by firing squad as a terrorist countermeasure in the event of any Partisan guerrilla warfare actions, as well as the guarantee of legal protection for the officers who would have adopted these measures clearly contrary to the legal rules of war.

> b) Where there are Partisans in considerable numbers, hostages will be taken from the local population and will be executed by firing squad in the event of acts of violence occurring. The population will be informed of this when the arrests will have been effected [. . .]. Execution by firing squad will also be immediate for: whoever helps the Partisan criminals and traitors, by giving them food and lodging, or carrying military messages, whoever carries arms (including hunting rifles) or explosives, whoever commits acts hostile to the German Armed Forces. I will protect any officers who could go beyond our traditional moderation in his choice of measures for confronting the Partisans, or in the severity with which these measures are applied. In this case what counts is the old principle that it is better to act and make mistakes rather than do nothing and be weak. Every forceful and immediate intervention is an essential punishment and a deterrent to stifle at birth excesses on a greater scale.[49]

The evidence of the almost literal similarity between the two formulations remained in abeyance for a long time among the documents of the preliminary investigation of general proceedings, for a long time catalogued as *Judge Advocate General Military Tribunal, London, War Crimes German Generals*, which should have given rise to a unified trial for the war crimes committed in Italy by German forces.[50] As we shall see, the evidence would only have surfaced *in extremis*, during Kesselring's trial in Venice. And yet the investigators had, a long time ago, arrived very close to the truth, as is clear from another document, the long report attached to the folder dealing with *War Crimes of German Generals* and drawn up, at the end of the war, with particular regard to the system of orders issued by the Army Headquarters. The British investigator comments:

> The severity with which the Commander-in-Chief of the South-West Sector examined the question of the Partisans and the measures he instituted to combat them can be seen in the directives of 17 June 1944, through which he instructed all the formations under his command. The first paragraph of this order is sufficiently exhaustive:
>
> [Here the investigator quotes from Kesselring's statement]:
>
> The problem of the Partisans in Italy, particularly in Central Italy, has recently worsened, and this constitutes a serious danger for the combat troops and the supplies, both as regards war materials and the economic potential. The war against the Partisans must be waged with all the means at our disposal and with the greatest severity. I will protect those commanders who could go too far in their methods of fighting the Partisans. In this case,

what is appropriate is the old proverb which says: it is better to err in the choice of a method, but follow orders rather than be negligent or not follow them at all. [. . .]

The file, found at the Headquarters of the Supreme Command of the South-West Sector, is not, unfortunately, complete for this period, but the detailed nature of the countermeasures can be deduced from the group of documents sent from the Bologna Military Headquarters to all the local headquarters, and found in the office of the Castiglione dei Pepoli Headquarters. These documents include a directive from the South-West Commander-in-Chief of 20 June 1944, in which it is stated that

[. . .] where there is a considerable presence of Partisan bands, a percentage of the male population of the area will have to be arrested and, in the event of acts of violence occurring, these men will be executed by firing squad [. . .].

Finally, in the Bologna file one finds a further list of orders of that period dated 1 August 1944, in which there are two interesting points:

(a) Relates an order from the Führer according to which civilians must not be tried, not even by a Court Martial, for acts committed in the course of Partisan activities (it appears with another order from the Führer found in Crete, and dated 10 July 1944).

(b) Specifically stated that if German soldiers fall victim to civilian attacks, ten able-bodied Italians will be shot for every German killed [. . .]

The investigator also hypothesizes a direct link between the terrorist measures envisaged in the orders given to the various army corps and the line formulated by the Field Marshal.

A further list of orders in force at the time, in the same form, appears in the directives issued by the 1st Parachute Corps on July 20, 1944, and turns out to be nothing other than a combination of the license to commit atrocities sent out by Kesselring on June 17, 1944, and the detailed directives issued by him on June 20, 1944. The repetition of the same orders in the directives for the 1st Parachute Corps confirms that these orders had been issued by Field Marshal Kesselring to all the troops under his command and, therefore, that they were not limited to the area of the Commander of the Bologna Military Headquarters.[51]

The British investigator went further, hypothesizing that the measures adopted against the Partisan movement and the civilian population in Italy should be traced back to the strategic turning point imposed on the anti-Partisan war by the Supreme Commander Keitel beginning in 1942, on direct orders from Hitler, and initially applied on the Eastern Front. After the "abrupt Italian volte-face" its consequences would have been extended to the Mediterranean Front and the peninsula.

There is no evidence in the files that can clearly indicate whether the orders for reprisals had been issued by the Commander in Chief of the South-West Sector under his own authority, or if they had come from the German High Command. It is, nevertheless, interesting to make a comparison with the order signed by General Keitel, Chief of the High Command, dated December 1942 and found in Crete. (The original of this order was sent to the Minister of War under cover of the Allied Forces Headquarters with the letter G1 [Br] 15012/A-3 of June 4, 1945.) It refers to an order of the Führer that, in the war against the Partisans in the Balkans and the East, authorized the unrestricted use of any means—even against women and children—in order to guarantee success, adding that the German soldiers employed against the Partisans would not be held responsible for their actions and therefore would not be subject to any disciplinary action or court martial. It does not seem an improbable deduction that similar orders had been given by the High Command to the Commander in Chief of the South-West Sector.[52]

The document also appears to be of great value because of further information relating to "the Duce's complaints, passed on by the Reich's plenipotentiary, regarding [. . .] the atrocities committed by German troops against innocent civilians."

In fact, the British investigator linked this initiative with the partial change of policy that would have been undertaken by the Field Marshal with the new order of August 21 and the letter dated September 24, a copy of which was found in the Headquarters of the XIV Army. These two documents presented new forms of safeguards for civilians, such as the creation of courts martial and "preliminary trials of the people who were to be the object of reprisals." Such measures were definitely established on February 8, 1945, without, however, their representing a real change in the strategy of the war against civilians. The British investigator's conclusion appears, in this context, unambiguous.

The deletion in the new order of all references to the execution of hostages could seem at first sight an instance of humanity and could undoubtedly also serve as a justification for all the German commanders responsible for massacres. But that this is not the case is clearly demonstrated in the first draft of the memorandum prepared for Sturmbannführer Wenner. In this one can clearly read that the reason for the change of policy lay in the fact that that method did not pay.[53]

The writer of the document showed that he also had very clear ideas as to where the responsibility lay:

> Germany was, at that time, involved in operations on four fronts: Russia, France, the Balkans, and Italy, and it was clear that the orders relating to

> anti-Partisan operations, as well as those against civilian populations, had undoubtedly been issued by the Army High Command, after the Führer and the High Command had, in their turn, imposed very severe measures. The directives issued by Kesselring had, therefore, originated from the Führer's Headquarters, after which Himmler had phoned Wolff several times, asking him to be more committed to the severity of the reprisal measures, while Keitel himself had stressed the need for extreme measures. [. . .]. The reprisals were not, therefore, carried out following individual orders issued by the commanders of German formations, but were the result of a campaign organized and directed by Field Marshal Kesselring's Headquarters.[54]

The belated protests of the head of the RSI in August 1944 would only have resulted in the embarrassing admission by the Germans that some excesses against civilians had perhaps been committed, but the Führer's new order of July 30 and the directives issued by Kesselring in August had not modified the procedures set in motion with the two preceding series of measures.[55]

It seems, therefore, that these documents offer indisputable evidence of the strategic viewpoint and attitude of the German commanders. And yet the interpretations of the massacres of civilians—which occurred during World War II and in particular those perpetrated in Italy—do not find complete accord among the historians who are concerned with this problem. For some, in fact, the phenomenon is not very different from the horrors that have occurred in the wars of every age. Marc Bloch, however, does not agree, noting that the bloody involvement of populations was a new phenomenon in the wars of the 1700s and 1800s, but World War II had spread it with the use of new destructive technologies.[56]

If it is Claudio Pavone's merit to have put back into the context of the drama of the Partisan and civil war the positions of all those who were involved—the occupying Germans, the Fascist collaborators, the Partisans, and the civilian population—more recently the drama experienced by the civilian population has become a historiographic subject. In the historiography dedicated to the catastrophe experienced by the civilian population, once again the duality between the experience of the Resistance in the North and that of the South seems to resurface.[57]

As has been said, the first massacres took place in Naples and its province at the end of September 1943—shortly before the Anglo-American troops entered the city—in the context of a gigantic roundup operation that aimed at the deportation of 30,000 adult men between the ages of 18 and 33. For reasons that can be traced back not only to the dynamics of those events but above all to the ways in which the public memory of those regions has developed, the Southern massacres sank into oblivion, while the slaughter of the civilian population, in Tuscany and in other regions of the North was already at that time remembered tenaciously in the local communities, even if that memory was sometimes at odds with the "official speeches" of the institutional celebrations of the Resistance promoted by the Republic.

In the course of over half a century of Republican history, the recollections of the massacres have not been handed down in a uniform way, thus hindering the formation of a unified memory. This conflicting and divided memory has, however, proved to be useful in deciphering the perception of the war in different parts of the country, as well as piecing together the fragments of the collective, individual and group psychology of those who were involved in various ways in the civil war. And it is precisely through the archaeological excavation of memory that the link with violence inevitably re-emerges. In fact, a massacre poses again the general question of violence in the context of a total war in which death is at the center of the daily experience of millions of people. It is in a massacre—however one defines it—that many unresolved questions re-present themselves distinctly in the context of war and civil war: the presumed legitimacy of the repressive violence exercised by the State or in the name of the State, the redefinition of the difference between legitimate and illegitimate violence, the problem of legal and moral responsibility, and the subjective perception of violence. This is a tangle in which historical contextualization can in no way resolve all the moral implications, even if it can serve to illuminate, at least in part, the link between the massacres, the Nazi occupation practices, and the dynamics of the civil war. This link was the object of clashes of opinion and feeling from the very beginning of the postwar period. It was, in fact, the civilian population itself, which was affected by the massacres that was totally split over who should shoulder the responsibility for the slaughter, and it sometimes called into question the political and military conduct of the Partisan units and expressed greater resentment towards them than towards the Nazi or Fascist perpetrators of the massacres.[58]

The presence of this attitude was certainly more marked in some quarters, such as among the non-combatants and other sectors of society, as well as in the middle classes and the upper ecclesiastical hierarchy, which was more inclined to wait for the arrival of the Anglo-American Allies and therefore to consider armed action as useless and harmful. Regarding the question of the massacres, the same political and cultural attitudes would, after the war, have become stratified, depositing conflicting individual and collective memories that would even cast doubts on the political value and the symbolic significance of the choice of armed Resistance.[59]

From this point of view, the moral conception that sees massacres as an "inevitability of war" is absolutely typical. Like a bombing raid, a massacre appears to be inevitable, but it is a fatality that could have been avoided if the Partisans' conduct had been guided by a "sense of responsibility."[60]

The memories of the women of the Tuscan villages of Civitella, Cornia, and San Pancrazio, which were struck by the massacres perpetrated on June 29, 1944, by a unit of the Hermann Göring Division, are, from this point of view, paradigmatic:

> in the local recollection, the German will remain [. . .] nevertheless, paradoxically devoid of a personality or moral and political responsibility. A sort of natural force endowed with enormous destructive power, which, however, would not have been harmful if it had been left undisturbed. The blame, instead, lies with those who have taken the responsibility of playing with fire.[61]

In its most extreme expression—precisely that of Tsvetan Todorov—a standpoint of this type leads to a facile rejection of any Partisan initiative "when the benefits do not justify it and the negative effect is foreseeable." Opposing the presumed "morality of the necessity of sacrifice" (the sacrifice of others or oneself on the altar of heroic devotion) that inspires the Partisan actions that resulted in serious consequences for the population is the "morality of risk," which instead remains mindful of the principle of responsibility. According to Todorov's perspective, the armed option thus risks being, in some way, reduced to a negative metaphor for revolutionary politics, which can easily be countered by the pattern of a calculated risk and the art of mediation. The white of the ethics of responsibility comes to be split too easily by the black of warlike ethics and sacrifice. But the ethical dualism put forward by Todorov does not resolve the question of the choice in favor of or against violence. In more general terms, awareness and moral freedom cannot be made to originate only from a careful examination of the context and the conditions in which the decision has to be made. One can be favorable to preventing pathologies, but this does not exclude the possibility that there may be conditions requiring surgery. To do otherwise would only mean washing one's hands of the necessity of offering aid in the face of the threat of death.

There is no doubt that, after September 1943, and above all after June 1944, the Germans organized punitive measures aiming at repressing all forms of opposition and resistance, even passive, by the population. The existence of what the investigators defined as "the mechanism of terror" makes the dilemma between the two presumed moral alternatives, at least in the terms in which it has been put forward by Todorov, absolutely abstract.[62]

My hypothesis is that the key to understanding the war waged by the Nazi system of occupation against the Italian population is to be found earlier on, in the punitive mechanism that began, above all, against the civilians living close to the Tuscan-Emilian Apennine chain, beginning on May 1, 1944. In the course of what Roberto Battaglia has defined as the "slow German retreat towards the Arno," which began after the liberation of Rome by Allied troops, the reasons for the opposition between the two strategies, which had until then been at odds—the "soft" line advocated by Otto Rahn, the representative of the Foreign Ministry, and the "military treatment" of the Partisan movement and the civilian population's resistance, supported by Marshal Kesselring—disappeared. The agreement reached between Kesselring and the SS General, Wolff, encouraged by Keitel and with Himmler's consent, definitively conferred upon the Wehrmacht the responsibility for initiating a real "war" against the Partisans and the civilians in the strategic area between the Apennines and Rome. From the agreement there emerged a repressive mechanism based on the system of orders issued by the German Army Command, which remained in force after the summer of 1944, when it was only partially modified and integrated with new directives, taking on board the negative reactions of some military quarters and Mussolini's protests.[63] The Army's confirmed responsibility in the campaign of terror compels us to consider the role played by the specialized SS units—which, instead, was emphasized at the time and in the postwar period—as less important: today it is assumed that not more than 30 percent of the massacres can be attributed to the two major SS divisions, the XVI Panzergrenadier Reichsführer and the "Hermann Göring." The responsibility for the majority of the actions that led to massacres and slaughters has instead to be ascribed to various units of the army (and it has not even been proved that the units commanded by officers coming from the Eastern European front or the Ost-Bataillone themselves—more used to the sanguinary experiences of the repression exercised in those countries—played a decisive role).[64] The homogeneity of the repressive procedures adopted by single detachments belonging to very different army units can only be explained by the fact that all the military units obeyed the same directives, namely the consistency of the orders issued by the divisional and army corps commanders. These orders—derived from those drawn up by the upper echelons of the X and XIV Armies, stationed, respectively, on the Adriatic and Tyrrhenian fronts—had, in turn, been written following the directives of the Supreme Command in Italy.

The general lines that inspired the reprisals lead back directly to the OKSW (Ober Kommando Süd-West) of Kesselring, who organized the control of the movements of the rebels and the civilian population living along the lines of the German Army's retreat from Rome towards the Arno Front; he paid particular attention to the railway communications between the Apennines and Pisa, Florence, Arezzo, and Ancona in order to ensure the completion of the work on the defense emplacements of the Green Line. Therefore, numerous and massive roundups of the able-bodied male workforce above fifteen years of age were organized, while severe punishments were prescribed for the Social Republic's draft dodgers. The evacuation of entire zones was planned with the aim of guaranteeing the security of certain areas of strategic importance; a typical example was the evacuation plan for the population of the province of Lucca.

The accord reached between the Wehrmacht and the SS-DS apparatus was defined by Allied observers as "a systematic policy of extermination, plunder, and terrorism," which would have been put into effect with procedures "envisaged by repeated orders and realized by an organization geared to the carrying out of collective reprisals (without distinguishing between Partisan fighters and the civilian population), the destruction of the population centers of entire regions, and the capture and elimination of hostages."[65]

The inquiries undertaken by the Allies during the conflict ascertained that the structures involved in the reprisal procedures and the war against the civilians had been the Supreme Headquarters of Kesselring, the commanders of the X and XIV Armies (Vietinghoff and Lemelsen, respectively), as well as the army corps and division commanders (respectively Schramm, Dorstler, and Herr; Conradt, Bölsen, Schrank, Bässler, Roth, and Crasemann). There was evidence that the commander of the SS, Wolff, and of the Waffen SS, Debes, as well as the heads of the Ordnung Polizei, Harster and von Kampf, had also been involved in organizing the mechanism of terror.[66]

On January 13, 1946, Colonel J. E. M. Cunning, Deputy Judge of the Military Tribunal, sent a confidential note to the Presiding Judge of the Tribunal itself:

> This Headquarters intends to bring to trial the German generals responsible for illegal reprisals directed against the Italian population. A report has already been compiled by the AG3, and has been entrusted to the British War Crimes Executive to be used in conjunction with the Nuremberg Trials [. . .]. In this context there are numerous German generals who should be indicted. There is a very large number of officers and non-commissioned officers who could testify as to the responsibility of the various generals with regard to the reprisals. For the moment I have not taken any initiatives about the interrogations, as I felt it was advisable to wait for your opinion on this matter. If you wish the suspects to be interrogated, let me know [. . .]. From

> the documents recovered and the depositions already obtained (app. B), it is obvious that Partisan activity, as early as the beginning of 1944, must have caused grave concern to the German Army. This activity increased following the fall of Rome in June 1944. At the moment we do not have other documents referring to Partisan activity as a serious danger for the German forces, prior to the letter of the Commander in Chief of the South-West Sector, dated 17 June 1944, even though this letter contains information dated 10 May 1944. The situation at that time is, however, reported by the statements of Wolff (B. 114), Roettiger (B. 119), Dollman (B. 121) and Harster (B. 112), and the correspondence regarding the organization of the anti-Partisan activities (from B. 1 to B. 30), which began on 29 March 1944. In particular, the first illegal reprisal took place, according to the information in my possession, at the end of March 1944, and is the subject of a long deposition by Kappler (B. 124) [. . .]. The directives of the Commander-in-Chief of the South-West Sector (Field Marshal Kesselring) regarding the reprisals became operative through two channels.
>
> (a) In the zone of operations and in the area which extended up to 30 Km inland from the coast, through the army commanders;
>
> (b) In the territory behind the front, through the Supreme Commander of the police and the SS.
>
> This was the situation after 29 March 1944 (see B. p. 1).
>
> *Note*: It seems that the responsibility for the anti-Partisan activities in the coastal area (in the above-mentioned 30 Km strip) and in the Adriatic Coast zone of operations (which included more than 30 Km of coastline), in March 1944, lay with the Commander of the von Zangen Army Group.
>
> On 30 April 1944, the Commander-in-Chief of the South-West Sector ordered that, in the Adriatic Coast zone of operations, the anti-guerrilla activities should (in accordance with the agreements reached) be conducted directly by the Supreme Commander of the SS and the Police and the Operational Commander in the zone of the Adriatic Coast (General Kübler) (B. p. 9). The anti-Partisan operations in the 30 Km coastal strip had been entrusted to the headquarters of the Adriatic Coast zone on 18 July 1944, but on 2 September 1944 the responsibility for this zone was transferred to the Supreme Commander of the SS and the Police.[67]

The hypothesis that emerges from this document appears, in my view, to be totally plausible. One can clearly deduce from this document that the reprisal of the Ardeatine Caves of Rome marked a real turning point, which would have been followed by the agreement reached between the Wehrmacht and the SS on May 10, 1944. The so-called " punitive mechanism" was therefore set in motion by Kesselring's order of June 17, 1944, and was further "enriched" with guidelines in messages to the commanders of the operational units sent on July 8 and 20 and in subsequent orders of July 31 and August 5, 6, 8, 12 and 22, regarding the definition of the areas for the anti-Partisan operations and the roundups in the Apennines.[68] Thus, the general line of conduct that emerges from these documents appears to be unambiguous: it envisaged razing to the ground the villages situated in the zones "infested" by the bands, rounding up all the male population and taking hostages to be eliminated in the event of Partisan initiatives, while guaranteeing legal protection for any excesses that could be committed by the commanding officers.[69] It was, in other words, a totally terrorist line of conduct, and it would have been applied systematically by many units subordinate to the Supreme Command, as for example, General Dorstler's LXXV Army Corps, as well as the headquarters of Lucca, Piazza al Serchio, and the Apuan Hills, under the command of the Waffen SS General Bürger, and that (by now well known to us) of the First Parachute Corps. In some cases, Kesselring's line was actually intensified, as in the order issued on July 29, 1944, by General Lemelsen, the commander of the XIV Army: noting that the peasants "participate in various ways in the activities of the bands," he resolved to "issue directives also in order to combat resolutely, with the harshest means, the civilian population."[70]

It was precisely on the basis of Lemelsen's order that in July, August, and September 1944 some major anti-Partisan operations took place in the Apuan Hills, in the northern part of the Garfagnana, and on the Apennine ridge from La Spezia to Parma (the Wallenstein I and II operations).[71] And it was Lemelsen who organized the mass deportation during certain extensive roundups of the civilian population along the Arno, with the aim of creating large, secure zones for the troops behind the front, in the area ten kilometers north and twenty kilometers south of the Gothic Line and in the zone between five and ten kilometers south of the Arno. These zones witnessed the imposition of the total evacuation of the population and the deportation of the men for forced labor in the Apennines: evacuations and deportations that were effected by means of drastic interventions that led to many massacres. In other words, it is clear first that a good part of the massacres that occurred in northwest Tuscany during the summer of 1944 were triggered precisely by the operations planned to guarantee the security of the western sector of the Gothic Line, which was defended by General Lemelsen's XIV Army, and to ensure holding the line of the Arno until September, and second that only in some cases were such operations directed against the presence of Partisan bands.[72]

The "reclamation" of the territory behind Lucca as far as the Lunigiana and the Cisa Pass was entrusted to the XVI Panzergrenadier Division Reichsführer SS; the LXXV Army Corps took on the task of safeguarding the coastal fortifications of the strategic zone between Versilia, Pisa, and the Gulf of La Spezia; and the von Zangen LXXXVII Army Corps had to complete equipping the Green Line.[73] The initial phase of the operations against the Partisans and the civilians, in these and other zones along the Cassia and the Aurelia, took up the long spring and summer period, and in particular the weeks following May 25, 1944, the last day on which those called up by the RSI's army could, of their own free will, report to military offices.

The statements made after the end of the war by captured German officers to Allied investigators and, in this case, particularly by the Military Judge Keller and Colonel Beelitz (who had both been members of Commander Kesselring's staff), confirmed the scale of the operations.[74] If the measures of ethnic cleansing and colonization, such as those applied in the East,[75] were not envisaged for Western Europe, nevertheless, the mechanisms adopted against the Partisan and civilian Resistance—which did not countenance distinctions between combatants and non-combatants—were no less ruthless than the "eastern" ones. [76] The eastern decrees were planned on the basis of Keitel's decrees, the first of May 13, 1941, which provided special measures for the troops in Russia, and the second on June 6, which provided the guidelines for the elimination of the political commissars of the Red Army. The policy of annihilation was based on the drastic decision to "consider any civilian who hindered or encouraged others to hinder the Wehrmacht a Partisan who had to be executed immediately."[77]

In Western Europe, measures analogous to those organized on the Eastern Front had been taken in 1942 by the OKW against the Greek Partisans of the Ellinikós Laikós Apeleftpericon Stratós (The Greek Popular Liberation Army); Harster and Kesselring had discussed their application in Italy as early as 1943, but it was only in the spring of 1944 that they adopted a modified set of measures.[78] A document entitled *Report on German Reprisals for Partisan Activity in Italy*, drawn up at the Mediterranean Forces Headquarters, conveys, for the first time in an explicit way, the evidence that the mechanism organized by Kesselring had taken as a model the measures adopted for Central-Eastern Europe and Greece.[79]

The spring of 1944 witnessed the first exchange of information between the British and American authorities about the war crimes committed by German troops against the Italian population. On March 15, 1944, the British Embassy conveyed to the American Secretary of War the proposal that the UN War Crimes Commission in London, charged with investigating possible war crimes committed by the army and police forces of the Third Reich against the military, the prisoners, and the civilian populations of Allied countries, could also deal with the crimes perpetrated against Italian civilians. The widening of the Commission's range of inquiry therefore occurred as a result of the status of "cobelligerent," which Italy had assumed since the declaration of war against Germany by the Badoglio government on October 13, 1943. The Allies' decision immediately appeared full of implications and consequences that would not be easy to handle: Italy could have produced, with the help of the Allies, evidence for war crimes committed against its own population, but, unlike the Allied nations, it could not have participated fully in the Commission's work because of its position as an enemy country until the first days of September 1943. The reason for the decision was obvious: the Commission also concerned itself with the crimes committed by Italian troops in the countries occupied by the Axis, and if the Italian government had been admitted to the Commission's work, it would have had to examine and judge not only the crimes committed by the Nazis against Italian civilians, but also the war crimes committed by the Italians themselves against Allied troops and the population of the territories occupied by the Axis in the period prior to September 8, 1943.[80]

Beginning in the spring of 1944, the Commission began to receive more and more frequently reports from American Intelligence and the British Special Investigation Branch operating in the peninsula.[81] In addition, it received news sent by the *carabinieri*[82] and Italian public prosecutors' offices, transmitted by the Foreign Minister of the Government of the Kingdom of the South.[83] By August the Allied Forces Headquarters had already drawn up a report entitled *Provisory Report on British Investigation of War Crimes in Italy*:

> On 18 August 1944, a conference was held at the Allied Forces Headquarters with the aim of reorganizing the investigation of war crimes in this territory.
>
> The directives previously issued by this Headquarters envisaged that the investigations would have been carried out by unit commanders, by themselves or with the assistance of the security sections. It was found, however, that the unit commanders did not have enough time to give to such investigations and that the sections lacked the specific experience to bring such investigative cases to a successful conclusion. It was, therefore, decided that, in future, the investigations would have been carried out by sections of the SIB (Special Investigation Branch) [. . .].
>
> The main sources from which the information emerged are the following:
>
> (a) The interrogations of our former prisoners of war who had crossed the lines.
>
> (b) The interrogations of enemy prisoners of war.
>
> (c) The reports of officers of the Allied Military Administration (AmGOT) based on information obtained by them from the civilian authorities.

> (d) The reports of the Partisans who operated behind enemy lines, obtained through the Psychological Warfare Branch [. . .].
>
> There are approximately 200 cases awaiting investigation, and of these 12 have been investigated in detail, while 7 inquiries are still in progress [. . .].
>
> In some cases, particularly when the information comes from enemy prisoners of war, the names of those responsible come to be known before the investigation begins, and these cases receive absolute priority, but even then it can happen that—because of the time which has elapsed between the incident and its reconstruction, or because the population could have abandoned the places in question—there are difficulties in obtaining concrete evidence against the people held to be responsible. Sometimes an entire village has been destroyed and all the inhabitants killed, so that there are no live witnesses or relatives to identify the victims. Once the bodies have been discovered, there are few possibilities of identifying them, except by means of the remaining clothes or some personal object which can be found together with the bodies.[84]

Some of the inquiries were once again referred to the Italian authorities, who were dealing with the trials of Fascist Republicans because in some cases Italians also appeared to be involved.[85] A further request for information about the political and military mechanism that had permitted the "functional organization" of the reprisals was forwarded on December 8, 1945, by the Supreme Military British Tribunal to the Allied Mediterranean Forces Headquarters, which replied by sending a new general report and a detailed investigation of the commanders held responsible for the mechanism of repression.[86] They were followed by other reports drawn up by the British War Crime Section, which had been charged with carrying out the investigations concerning Italy in the context of the inquiry initiated by the UN War Crimes Commission against the "major criminals" of the Axis.[87]

This Commission had been called for by Roosevelt and Lord Simon, the Chancellor of the United Kingdom, after the Allies had already made the decision to proceed with the setting up of a major trial against the leading culprits of the Axis Powers and the Tripartite Pact. As the basis for the judicial action, the definition of "war crime" ratified in 1919 by the Responsibilities Commission of the Paris Peace Conference had been adopted. The UN Commission had defined the extradition procedures, the organization of the tribunals, the classification of the crimes, and the order of the most important trials: after the International Military Tribunal's judgement of the main Nazi and Fascist culprits, there would have been some major trials, for which the Allied Authorities in the single States would have been responsible. The British Government agreed with the American Secretary of State about the setting up of a UN Court charged with trying the major war criminals, "not only in the interest of justice, but in the interest of world security in general":[88] this formula proves that from the beginning the setting up and conduct of the Nuremberg Trials followed not only legal criteria, but also moral and political criteria that aimed, in the first place, to punish Nazism for having unleashed the war and launched an "attack on peace and the world order." The judicial debate was intended to offer a historical interpretation of the political responsibilities of the war, which would have formed "a general guide in dealing with individual war crimes, without unduly restricting the Government."[89]

The juridical basis of the international Nuremberg Trials was, therefore, rigorously established by setting the rules for the investigations and the gathering and the recording of evidence from witnesses, as well as through the drawing up of charges for thirty-three types of crimes, including systematic massacre, killing of hostages, torture, deportation, condemning to starvation, internment, forced labor, plunder, confiscating property, illegal requisitions, the destruction of religious buildings, indiscriminate mass arrests, the directives of a war "without quarter."[90] On the same basis, the War Crimes Commission for Italy began in May 1945 to collaborate with the Italian Government's War Crimes Central Commission, which included the Undersecretary of State, Aldobrando Medici-Tornaquinci; the Divisional Presiding Judge of the Court of Cassation, Saverio Brigante; the Rector of the University of Padua, Prof. Concetto Marchesi; the First Secretary of Legation of the Foreign Ministry, Antonio Cottafavi; the Councillor of the Ministry of the Interior, Francesco Ferrante; Colonel Sormanti of the War Ministry; Dr. Pietro Berretta, a judge; and a lawyer for the CLNAI (*Comitato di Liberazione Nazionale dell'Alta Italia*, the National Liberation Committee for Northern Italy), Arturo della Scala. Mauro Scoccimarro, the Minister for Occupied Italy, in a June 1, 1945, letter sent to Rome to Brigadier General Richmond, Judge Advocate of the US Army, and to Colonel Passingham, of the group belonging to the Allied Army, asked

> that the Allied Authorities would be so good as to give the said Central Commission the documents of the investigations, in their possession, relating to such crimes, as well as the reports or simply the information about them, on the basis of which the Central Commission would carry out a thorough preliminary inquiry.[91]

Beginning immediately with this exchange of letters, the Allies revealed strong misgivings about granting the Italians the possibility of trying Nazi war criminals indicted for the massacres of the civilian population. The main point of the reply drawn up by General Richmond and then sent to Scoccimarro in concise form by Colonel C. W. Christenbury on June 27, 1945, appears unambiguous:

> The majority of war crimes perpetrated in Italy are outrages against Italian civilians carried out by Germans and by Italians under German command. Legal proceedings against such criminals are of primary importance to the Italian authorities and the relative inquiries should be the concern of the Italian Government. Nevertheless, in the absence of an Italian body dedicated to this function, the English and the Americans have carried out the investigations of the cases which occurred in their respective areas of jurisdiction. This department is, therefore, in possession of numerous notifications of the crimes perpetrated in the area occupied by American troops and proposes sending these notifications, bearing the signature of the Adjutant Major of the Allied Forces Headquarters, to the Secretary of the War Crimes Central Commission and conveying, without further investigations, all the information, so far received, about each case.
>
> The crimes committed by the German and the Italians against American and British forces will be investigated by the respective departments, and the criminals brought to trial. None of these cases will be handed over to the Italians.
>
> The scope of the cooperation with the Italians, which has been proposed, following Signor Scoccimarro's letter, will be solely limited to the investigations. In the event that the English and the Americans were, still, to have in custody the accused—sought by the Italians—they would not be handed over unless the transfer is authorized by those jointly responsible for the personnel.[92]

On August 11 of the same year, the Allied Supreme Commander of the Mediterranean theater of war sent a detailed account of the slaughters and massacres suffered by the civilian population in which it was specified that

> It would be fair to think that these trials are the concern of the Italian government, but it is known that that government does not have either the facilities or the energy to bring to a conclusion trials of such significance, and there would be good reasons for fearing that, if the question of responsibility were to present strong legal difficulties, the accused might not receive a fair trial. If the high-ranking German officers have to be tried with impartiality, then it should be the English courts which should do so, and this depends on the fact that the issue is our concern, since we have played a primary role in encouraging the Partisan actions which led to the reprisals.[93]

Apart from the objective factor referred to in the last part of the text (the Allies thought that some of the massacres of the civilian population were a

German reaction provoked by the actions of the Partisans urged by the Anglo-American Command), the reluctance of the British to hand over the accused can only be explained by the political design of reserving for themselves the legal proceedings for the two most important cases, the massacre of the Ardeatine Caves near Rome and the planning of the campaign of reprisals in Italy.[94] From August 1945 to April 1946, the Allied authorities, in fact, thought it possible to prepare cases for those two trials,[95] and they should have taken on the scale of a "second Nuremberg."

> The resources which will be available in this theatre of war depend entirely upon the date of the trial. If, as is expected, it were not to take place until after August 1946, it is thought that its organization will require notable assistance.
>
> It is confirmed that there are expected to be about 50 defence counsels. Since, at the moment, in this area, there are no officers with legal qualifications and in anticipation of a general lack of officers, it would be indispensable for the latter to assist the accused by providing a defence from elsewhere, for example by utilizing German lawyers as counsel for the defence.
>
> As the trial will be rather complex, it is probable that a certain amount of time will be required for it to be concluded. It is felt that the court should be exclusively composed of high-ranking officers, and it is highly improbable that it will be possible to find, in the area, enough officers prepared to dedicate many weeks to the sessions of the war crimes court [. . .].
>
> Using the simultaneous-translation apparatus employed in the Nuremberg Trials would save time, but it would be absolutely impossible to find the technical staff to install such a system. In the event of the Nuremberg Trials already being concluded, we could transport the entire technical apparatus, but we would require the assistance of highly specialized staff and interpreters.[96]

What were the reasons for abandoning the project of holding a major trial for the planning of the terrorist campaign of reprisals against and massacres of the civilian population? Why was attention concentrated (at least apparently) only on the expiry term of the imminent transfer to the Italian authorities of the investigative documentation gathered against the so-called "minor war criminals"? Let us once again turn to the words of the English authorities, in this case Colonel Cunning, who—as has been seen—was at the time the Deputy Presiding Judge of the Supreme Court:

> Since the investigations in loco of the reprisals by the German Army have been completed and those regarding the German SS and Police are well advanced, I am anxious to know your opinion about the conduct to be followed in relation to the lower-ranking German officers and troops who were involved.

> As you have observed, from a careful examination of the investigations sent to you in their entirety, in many cases the actual perpetrators of the atrocities and illegal reprisals are known. It is common knowledge that the Allies are limiting their punitive actions to the higher-ranking German officers responsible for the orders on the basis of which such incidents took place. The Italian Authorities and the people of many regions, nevertheless, strongly desire that the small fish, in many cases particularly brutal men with sadistic tendencies, should not go unpunished if their culpability is established and they themselves have been identified.
>
> So far, the results of the inquiries carried out by the Special Investigation Branch have not been made known to the Italian Authorities. Do you think that the time is right to convey such results to the Italians, so that they can bring to trial the greatest possible number of Germans, whom we are not interested in prosecuting on our own account?
>
> If such an option were to be adopted, it would obviously be necessary to obtain the guarantee that no Germans would be brought to trial without a previous consultation with the Allies, in case any of them could be required as a witness in the trial against the German generals.
>
> There is, at the moment, no doubt that a substantial percentage of the Italian people is hostile to such war crime trials, inasmuch as they also involve Italian citizens and, since the Italians have suffered so terribly at the hands of the Germans, presumably many months will have to pass before the German generals are tried. Do you think that adopting such a line of conduct could be a positive thing for the morale of the Italians?[97]

Understanding the change in the Allied attitude appears, in my view, vital in order to interpret their political and judicial perspective vis-à-vis the evolution of the Italian situation between June 1946, when the prospect of an Italian Nuremberg was still viable, and February 1947. The beginning of the trial of Marshal Kesselring, which was followed by a few other trials of less important figures, in fact, marked the end of the possibility of holding a single major trial of all the military commanders of the occupation system. We must therefore go back to an important document, the letter of the Commander in Chief of the Central Mediterranean Allied Military Forces Headquarters, sent to the Undersecretary of State for War on April 19, 1946. Apart from the aspects already quoted, the letter contains an extremely significant clue regarding the concern felt by the Anglo-American authorities about the effect that the legal prosecution of Nazi war criminals would have had on Italian public opinion.

> Since one of the main objectives of this trial is, presumably, to favour Anglo-Italian relations thanks to the impact it will have on public opinion in Italy, it is considered appropriate that, through diplomatic channels, the Italian

> government's opinion should be sought as to whether the trial should be held in Rome, Milan or another city.[98]

In the document it is stated that the impact on "public opinion" that the Allies were expecting from the trials should have tended "to favour Anglo-Italian relations." But what was the exact meaning of such a statement in April 1946?

To answer this question it is necessary to recreate the context of the spring of that year and, in those circumstances, the causes of British concerns for "Anglo-Italian" relations. There appear to be two reasons why the English continued to exercise control over the Italian political situation: the strength of the Liberal, Catholic moderate political parties, which, it was hoped, would succeed, as soon as possible, in gaining power and forming a government, and a favorable outcome for the monarchy in the constitutional referendum on the form of the State. For both of these objectives, from a British point of view, the spring of 1946 represented, instead, a negative outcome. In April, in fact, local elections were held. They were the first to which Italian citizens had been called to participate since the Fascist regime had replaced town councils and elected mayors with government-nominated *podestà* (even if during the Resistance, in certain parts of Northern Italy, some local elections, having a purely political significance, had been held). The local by-elections of spring 1946 preceded, by a few weeks, the general election and the June referendum, and they began to provide important pointers to the relative strength of the parties in the country and their territorial distribution, revealing that in Italy the political contest, at this point, revolved around the clash between the Christian Democrat Party, which had won about 2,000 of the 5,596 municipal districts, and the parties of the Left. In particular, the Socialists and the Communists had won 2,256 municipal districts, while the other parties, starting with the Liberal Party so dear to the British authorities, had achieved very disappointing results. The "popular bloc" of the left-wing parties gained a majority in all the big cities of the North and Center, Milan, Turin, Genoa, Bologna, Florence, Rome, also winning in the industrial North-West (Piedmont and Lombardy), Emilia-Romagna, Tuscany, Umbria, the Marches, Rome, Apulia, Calabria, and Sicily: a result, therefore, of great importance.

The possibility that Italy could have a parliamentary majority and hence a government of the Left was not, consequently, too remote: the general election confirmed the relative strengths of the parties that the local elections had begun to outline in the various regions, at least in the North and the Center (while in the South there had been a certain recovery by the Christian Democrats and the politically "indifferent" parties). The Christian

Democrat Party, in fact, obtained 35.2 percent of the votes, but the result obtained by the Socialists and the Communists reached the important figure of 39.7 percent. The victory of the Republic, the most marked result of the impetus of political renewal generated by the Resistance, reinforced yet again British concerns.

The new political climate of 1946 can, therefore, explain both the references in the letter to the state of public opinion and the evolution of British judicial policy, which from that moment on was directed at avoiding any choice that could favor even indirectly a mass mobilization, which would have been completely to the advantage of the most radical political alignment. It was hoped to prevent the exploitation of the emotions that would have been aroused by the trial and tied to the very recent memory of the occupation, the Partisan war, and the Nazi terror. It was certainly for this reason that the prospect of holding an Italian Nuremberg was definitively shelved, while the references to the appropriateness of preparing a few cases for the trials of some minor accused figures became more and more frequent. But, in fact, there were also other reasons that complicated the question of trying the Nazi war criminals.

One must go back at least as far as the autumn of 1945. A few months after the end of the war, two different requests had been made, which were very soon at variance: the British Government had, in fact, formally asked for the arrest and handover of the Italian military accused of having committed war crimes against the people of the countries occupied by Italy or against the Allied armies; on the other hand, the Italian Ambassador, Count Carandini, had formulated an official request asking for the recognition of the Italian Government's right to try the Nazi military accused of having committed crimes against the Italian civilian population.[99] The situation was further complicated by the Yugoslav authorities' formal request for the handover of General Roatta and other Italian military personnel held to be guilty of atrocities in the Balkans.[100]

As far as Italy was concerned, the excessive insistence on dealing directly with the trying of Nazi war criminals, therefore, risked triggering a dangerous reaction and creating the conditions for Italian military personnel to be tried by the Allies or, even worse, by the Yugoslav authorities. Relations with the latter remained extremely tense because of the tangled web of reciprocal accusations regarding the Fascist persecution in the Balkans and the massacres by the Yugoslav Army in the Istrian *foibe*, as well as the diplomatic dispute over the destiny of the city and territory of Trieste.[101] The diverging views divided the British judiciary itself: while the Presiding Judge of the Supreme Military Tribunal was still proposing in the spring of 1946 to commit about fifty high-ranking German officers to trial,[102]

Colonel Cunning, responsible for investigations in Italy, was afraid of "stirring up the Italian civilian population and creating serious problems of public order both for the Allies and the Italian Government."[103]

The trial would easily have become "a matter of policy," by also creating a rather artificial clash between the Italian Courts of Assizes, having the task of trying the Fascist collaborators, and the English Military Tribunal appointed to try the German commanders. However, in putting forward their misgivings, the English authorities inadvertently revealed their intentions in preparing cases for trial: the Italian courts were considered "popular tribunals which acted too summarily," while it was all too easy to foresee Italian public opinion's resentment towards Allied procedures and their presumed laxity vis-à-vis the Fascist collaborators.[104] A comparison between the two types of "justice" appeared inevitable, since the Italian Commission, presided over by Medici-Tornaquinci, would have worked utilizing, above all, the preliminary investigations carried out by the Allies.

The difficulties of preparing a case for a single major trial of the German commanders and the complexity of the Italian political situation constituted two sets of problems that raised fears of serious consequences in a very delicate political phase. Weighing in favor of abandoning a single trial were—definitively, but not solely—questions of political judgment: in fact, in those months, a new factor intervened, the disagreement that had erupted between the Soviets and the Anglo-Americans regarding the right of each State to try the Nazi military accused of war crimes and crimes against humanity perpetrated in the respective countries. The Soviets claimed this right, while the Allies maintained the advisability of unifying laws and procedures and committing the accused for trial at the UN War Crime Commission.[105] The Communist press was accused of spreading the suspicion that a trial held under the authority of the UN would have avoided punishing the criminals too severely.[106]

Thus an Italian Nuremberg did not take place. It was decided to hold a few separate trials, in fact withholding the most important items of evidence that had emerged from the investigations, which was the discovery of the mechanism of terror and the systematic series of orders issued by Kesselring and transmitted and duplicated by the army corps, army and divisional commanders. Those orders constituted "the clear proof of a policy"—as Colonel V. A. Isham had written—guided by the criterion of "collective reprisals conducted without respecting the distinction between the guilty and the innocent."[107] That the key to the whole question lay in the system of orders and in the mechanism of planning terror was the very strong conviction of a few, but qualified, investigators: Colonel C. L. Sterling, in the department of the Presiding Judge of the Supreme Military Tribunal, had in fact concluded that the orders of the German General Staff had correctly interpreted "the meaning of an occupation policy, conducted for over a year by the Supreme Command, the commanders of army groups, armies and divisions, SS units and the Italian Divisions Monte Rosa and San Marco."[108]

The Presiding Judge of the Supreme Military Tribunal himself, Sir Foster MacGeagh, had logically concluded that, apart from Kesselring, those military figures who were primarily responsible for the occupation system—Generals Westphal, Roettiger, Westzell, Hauser, Nagel, Pemsell, Simon (XVI Panzergrenadier Division), Bässler (XIX Luftwaffe Infantry Division), and Crasemann (XXVI Panzergrenadier Division), as well as, obviously, Lemelsen, Commander of the XIV Army, and Vietinghoff, Commander of the X Army[109]—should have been tried. But the decision made by the occupying authorities, and approved by Foster MacGeagh himself,[110] led to the indictment only of Kesselring, while later, in November 1946, the names of Generals Schmalz and Conradt (Hermann Göring Division), Bölke (344th Infantry Division), Feurstein, Treiber, and Schultz (First Parachute Corps) were added to the list. However, none of them were brought to trial.[111]

The change in the Allied judicial policy had drastic consequences for the possibility of knowing the exact nature and causes of the war conducted by the Nazi occupation system against the civilian population. The investigation of the mechanism of terror was abandoned and the whole issue was reductively centered around the figure of Marshal Kesselring. From that moment on, there began a political and communications struggle between those who were ready to recognize in the Marshal the features of a "human monster" troubled by "growing feelings of brutal hostility towards the Italian people after the betrayal of the Axis alliance,"[112] and those who, instead, accorded him the behavior of a soldier and fair conduct.

But it had been Kesselring himself, after the end of the war, who admitted that the main reason for such a situation was,

> in my view, the totally unscrupulous partisan actions on the part of the Italian population and the atmosphere of hatred and growing revenge that were gaining ground in a large section of my soldiers, because of the cowardly and criminal ways of fighting on the part of a civilian population, formerly friendly and in our debt because of our general conduct. In an uncertain situation, we were forced to view every civilian as a fanatical assassin and to expect to be struck from every house.[113]

The document from which the quotation is taken is a deposition voluntarily made by Kesselring. It is significant that in a text of this nature

Kesselring uses terms such as "cowardly and criminal ways of fighting" and attributed this behavior to the Italian people *en masse*: these are eloquent pointers to the way in which he had considered, not the Partisans, but all the civilian population, as an enemy. It was, in fact, the population, according to the Field Marshal, which was conducting "a cowardly and criminal partisan activity."

The Field Marshal thus maintained that the commanders were forced to adopt a "policy of total destruction," in which military limits "could easily be exceeded," while, in fact, it had been Kesselring himself who had established the premises of that policy, as may be seen from admissions of this type:

> There were localities and even regions in which everyone, irrespective of being a man, a woman or a child, was in some way linked with the Partisans, as a combatant, a collaborator, or an occasional supporter. In this context it was totally irrelevant whether these people were acting by conviction or cooperating with the Partisans under duress [. . .]. Therefore, the considerations which had to be made were of a military, and not human, nature.[114]

In Kesselring's perspective, Partisan activity had, therefore, to be considered a war crime with which the population itself could be charged and, consequently, the civilians had been deprived of those rights guaranteed to the population of an occupied enemy country. It was a question of a political-military logic that had ended by legitimizing the mechanism of terror with the aim of "forestalling the criminal and treacherous behavior of the civilian population of an allied country that did not respect the laws of war." The destruction of villages and the deportation and execution by firing squad of hostages thus became the measures necessary to "prevent more serious excesses,"[115] in accordance with the principle "that an error in the choice of means had to be considered preferable to no action or to negligence in one's actions."[116]

On the eve of the trial of Generals Mältzer and von Mackensen, who had been indicted for the massacre of the Ardeatine Caves, Kesselring yet again reasserted his own convictions:

> I am, Your Honor, still today convinced that the killing of Italians in the ratio of one to ten, as an act of reprisal, was necessary in the context of the entire military situation at that time, and that it did not constitute an excess in terms of legitimate limits. Other measures, including killings on a smaller scale, would not have been sufficient for the pacification of Rome or to safeguard the front line in the situation which was developing.[117]

Sir Foster MacGeagh, Presiding Judge of the Supreme Military Tribunal, repeated a few months later that "those massacres of civilians" had to be considered "the natural consequences of the orders wanted by Kesselring." He had, in fact, organized not simple "anti-Partisan operations, but deliberate indiscriminate reprisals against the population," following the model suggested by Keitel in order to unleash the "total war applied in the Balkans and in the Ukraine without regard for the civilian population."[118]

That such a strategy had been a "deliberate choice" was also confirmed by further evidence: the procedures of the war against civilians had been homogeneous throughout the country:[119]

> The reprisals took place not only in the operational areas, but also behind the lines [. . .]. The same distribution, on the map, of the cases of massacres indicates, in itself, that they were not carried out on the orders of the commanders of single formations and units, but that they were examples and instances of a campaign organized and directed by Field Marshal Kesselring's Headquarters.[120]

After all, Kesselring himself had admitted to having foreseen the bloody consequences of the terrorist mechanism put into effect:

> Calculations [of victims] which gave about a hundred or more dead would have been and were considered, on my part, acceptable or at least not at all surprising; at the front, unfortunately, I had got used to totally different figures.[121]

But conclusions of this type had not always been calmly received within German Headquarters itself: the records of the preliminary inquiry prove that the acceptance of the terrorist approach of the anti-Partisan war and the treatment of the civilian population had been neither unanimous nor painless, and that considerable doubts had also been formulated at the highest levels of the German Army, for example by the commander of the XIV Army, Joachin Lemelsen. In a statement given on February 26, 1946, the latter remembered having expressed an explicit criticism of Kesselring's order of June 17, 1944:

> This order, which covered every officer who had exceeded the measure prescribed in the choice of means for fighting the Partisans, contained, in my opinion, a serious threat for discipline and order, bearing in mind the critical situation and the nature of the tension affecting the troops' morale.[122]

Lemelsen indicated precisely the "excessive freedom" that those orders had given the troops as the main cause of the massacres, such as that of

Fucecchio or other Tuscan localities; General Frido von Senger und Etterling, who had commanded the XIV Armored Army Corps, also admitted that the brutality shown by the troops on those occasions had to be considered the result of Kesselring's orders, which had imposed "the adoption of the severest measures."[123]

During the trials held in the postwar period, the investigators pointed out that it would, nevertheless, have been possible to question those orders or not follow them: Frido von Senger und Etterling also remembered having provided "verbal instructions" with the aim of limiting the impact of Kesselring's orders. In fact, the General's units did not behave differently from the others and were responsible for one of the most ruthless massacres, that of Padule di Fucecchio perpetrated in August 1944.

Actually, von Senger had waited until September and October to draw up a memorandum "with the aim of obtaining the cancellation of the orders that had been issued by the highest commanders and were contrary to [my] point of view"; instead, he advised his underlings to "continue the fight against the Partisans in a way more in keeping with the rules of war."[124] As a matter of fact, he was aware of having had the possibility of changing the overall approach of the orders much earlier on. He had not implemented any effective countermeasures, and had agreed—together with almost all the commanders of divisions and subordinate units charged with the responsibility of the roundup operations in Padule di Fucecchio—with the orders that had led to the massacres. None of these commanders had considered the question of verifying if Kesselring's orders, which organized the anti-Partisan operations in such a way that the civilian population's involvement was inevitable, were appropriate and acceptable. The only example of a partial, corrective intervention appears to be that of the Chief of Police of Rome, Harster, who had insisted after the incident of Via Rasella that the hostages destined for the Ardeatine massacre, should only be chosen from among "those condemned to death or at least among those guilty of crimes punishable by death."[125]

The Military Judge, Hans Keller, who had been the legal attaché of the German Army's Supreme Command in Italy, had considered Kesselring's directives, inspired by the anti-Partisan war in the Balkans and Russia, to be "inapplicable"; nevertheless, he admitted that Kesselring, in the summer of 1944, found himself in a "condition of necessity" and attributed to this his decision to issue orders that "did not provide clear instructions and thus gave rise to the risk of arbitrary and irresponsible actions."[126] The SS Commander, Wolff, in turn, unloaded all responsibility on the Field Marshal, satisfied by assurances obtained for his own immunity at the time of the surrender of German troops.[127]

This was also the course of action followed by General Trettner, former Commander of the IV Parachute Division, who declared that he had criticized the systematic and indiscriminate repression of the civilian population wanted by Kesselring, claiming for himself the merit of having initiated disciplinary countermeasures against the military guilty of excesses; only twenty years later would it be possible to judge how credible his position was, when his responsibilities in the war in Italy emerged clearly during the furious controversy triggered by his taking on an important role in the army of the Federal German Republic.[128] In fact, in Italy "a complete integration of the *Wehrmacht* in the war practices of the *Führer*"[129] had taken place.

Chapter 3

The Kesselring Trial

The first trial held in Italy by the Allied authorities was that of General Eberhard von Mackensen—the commander of the XIV Army of the Wehrmacht in spring 1944, whose operational area, at that time, included the capital—and of General Kurt Mältzer, commander of the Rome Military Headquarters in the same period. They were indicted for the massacre of 335 citizens of Rome, which occurred on March 24, 1944, at the Ardeatine Caves as a reprisal for the attack in Via Rasella in Rome.[1] Those proceedings were the first in an extremely short series of trials: in fact, after Mackensen and Mältzer, the Allies only brought to trial the Commander in Chief of the Wehrmacht in Italy, Field Marshal Albert Kesselring; SS General Simon; and General Crasemann, while other minor defendants, including Captain Strauch, *Obersturmbannführer* Kappler, and Captain Reder, were tried a few months later by Italian military courts.

From the records of the Mackensen-Mältzer trial, one can see the elements of the plan that aimed at laying the juridical foundations of the Field Marshal's conviction: the British military judges tried, first of all, to provide the framework within which to place the massacres of the civilian population, starting with that of the Ardeatine Caves. On the opposing side, the defense tried to present the German Army's conduct towards the civilian population as a strategy of extreme caution executed by a command that had found itself adopting extreme measures of reprisals that were wholly legal in the case of the massacre of Rome. Nevertheless, the defense's strategy worked against the defendants themselves when some witnesses, such as Sergeant Ammon and the former editor of the newspaper *Il Messagero*, did not succeed in demonstrating that the population of the capital had been warned of the danger of reprisals in the event of terrorist attacks.[2] Nor did the judges believe the interesting scenario presented by another defense witness, Colonel Beelitz, who tried to exculpate Kesselring, Mackensen, and Mältzer by maintaining that the occupation system had depended upon three independent lines of command: from Himmler to Wolff, from Keitel to Kesselring, and from von Ribbentrop to Rahn.[3] His hypothesis—that the order for the reprisal issued by Hitler for the attack in Via Rasella had been transmitted via Himmler to Wolff and from the latter directly to Kappler (therefore bypassing Kesselring)—did not, however, find any corroboration. In reality, even in such a situation, Kesselring (as Army Commander in Chief), Mackensen and Mältzer (as, respectively, commanders of the XIV Army), and the Rome Military Headquarters could have intervened to countermand the order.[4]

The sentence took up the prosecution's requests and convicted the two high-ranking army officers for not having tried, as was, in fact, their duty, inasmuch as they were in charge of the military zone of Rome, to verify the legality of the order and the justness of the actions of Kappler, the officer directed to carry out that reprisal which proved to be, in the opinion of the judges, "exaggerated and unjust," as it had not been inflicted on prisoners already "sentenced to death," but on those awaiting trial for different offenses, of which only a few were "death worthy."[5] A not insignificant role was played by the person who would have proved to be one of those principally responsible for the episode, Kappler, who obviously had every interest in making his actions appear totally consistent with the directives received from Kesselring and, via the hierarchical order, from Mackensen and Mältzer. Believing Kappler, the judges laid the foundations for the conviction of Kesselring in the trial that would have taken place a few months later.

In fact, the trial records reveal not only the evident difficulty of the high-ranking British investigative officers in understanding how the structure of the German military command and the police forces really worked and, therefore, the hierarchy of responsibility. (The German witnesses themselves, for obvious reasons, tended to exaggerate the occupation system's disorder.) However, the investigation of guilt was also not helped by the fragmentation of the inquiry findings in different trials, which had been the result of the decision not to hold a single major trial, an "Italian Nuremberg." In 1947 there were many who had an interest in seeing that the punishment of the war criminals should no go too far beyond the sphere of the high-ranking Nazis already tried in Germany.

The clash between a few judges, nevertheless determined to prosecute those responsible for the Nazi massacres, and British politicians flared up again soon after the trial of Mackensen and Mältzer. The Vatican also intervened: Father Alfonso Hiemer, an authoritative member of the Pontifical Biblical Institute, forcefully advocated the granting of a measure of leniency, bearing witness that "in those days Rome could not have had a better commander than General Mältzer."[6] The issue would only have been resolved in December 1949 with the rejection of the appeal.

The trial of Field Marshal Kesselring began only a few months later, on February 17, 1947, and sentence was passed on May 6 of that same year.[7] The overall situation in which the trial was held appeared more reassuring for the Allies. On his return from a trip to the United States at the end of January 1947, De Gasperi had set up the last cabinet of the unified coalition; this, however, forced the left-wing parties to give up the two important ministries they still held: Foreign Affairs and Finance. At the end of May, when the trial had just been concluded, De Gasperi would have completed a decisive change, forming his fourth government and excluding the socialists and the communists. A new era had begun.

For the Kesselring trial, the court convened by General John Harding, the Commander of the Mediterranean Allied Forces, was composed of a senior officer who had commanded a combat division during the war, General E. Hakevill-Smith, and four officers with the rank of lieutenant-colonel (P. M. Marjoribanks-Egerton, A. W. Gibbon, W. M. Medlam, and W. Turner-Coles).[8] While the prosecutor was Colonel R. G. Halse, the counsel for the defense was Dr. H. Laternser, who had already defended the accused at the Nuremberg Trials, together with Dr. E. Schwinge, formerly a professor at the Universities of Halle, Marburg, and Vienna, assisted by Professors F. Frohwlin and A. Schutze (a high-level team that knew how to exploit fully its qualities in the course of the trial). C. L. Sterling was appointed Presiding Judge of the Military Tribunal.

Kesselring was accused of the massacre of the Ardeatine Caves (for which Mackensen and Mältzer had already been sentenced) and also for having

> between June and August 1944, in violation of the laws and customs of war, as Oberfehlshaber der Heeresgruppe SüdWest (Commander-in-Chief of the South-West Sector Army Group), incited and ordered the German Armed Forces and Police Forces, under his command in Italy, to eliminate, as a reprisal, a considerable number of civilians of Italian nationality.[9]

The first three weeks were taken up with the examination of the documents concerning the evidence presented for the two indictments, the interrogation of the accused, the examination of the witnesses: nine for the prosecution and twenty-one for the defense. Among the former, the most important were undoubtedly Lieutenant-Colonel A. P. Scotland, a British Army espionage officer who had infiltrated the German Army, Herbert Kappler himself, and the German Army military judge, Hans Keller.

Scotland had played a decisive role in the committal proceedings, having interrogated Kesselring and taken his testimony while he was in the military prison in London and so producing documents that constituted, as will be seen, the conclusive evidence for the indictment and sentencing of the Field Marshal.[10] At the trial, Scotland underlined the role of the orders issued by the German Army Headquarters in Italy and in particular those of June 17 and July 1, which had contributed to unleashing anti-guerrilla warfare conducted "with the utmost violence even against women and children," in this way giving the go-ahead "to all the excesses against civilians in which the subordinate commanders would have indulged."

Kappler himself played his part in compromising the Supreme Commander's position, as he had done in relation to Mackensen and Mältzer, reasserting that he had explicitly stated—when the reprisal of the Ardeatine Caves had been decided upon—that he had in custody people charged with crimes carrying the death penalty and not yet sentenced to death and that he had spoken of this to Kesselring, who would have personally confirmed the absolute necessity of immediately carrying out, and under any conditions, the reprisal order imposed by Hitler. This aspect of his testimony was distinctly at odds with that of other officers of the General Staff, and in particular with that of Colonel Zolling and the Military Judge, Keller. And yet the latter's evidence also ended up by damaging Kesselring's position.

In his capacity as Supervisory Judge of courts martial and assistant to the authority in charge of committal proceedings (even if dependent upon, and limited by, the non-intervention directive in internal issues relating to divisions and minor military units), Keller had found himself in an excellent vantage point, in the Field Marshal's General Staff, from which to view events. At that time, in fact, Kesselring had reserved the exclusive right to confirm the death sentences passed on Italians, and Keller was the officer of the General Staff best placed to follow, at close quarters, the punitive procedures. In spite of this, he was unable to give the Court any plausible figure for the death sentences carried out or not confirmed and, though claiming to have issued the order that "compelled every combat battalion to provide itself, as a precautionary measure, with courts martial in the field,"[11] was forced to admit that such courts lacked any instruments with which to operate effectively, starting from the codes and textbooks dealing with the laws of war. Thus, Keller ended by admitting that the very order issued by Kesselring on June 17, 1944, "by granting protection to any officer who might have been responsible for excesses in his choice of measures and methods, in the hands of a young officer, could have appeared ambiguous and could have been misunderstood."[12]

Nor was the judge able to provide evidence of the arrangements for the instructions for the holding of "normal trials" of captured Partisans and civilians suspected of collaborating with them.[13] Why, in fact, would there have been any need to issue those instructions, which would immediately have been at variance with the numerous meticulously prepared orders regarding the procedures for the reprisals? Some of those instructions envisaged contrary measures, such as the taking of hostages, from among the workers recruited by the Todt organization and destined for the firing squad.[14] How could the same commander have proposed prompt and hasty methods and at the same time procedures guaranteeing civil rights? Another witness, Captain Victor Krumhaar—the officer in charge of the massacre of Borgo Ticino on June 13, 1944—also denied having received instructions about the setting up of courts martial to try Italian civilians.[15]

Colonel Scotland, instead, documented how, from 1 May 1944 and subsequent to an order of the Wehrmacht Supreme Command sent directly by Marshal Keitel, Kesselring was given supreme authority over the anti-Partisan operations, the command of the SS and police forces of General Wolff, as well as the supervision of the territorial coordination of the lines of communication with the rear, which were assigned to the plenipotentiary General Toussaint (who was later to be replaced by Wolff himself). On this basis, the SS Headquarters would have been in charge of anti-Partisan operations at the rear on condition that "the conduct of such operations, on the part of Wolff, had been coordinated with Kesselring [. . .] and any plan of attack had been approved by Kesselring's headquarters."[16]

Colonel Beelitz himself, who had held the position of first officer in Kesselring's General Staff from November 1943 to November 1944, added further details to the picture presented by Scotland. He explained that Wolff's subordination to Kesselring had not signified the total subordination of the SS to the Wehrmacht but had led to the formation of a pyramidal command structure. As in the case of the security police and the SD (Sicherheitsdienst), the Headquarters of the Ordnungspolizei and the Waffen SS also enjoyed a measure of relative autonomy.

> In a certain number of local SD headquarters, for example in Rome, Bologna and Florence, and in the relationship between the Wehrmacht and the SS headquarters, [. . . .] there was not an actual subordination, but only a collaboration which, generally, extended to the army commanders, but was usually only in force at the higher levels, as for example between the military headquarters in Rome and the local SD headquarters. The collaboration was, however, always limited to reconnaissance operations, the war at the front or against the resistance movements. [. . .] It was only from 1 May that

> General Wolff was ordered to follow the orders of the *Oberkommando Sud West* of the army inasmuch as they concerned the anti-Partisan war [while] the security commanders of the different zones received orders from the Supreme Head of the SS and the police for the areas behind the operational zones.[17]

Beelitz, even though wanting to clear Kesselring of the most serious charges, confirmed the role assumed by Army Headquarters and the existence of organic links between it and SS Headquarters that had enabled Kesselring to be constantly kept abreast of all the aspects of the operations conducted by the troops commanded by Wolff. Hence the question arose as to how much Kesselring had actually known about the brutal actions of some units of the Waffen SS placed under direct orders from Berlin—for example, the XVI SS Panzerdivision, the Hermann Göering SS Division, and the Cossack Division of Debes—which had been responsible for some of the worst massacres, from Sant'Anna di Stazzema to Marzabotto.[18]

Thus the hypothesis that the SS had really been subordinated to the Wehrmacht, in the operations against the Partisans and the civilian population, was confirmed.

Kesselring defended himself by maintaining that the measures he had ordered against the Partisans and the civilian population were understandable in the context of the very difficult situation in which the German Army found itself after the fall of Rome on June 4, 1944. But it was precisely his own statements (as had already been the case with the depositions he had made in London during the committal proceedings) that dramatically revealed the feelings of rancor he had been harboring towards the Italian army and people that had been the premise of his policy.[19] The withdrawal towards the line of Lake Trasimene and then towards the Arno had been a very slow march, punctuated by Partisan ambushes and attacks. But that slowness, which had exposed the army to the greatest dangers, had been a necessity that allowed the army to complete the construction of the final and extreme line of defense in the Apennines, which they would have occupied at the beginning of August 1944. Thus, that retreat had been racked by Allied bombing raids, against which the Wehrmacht was by then defenseless, and by the "unexpected attacks of the resistance that suddenly began to rain down, from every corner and every house, on my men from a guerrilla warfare that was the result of a degenerate conduct of war and contrary to international law."[20]

But it had been the Fascist officials of the RSI—according to Kesselring—who had made the policy decision of "unleashing the civil war," committing "countless atrocities," which he had opposed with his moderation and the wisdom of the German authorities. His testimony was also substantiated by Rahn's aim of "softening" as far as possible the deportation of the male workforce and forced population transfers.

The orders issued by Army Headquarters regarding the anti-Partisan war, starting from that of June 17, would have been conceived—according to his testimony—with the aim of avoiding a situation in which every "unit, perhaps badly commanded, should dictate its own rules of war," as well as to form a sound reference framework for the commanders of subordinate units in order to avoid any arbitrary decisions. Kesselring was, however, forced to admit that "some atrocities" had, in fact, also been committed by the Germans. In the areas infested or occupied by the Partisans, the population fought at their side or collaborated with them, voluntarily or otherwise. The army was, therefore, forced to consider the population as Partisans.[21]

Without realizing it, Kesselring had made an admission that would prove to be fatal for the outcome of the trial by introducing an artificial distinction between the population of the "areas infested" by Partisans—which could be rounded up, deported and even "executed" in the event of repeated attacks—and the reprisals against Partisan combatants, who could be eliminated under any circumstances without regard to the rules of war. The Presiding Judge interrupted him, pointing out that in both cases there had been executions by firing squad and indiscriminate massacres lacking any legal sanction, and that therefore his distinction appeared to be a mere turn of phrase.

Trial records are insidious documents and are certainly inadequate to convey the actual reality of the events they refer to, but in reading them one can detect—as in this case—extremely revealing indications: from the Field Marshal's words, in fact, all the evidence points to no execution of civilians having ever been preceded by a trial. As a matter of fact, in none of the offices of the Supreme Headquarters was any evidence ever found relating to trials or the recording of sentences, by means of which the Supreme Commander could, however, have given his assent to the executions.

Kesselring's defense was very clearly reeling. That the procedures had been anything but lawful, even from the point of view of the military codes, was confirmed by an additional factor. After Mussolini's protests at the end of the summer of 1944, Kesselring himself had felt bound, as has already been mentioned, to issue two new orders, on August 21 and September 24, 1944, which envisaged—this time clearly and explicitly—"the setting up of military tribunals in the field," a measure never previously mentioned. Despite the quibbling insinuations of Beelitz, up to the end of August the army corps, like that of the parachutists commanded by von Hoffmann, had, in fact, operated without utilizing courts martial and by following hurried procedures, sometimes keeping the Supreme Headquarters in the dark as to the extent of the massacres of civilians, whose scale was concealed by including the civilian victims in the number of Partisans killed in battle.[22] At his trial, the Field Marshal therefore found himself in the grip of an irreconcilable contradiction: on the one hand, he maintained that his own orders had been consistent with the laws of the usage and customs of war; on the other hand, he tried to convey the image of an army that had plunged into chaos and ascribed the cause of the massacres to the "incredible delay" with which his orders would have reached the various units: the adoption of indiscriminate measures would, therefore, have been the result of a communications system that had plunged into chaos.[23]

The documents show, however, that Kesselring had taken action beginning at the end of 1943, at the suggestion of Keitel, and in issuing his orders had indicated the use not only of traditional military measures of anti-guerrilla warfare, but also of "all available means," including the use of terror against the civilian population.[24] From the cross-examination by the prosecution and the presiding judge, it emerged, in fact, that the suggestion of indiscriminately killing "suspected" civilians had been the direct result of his promise of granting special protection to whoever had struck without going through judicial procedures. Resounding evidence also resulted from his bureaucratic justification of the slaughter at Bardine San Terenzo and the massacre of Fucecchio,[25] as well as the *volte-face* recorded in his orders from the end of the summer of 1944 and, even more, after February 8, 1945, when he had intimated "with the aim of avoiding errors, that decisions should only be taken by the courts martial."[26]

At the beginning of the twenty-first day of the trial, Colonel Halse finally succeeded in challenging Kesselring about the text of the order of July 1, 1944, which contained the passage already referred to: "A section of the male population of the area (infested by Partisans) will be arrested and, in the event of acts of violence occurring, these men themselves will be killed."[27]

The accused tried to defend himself, arguing that he had considered as hostages not all the inhabitants of the areas infested by Partisans, but only the civilians detained as a preventative measure, and that the order in question concerned, instead, the civilians "guilty" of direct collaboration with the Partisans and their leaders, who could have been eliminated even if not directly involved in attacks. Invited to demonstrate how it would be possible to detain as hostages only the civilians already "considered guilty of collaboration," Kesselring replied that his subordinate commanders "usually proceeded, in the first place, to arrest the category of people in some way involved in collaboration." But in the face of a new objection, that "the order did not present, in absolutely explicit terms, the indication to arrest only the civilians clearly guilty of collaborating with the Partisans," he was forced to fall back on an incredible syllogism: "in those areas I define as being under Partisan occupation, the entire population pursued the same aim as the Partisans and therefore those arrested could only be Partisans and some of them even their leaders."[28] The Field Marshal, in other words, went so far as to maintain that even the innocent civilians wiped out as hostages had been killed because they were, in any case, guilty of "not having distanced themselves in time from the Partisans."

In this sense, some of the indisputable orders had, after all, come directly from Hitler: the most explicit directive issued by the Führer on the anti-Partisan strategy had, in fact, been the order of October 18, 1942, concerning Central-Eastern Europe, but it also had to be considered a guideline for the Italian theatre of war.

> On the Eastern Front, this type of guerrilla warfare has, until last winter, seriously impaired our combat capability [. . .]. All the measures adopted to counter the sabotage, as cruel as they were indispensable, have failed solely because the German officers and their men did not grasp the gravity of the danger [. . .]. It therefore becomes necessary to set up, in the East, special units to tackle this danger or assign the task to special SS units. Only where the war against the guerrilla fighters has been initiated and conducted with inflexible severity have the results improved our army's front-line combat situation.[29]

Among the documents discovered at the Command Headquarters in Verona, Italy, after April 25, 1945, there was the proof that this text had been considered the most important guideline by the Wehrmacht Supreme Commander, Keitel, in order to tackle the problems that the Partisan war had posed in the Balkans, Greece, and Italy. After having been transmitted to Crete to direct the conduct of the war against the Greek and Balkan Resistance, it had also been considered by Kesselring since December 1943 as a valid reference point for the Italian Front.[3]

In other words, the position on which the Field Marshal chose to make his stand ended up by producing a tangle of contradictions: having explicitly admitted that the Führer and Keitel's directives could be corrected "with some freedom of movement," he could not therefore maintain (as he had in fact done) that that strategic approach of the war against the Partisans and civilians could not have been modified. If, therefore, the relative freedom of movement of which he had boasted on several occasions had existed, then Kesselring would have had difficulty in demonstrating that the strategic approach of the anti-Partisan war and Hitler's own dispositions for Rome between March 23 and 24, 1944, could not have been discussed and disputed.[31]

The evidence for the defense, provided by Colonel Beelitz, also failed in its aim. He wanted to maintain that the "general guiding emergency rules prepared for the Eastern Front" had been applied from before the summer of 1944 (a statement that, as has been seen, corresponded with the truth),[32] but he could not demonstrate that the new orders issued by the German Army Headquarters in Italy had been consistent with international legislation and the laws of war.[33]

Pressed by the questions from the judge and the public prosecutor, Beelitz ended up by contradicting himself, which would prove to be fatal for Kesselring. Faced with the sequential order of some documents—Kesselring's orders of June 17 and July 1 and that of the commander of the First Parachute Corps, von Hoffmann, of July 20, 1944—he was forced to admit that the last-mentioned order was nothing other than an adaptation of the earlier ones and that therefore there had been neither a delay in carrying them out nor any modification of the strategy worked out by Kesselring on the part of subordinate commanders. Colonel Halse first presented Beelitz with the order of July 1, signed by Kesselring.

> In my appeal to the Italians I had declared that severe measures against the Partisans would have been established. This new announcement must not appear to be an empty threat. It is the precise duty of all the police forces placed under my command to order the severest measures. Every act of violence committed by the Partisans must be punished immediately. The reports will have to detail the countermeasures undertaken. Where there is a marked presence of Partisan bands, a percentage of the male population of the zone will have to be arrested, in the event of acts of violence occurring, these men will have to be executed by firing squad. The population must be informed of this.[34]

Halse then invited Beelitz to examine the document of June 17 and, finally, the text signed by von Hoffmann, which stated:

> The situation of the Partisans behind the lines continues to represent a serious threat to the combat troops and supplies. The fight against the Partisans will have to be conducted with the utmost severity. The good character and moderation, so common among German troops, must be guided by continuous instructions.
>
> Every act of violence on the part of the Partisans must be punished immediately. The report on the incident will indicate the appropriate countermeasures: where there are Partisans in considerable numbers, hostages

will be taken from the local population and immediately executed by firing squad in the event of further acts of violence occurring. The population will be informed of the threat when the arrests are made. In the event of German soldiers being killed in the proximity of a village, it will be burnt down and the perpetrators and their leaders will be publicly hanged.

In the event of sabotage to telephone lines or of damage to tyres, the villages in the immediate vicinity will be held responsible [. . .].

The members of the Fascist Party will be excluded from all the reprisal measures [. . .].

The following will also be immediately executed: anyone giving aid to Partisan criminals and traitors, by giving them food and lodging, or carrying military messages; anyone carrying arms (including hunting rifles) or explosives; anyone committing acts hostile to the German Armed Forces. I will protect any officer who exceeds our traditional moderation in the choice of measures for tackling the Partisans, or in the severity with which they are applied.[35]

Faced with these texts, Beelitz dramatically contradicted himself under the pressure of the questions.

Question: Read von Hoffmann's order.
Answer: I think this order is only slightly based on Kesselring's order of 1 July.
Question: Witness, you are not a very wise officer: it is always a good rule to read an order in its entirety, before replying. That is my advice.
Answer : It is an aggregate of different orders.
Question: But it doesn't deal with tactical orders, does it?
Answer: Part of it deals with tactical matters, part of it with orders for reprisals.
Question: Look at paragraph 2. Do you admit that the first part deals with something which is related to Kesselring's order of 1 July?
Answer: In many respects it certainly does ("hostages will be taken from the civilian population and immediately executed by firing squad in the event etc. etc.").
Question: And do you therefore admit that the second passage is nothing but an extract from the orders issued by the Field Marshal?
Answer: The copy is difficult to read.
Question: Then take the original, which is no better. Or do you want the English version? Do you understand English?
Answer: I would prefer the German text.
Question: All right, do you see that passage [. . .]. Isn't it a passage from the Field Marshal's security instructions?
Answer: I don't know, but it's probable.

> **Question:** And what about the last passage of paragraph 2 ("I will protect any officer etc."). Do you remember these words?
> *Answer*: Yes.
> **Question:** Are they taken from the order of 17 June?
> *Answer*: Yes.
> **Question:** Colonel Beelitz, I put it to you that the 1st Parachute Corps interpreted the Field Marshal's order of 17 June as the basis for the guidelines concerning reprisals.[36]

The Supreme Commander's direct responsibility had been incontrovertibly proved and his conviction was inevitable.

Chapter 4

Judiciary Oblivion and the Sins of Memory

There were, therefore, very few trials actually held of those in charge of the German system of occupation. Apart from those of Mackensen, Mältzer, Kesselring, and Simon, conducted by the Judiciary of the Allied Military Government, the only other trials held subsequently were those of lower-ranking officers—including that of Herbert Kappler for the massacre of the Ardeatine Caves, which provoked extraordinary tension in public opinion—conducted by the Italian Military authorities. Hence, not only was there no "Italian Nuremberg," or major trial of the "mechanism of terror," but the individual trials themselves proved to be very few in number. In order to resolve this new issue it is once again necessary to go back in time, specifically to 1946, and retrace some decisive aspects of this question to the indirect consequences of the outcome of the international trials of the supreme authorities of the Third Reich held at Nuremberg. It is equally important to go back to the evolution of the situation in Italy and the clash between the Allies and the Italian Government over who had the right to try the Italian military guilty of crimes in the territories occupied by the troops of the Royal Army and governed by the regime's authorities prior to July 25, 1943. This second issue was linked to the diplomatic confrontation between the Allies and Italy over the Armistice and subsequently over the peace treaty, including questions regarding safeguarding the national territory, the peace terms, and Italy's international status within the context of the difficult relations between the Allies of the international anti-Fascist coalition after the end of the conflict.

Let us begin with the second aspect. From October 13, 1943, the date of the declaration of war against Germany by the Badoglio Government, Italy, subject to the regime of the Armistice and deployed at the side of the UN[1] as a "cobelligerent" against its former German ally, had come to find itself—as has been said—in an ambiguous diplomatic situation. The terms of the Armistice (and predictably of the peace treaty) would not have spared Italy from the consequences of its intervention in the war of aggression at the side of National Socialist Germany on the basis of the provisions of the alliance of the Rome-Berlin Axis. Nevertheless, the new cobelligerence at the side of the UN had enabled the government in Rome to claim the right to participate in future negotiations with Germany, putting forward demands for reparations for the purloining of industrial assets and works of art, as well as for judicial and punitive proceedings for the massacres of Italian civilians and troops.[2]

For its part, the Committee of National Liberation for Northern Italy had taken the initiative of collecting the evidence of crimes chargeable to the National Socialist military, and in November 1944 the Foreign Ministry had initiated an inquiry that also involved other ministries (Interior, Justice, and War). The documents had been sent to the central commission for the investigation of atrocities committed by the Germans and the Fascists after July 25, 1943, set up at the Ministry for Occupied Italy, formerly presided over by the Undersecretary of the same ministry, Medici-Tornaquinci, and subsequently under the authority of the Prime Minister's office.[3] The documentation would have been examined by the Chief Military Prosecutor, while the charges would have been forwarded to the UN War Crimes Commission.

In the clash between the Allies and the Italians over the reciprocal handing over of those suspected of war crimes, the stakes were evidently totally political, and justice certainly did not constitute the primary concern. It was a question of winning, even in this way, Italy's right to different treatment than Germany would have received. The plan also included the demand of seeing an image of Italy—which would be accepted and legitimized—as largely contrary to the regime and the war from much earlier than 1943 and dissembling the consensus that the Fascist regime had enjoyed well beyond the entry into the war, precisely in order to avoid paying the consequences of the choices made by the ruling class and the monarchy up to July 25, 1943. However, the question as to who could and should try "the war criminals"—with which we have already dealt—began to become intertwined with different and much higher stakes.

In this regard, one of Benedetto Croce's texts offers us a clue, a note that was published in the newspapers on October 27, 1945, in which Croce proposes collecting and publishing the evidence and documents of the destruction and massacres brought about by both the military and the politicians in charge of the German system of occupation during the war years.

The advisability of publishing such material—wrote Croce—is threefold:

> 1) to preserve an exact record of a period of the history of our Italy, of which, with the passage of time, the eye-witness accounts and the documents would become scattered and, to a great extent, lost, even though the memory of the horrors suffered would not be extinguished, and to which the ruins and mutilations of the historical and artistic monuments would bear witness [. . .]; 2) to lay before the eyes of the world with how much terrible suffering, with how much dreadful and irreparable damage, Italy has paid the penalty for the Fascist folly, to which it submitted; 3) to give the German people, who have, for the most part, been unaware of the degree and extent of those horrors, a mirror in which to look at themselves (and in which we will all look, being horrified at the fearful forces which were stirring in the depths of man); which will perhaps help that nation to the conversion which it must spontaneously achieve to free itself of the instincts and concepts pernicious to itself and the world.[4]

Croce was probably referring to the documents and evidence of the National Socialist massacres and the war against civilians collected and deposited at the Foreign Ministry and was, obviously, not proposing its utilization for a trial or for material compensation. Instead, his aim was that of preserving an "exact record of a period of history," namely, the public memory and its legitimate political use also with regard to the UN, with the aim of demonstrating, to the Allies, the scale of the suffering undergone during the German occupation and therefore the inadmissibility of the most punitive terms of the Armistice. The intention itself, of offering evidence as an opportunity for reflection for the German conscience, revealed the implications of the proposal: a political operation on the memory, which would have corroborated the reduction of Fascism to an episode of a parenthetic nature in the history of the unified Italian State, exonerating the ruling class and the monarchy, attributing the moral and political responsibility for Italian suffering exclusively to Nazism.

While other exponents of European culture tended, at that time, to effect a break between the war and the preceding period, forgetting the compliance and the collaboration of the ruling classes in their own countries towards the authoritarian regimes and the new Hitlerian order, Croce, with greater subtlety, hinted at Italy's almost feminine—but fatal (that "to which it submitted")—weakness in the face of Fascism, which diminished its responsibility but at the same time ignominiously stigmatized its moral conduct.

Throughout Europe, the most recent past was almost detached from the distant past, while every national community tried to differentiate between its own identity and Nazism, which was condemned and demonized as absolute alterity. The suppression of the most inconvenient past thus served to select memories and forge a purified, but fictitious, image of the conscience of every European nation and of Europe itself: rather than an act of justice, it proved, in the end, to be an integral part of the culture of oblivion operative in the construction of a new European identity.

The Italian call to exercise the right to try "the human monsters," from whom there had been, at the opportune moment, a break, risked, however, becoming counterproductive and pushing the Allies to react by resolutely pursuing those responsible for the "Italian atrocities" in Greece and the Balkans.[5] During 1946, the national authorities began to act with greater prudence without making too many demands that could provoke sharp reactions in countries like the Soviet Union, Yugoslavia, and Greece, which were determined to insist on the handing over of the Italian military guilty of war crimes. In 1946, Italy limited itself to asking quietly for the handover of those responsible for the massacres of soldiers in Cefalonia and Léros in the Aegean and of civilians in the Ardeatine Caves, without insisting too much. In the course of time, the demands for the Nazi war criminals faded away. The UN War Crimes Commission, through the Allied Commission of Rome, definitively denied the handing over of higher-ranking German officers, permitting Italy to try only some of the lower-ranking officers, as long as they were not subject to legal proceedings in other countries. Neither did the action taken against the latter prove to be decisive. The opportunity to obtain the evidence necessary to apply for the handing over of the lower-ranking German war criminals was not adequately exploited, since the documentation collected by the English and American special services, once handed to the Chief Military Prosecutor of Rome, was not utilized, except in very rare cases: the proceedings against Kappler for the Ardeatine Caves, against Captain Reder for the slaughter of Marzabotto, against Captain Strauch for the massacre of Fucecchio, and then the trial of Krake, Fenn, Egmann, and Wagner.[6] Many investigations of "minor" war criminals were filed away and forgotten to avoid raising, in retaliation, the issue of Italian war criminals. For the same reason, the animated press campaign conducted by the main Italian daily newspapers during Kesselring's trial was, surprisingly, not followed by any official protest against the commuting of the death sentence, which occurred a few months later. The impression is that by then the Italian government was determined to smooth down every controversy and to delay the most troublesome decisions. Thus, no less than two thousand investigations of massacres, which would have given rise to as many trials in Italian territorial military tribunals, were slowly put out of mind utilizing the mechanisms of bureaucratic routine.[7]

In the second half of 1947, the international situation had also profoundly changed. The extremely resolute commitment of the Anglo-Americans to supporting the reconstruction of the German economy and institutions in an anti-Soviet context made it expedient to slow down the preliminary investigations of and the judicial proceedings against war crimes. After the setting up of the Federal Republic in 1949, the Italian government also committed itself to definitively suspending legal proceedings and initiating the procedures for pardoning the few war criminals detained in Italian prisons.

The parallel issue of the Italian war criminals had an analogous outcome. The first Badoglio government had, at that time, begun, only formally, to investigate those in charge of the Italian occupation of the Balkans: Generals Roatta (who had been tried but escaped prior to sentencing in March 1945) and Robotti; the Chief of Police, Messana; and the High Commissioner of Lubiana, Lombrassa. But the inquiries had been curbed by the strong resistance of the upper echelons to the ascertaining of the Army's complicity with the Fascist regime and to the purging of the military organizations. The clash between government officials, the High Commission for Sanctions against Fascism, and the High Commission for Purging had already led to a crisis at the time of the Bonomi government in November 1944.[8] But in 1946 the purging had, by then, already been blocked, and the few remaining inquiries were conducted very slowly, while there was still the pretense of continuing to claim, on the opposite front, the right to try the German war criminals.[9]

Officially, the conduct of the Italian Government had followed the principle of distinguishing between the role of Germany and that of Italy sanctioned by the Declaration of Moscow of October 30, 1943, which had envisaged the handing over of German war criminals to the countries in which they had committed their misdeeds. Thus, capitalizing on their favorable treatment, Italian governments desperately tried both to cancel the historical memory of a State that had shared, at least until 1943, in the decisions and crimes of its National Socialist ally, and to create a new public image.

Until the peace treaty came into force on September 15, 1947, the Italian Government tried, in other words, to operate on two fronts. On the one hand, with the Allies it avoided handing over Roatta, Robotti, Magaldi, Sorrentino and all the other generals suspected of war crimes until it could gain the acknowledgement of its right to try them directly (even though the opposite was envisaged by article 38 of the peace treaty), using the tactic of filing away and forgetting. On the other hand, the government was officially urging the Italian Chief Military Prosecutor to take action against the Italian military themselves while, in effect, inviting him to delay trial proceedings and, if anything, gather evidence of the war crimes committed by the Yugoslavs during the civil war, with the aim of countering the demand of Marshal Tito's Government to try high-ranking Italian officers.[10]

The Germans suspected of being responsible for the massacres of Italians in the Aegean islands were, therefore, not brought to trial, precisely in order to avoid a "boomerang effect" leading to the prosecution of the Italians under investigation. And not even one of the 1,200 Italians suspected of war crimes had to face trial. The Anglo-American Allies willingly cooperated with the "oblivion" solution, limiting themselves to holding only a few trials of those in charge of the Nazi occupation system in Italy and aiming at gradually reducing concern with the whole issue. The highest echelons of the Italian judiciary played a decisive role by, in the end, filing away and forgetting the applications from the local prosecutors' offices. The then General Military Prosecutor, Borsari, was probably involved in this episode, but there is no doubt as to the part played by the government, which went as far as to permit many of the accused to avoid being served with arrest warrants. The division itself, among the anti-Fascist parties—between, on the one hand, the Communists, who were in favor of handing over the Italian generals to the Yugoslav Government and, on the other hand, the members of the Action Party, the Socialists, and the Republicans, who were determined to support on moral and national grounds the Italians' right to judge their own offenses—favored the erosion of the purging procedures and the Government's own maneuvering, which was increasingly directed at ensuring the continuity, in a military context, of men and institutions, as well as the impunity of the commanders.[11]

Sixty years later, the dusty trial records permit some balanced considerations, far from the echoes of those proceedings that took place in the courtrooms of cities still in ruins. Returning to the documents forces one, above all, to face a preliminary issue, namely, whether the questions posed in the postwar period were the right ones.

Certainly the charges made against the accused were proved, and the link between Kesselring's orders and the massacres in the summer of 1944 were amply substantiated. Six decades later, however, the historical interpretation of the war against the Partisans and the civilians cannot simply confirm or dispute the sentences of the judges of those times: on the contrary, it is the sentences that have to be placed in the historical context of the immediate postwar period and critically assessed, not only as documents useful for reconstructing and interpreting the war, the Resistance, and the German occupation, but also as indications of politically influenced procedures geared to the construction of a propaganda-orientated public memory.

The trial records constitute documentation that can have a multiplicity of meanings. If we consider the trials as documents about the war, the National Socialist occupation, and the Resistance, the evidence of the waning of the intensity of the massacres during the winter of 1944–45 shows that the German commanders themselves had understood the need to modify the harsh repressive policy defined by Kesselring's orders. At the urging of Rahn and Mussolini, the system had been modified to a not inconsiderable degree.

In a document drawn up by the German Air Force Headquarters one actually finds the explicit admission that the massacres of civilians have been inducing even the honest and well-disposed elements of the population to pass to the enemy camp or the ranks of the Partisans, and for the first time there is an explicit reference to the necessity of holding trials before proceeding with the executions. The document, dated October 21, 1944, therefore proves that there had been a change of policy at the end of the summer of 1944: "all the measures against the Partisans had to be directed solely against the Partisans and their civilian collaborators, since every error was considered, by the population, as an unjustified excess."[12]

On February 8, 1945, it was finally laid down that "the death sentences had to be pronounced and carried out immediately only in exceptional cases by the military courts."[13] All this also constitutes a countercheck that, in the preceding period, the system of orders in force had favored indiscriminate massacres. It appears more difficult, however, to resolve the problem of whether there were really any differences between the divisional corps commanders and those of the army and whether these differences could be traced back to different conceptions of the relationship with the Italian civilian population held by the highest echelons of the Wehrmacht and the SS on the one hand, and Otto Rahn's political apparatus on the other hand. Did the so-called "soft strategy" towards the civilian population represent a real alternative, or did Rahn, following the agreement in May 1944 between Kesselring and Wolff, also fall into line with the military repression of the civilian population?

A letter written by the plenipotentiary to Kesselring, dated September 18, 1944, constitutes, from this point of view, an extremely ambiguous document. Conveying Mussolini's protest at the large-scale massacres in the summer of 1944, Rahn in fact stressed that the German reaction "to the furtive attacks against the lives of the soldiers" had been "inevitable." The statement can, however, be read as a precautionary formula to avoid clashing with Kesselring. The following sentence does not seem to leave any room for doubt: Rahn does not challenge the system of orders issued by Kesselring, nor does he suggest "altering the means of carrying out the reprisal measures, in conformity with the orders previously issued by you [Kesselring]." Rather, he limits himself to suggesting a series of measures useful in modifying, as far as possible, the attitude of a population traumatized by the reports of the massacres by adopting procedures officially more in tune with the laws of war, always aiming at "calming" public opinion. "The setting up of 'legal' courts martial, even if it is a question of pure form, could even have a favorable effect."[14]

Hence there is no proposal of an alternative approach for the war against civilians. However, the most important questions we have to ask of the documents concern a third aspect, namely, the judicial dimension and the framework of rules of international law within which the trials took place and, in particular, the gap between German judicial culture and that of the Allies, which had already emerged at Nuremberg and was also highlighted by the trials in Italy. The defense plan of the German military was, in fact, to take refuge behind the differences between the Nazi code of war, the laws of the Allied countries, and international regulations. But the existence of an actual divergence between those laws remains a problem that cannot be ignored because of its attempted exploitation by the lawyers of the Nazi defendants.

After all, Kesselring himself, in the course of his trial, asserted the consistency of his own orders with German legal doctrine in the context of the rules of war, in particular with the List Code of 1925 and the Waltzoog Code, published in 1941. These two authors had accepted reprisals against unarmed civilians and had defined partisan guerrilla warfare as criminal wartime behavior.[15] Apart from these authors, the defense had also proposed a particular interpretation of international law, especially of the second Hague Convention, also signed by Germany in 1907 and updated in Geneva in 1929, in which partisan warfare had been condemned as an illegal form of war. The approach of the Field Marshal's defense was not without arguments and legal bases, because for many years there had actually been no unanimity regarding the issue of reprisals. International law, and in particular the first and second Conventions signed at The Hague in Holland in 1899 and 1907, had been updated by four additional texts (the most important of which was certainly the one signed in Geneva in 1929, concerning the treatment of prisoners of war) that considered reprisals, taken to mean the indiscriminate killing of hostages, as unlawful, even if put into effect with the intention—in itself not unlawful—of forcing the enemy to interrupt partisan guerrilla warfare, itself also considered a violation of the rules of war.

In particular, the Hague Convention of 1907 had paid scant attention to the question of reprisals, confining itself to the articles of law 46, 47, and

50, which excluded the possibility of "any sanction" of a "pecuniary" type or of any other kind being inflicted on the communities and the population of a region because of the illegal actions committed by single individuals belonging to them. At the same time, the Convention had granted the occupying army the right to maintain order as long as wholly "legitimate" means were adopted, including reprisals themselves, "proportionate" to the injury sustained. In other words, reprisals had been defined as lawful only in the event of their being directed against those responsible for the attacks, which never permitted, under any circumstances, the execution by firing squad of innocent hostages and of civilians unconnected with the events. At the same time, bombing raids, fires, expropriations, putting a price on someone's head, and the detention of hostages constituted legitimate practices only on condition that they did not lead to the killing of people unconnected with the events or to the punishment of entire communities.

The international regulations in the military codes of war of individual countries had not shown themselves to be at all homogeneous. In some texts, the French, the English and the Belgian (Fouchil, Gall, Wosley), it had been excluded that unarmed civilians could constitute the object of an occupying army's reprisals, but it had also been pointed out that, in order to avail themselves of the protection of international law, the civilian population would have had to respect "the usages and customs of war." For example, partisan forces would have had to make themselves known through insignia, uniforms or identification marks.

The divergence between the English and French codes, on the one hand, and the German codes, on the other hand, had emerged from a long juridical reflection on the experiences of World War I: in the German codes, such as Fleischmann and List, both of 1925, reprisals had been categorized as legal, in order to justify *a posteriori* wartime episodes in occupied Belgium for which the Kaiser's Army had been responsible. In 1941, Waltzoog, a judge with the Wehrmacht Supreme Command, had authorized the overriding "on the grounds of military necessity" of the regulations laid down in the article of the Convention itself and granting the occupying army the right to capture hostages and make known to the population the detention of the hostages and the possibility of their being executed by firing squad in the event of attacks (provided that it was at least a divisional commander who issued the order).

At the Kesselring trial, the defense explicitly disputed the interpretation of the international regulations proposed by the Venice Tribunal based on British Codes, which it countered with the different juridical tradition codified in the texts of Fleischmann, List, and Waltzoog. The prosecution itself had to admit to a divergence between the two juridical cultures and the evident contradictions in the American and British Codes themselves: the Lauterpacht Code, in the 1935 edition, for example, had not explicitly banned reprisals, nor had it distinguished between the destruction of possessions or buildings and so-called punishments. Nevertheless, the interpretation of articles 46, 47, and 50 of the Hague Convention that had been proposed by the *Manual of British Military Law*—particularly in chapter 14—was clear, prohibiting the killing, as a reprisal, of innocent civilians and formally excluding the possibility of killing, for any reason whatsoever, a detained hostage. (In paragraphs 455 and 456 it was specifically pointed out that an individual soldier could never have resorted to reprisals, unless it was under the explicit order of his own commanding officer.)[16] In his order of July 1, Kesselring had, on the contrary, granted carte blanche in carrying out reprisals to every officer and every unit, giving guidelines that went well beyond a departure from the principle that entire communities could not be punished, which was accepted both by the Hague Convention and by the English Code. (According to the former, a population involved in attacks against an occupying army could be collectively punished; the occupying army, nevertheless, could not go so far as to kill hostages indiscriminately or take action against the civilian population living in areas bordering those in which the attacks had occurred.)

The Oppenheim Code of international law, which was invoked on several occasions by Kesselring's defense, itself only defended some forms of reprisals, such as the bombing of villages from which partisan attacks had originated (a case in point being the shelling of Alsatian villages during the Franco-Prussian War of 1870), or drastic retaliation, such as the setting on fire of the Belgian University of Louvain in 1914. At the same time, it rejected retaliation against entire communities and the execution by firing squad of hostages.[17]

The prevailing trend in international law had gone in the same direction: the Committee of Responsibilities of 1918 had codified some regulations of the rules of war, on the basis of which the subsequent Versailles Peace Treaty had been drawn up, explicitly including, among war crimes, killings, the massacre of civilians, systematic terror, and "the execution of hostages."[18] In the trials of Kesselring, Simon, von Mackensen, Mältzer, and Crasemann, the defense could therefore try to prove the legitimacy of the decisions taken by the German commanders on the basis of their coherence with their own military codes of war, which had included reprisals, as "legitimate means of safeguarding the security of the troops from attacks by illegal troops such as partisans." In the hypothesis suggested by the German lawyers, the slaughters and massacres of the civilian population would therefore not have been provoked by "individual" excesses, but by wartime procedures legitimized by law and the strategic situation. Even accepting that premise, it nevertheless remained difficult to maintain that international law (the text of article 50 of the fourth Convention attached to the second International Hague Peace Conference of 1907) could leave the way open to the interpretation of reprisals provided by the German Military Code. But it is equally certain that international law, at that time, was not immune from the possibility of ambiguous interpretation. In order to have an absolute and explicit ban on reprisals it would have been necessary to await the text of the Convention for the protection of war victims signed in Geneva in 1949.

The Allied officials who found themselves having to judge the German commanders were aware of the ambiguous nature of the international legal framework and of the differences between the Allied Codes and the Waltzoog Code. At the Nuremberg Trials, in discussing the responsibility for the massacres of the Balkan civilian populations, the Allies had already specified under what conditions reprisals were to be considered admissible: public notification, the exercise of the criterion of proportionality between the injury sustained by the occupying army and the responses inflicted on the population, the failure to find the real perpetrators of the attacks, the existence of a link between the hostages and the guilty parties, and the issuing of an order from the top.[19] In the light of such criteria, a guilty verdict for Kesselring therefore appeared inevitable, both for the indictment for the Ardeatine massacre and for the charge of having promoted an indiscriminate policy of war against the civilian population, even if the legal uncertainties and contradictions would have rendered the carrying out of the sentence improbable. General Harding, the judge who commuted the death sentence to life imprisonment, in fact went so far as to justify, to a certain extent, the reprisal orders, defining them as "instantaneous reactions" dictated by contingent military requirements and imposed by Hitler's superior orders. It was Harding who laid the foundations for Kesselring's subsequent release, agreeing in 1950 that the life sentence should be reduced to a twenty-one-year term of imprisonment.[20]

In the British Military High Command and ruling class, a very different opinion from the one formulated by the harsh judgment pronounced in Venice had taken shape in the meantime. General Archibald, for example, repeatedly maintained that Kesselring had conducted his war campaign in Italy in a way that was "fair and respectful of Italian culture,"[21] and Field Marshal Alexander, for his part, added: "I am not satisfied with Kesselring's sentence and hope that it will be commuted. Personally, as his old adversary on the battlefield, I have nothing with which to reproach him. Kesselring and his soldiers fought against us tenaciously but fairly." The target of this pressure was the then Prime Minister of the Labour Party, Attlee. Winston Churchill's interventions were particularly eloquent and insistent.

> My Dear Prime Minister,
>
> Thank you for your letter of 12 May. Regarding Kesselring, I obviously intend leaving the issue in abeyance while the case is *sub iudice*, provided that there is an appropriate interval between his conviction and the carrying out of the sentence. In my judgement it is a question of political policy: condemning to death the leaders of a defeated enemy has today ceased to have the usefulness which it could have had in the past.
>
> I would be grateful if you could let me know if there will be a sufficient interval of time between the verdict and its implementation in order to permit that the question be brought before Parliament. Otherwise I will put a parliamentary question, as a matter of urgency, tomorrow, Wednesday, 14 May, at the usual time.
>
> You will probably have noted the views of Sir Oliver Leese.
>
> I remain,
>
> Yours sincerely,
>
> (signed) *Winston Churchill*[22]

There was a succession of interventions by political figures and Members of Parliament, all in favor of the commutation of the death sentence: among these, mention should be made of the messages of eminent Conservatives such as Lord de l'Isle, Lord Dudley, and Lord Henderson.[23] In the British Establishment, by the second half of 1947, there was the prevailing opinion that can best be illustrated through another very interesting document, an anonymous and "confidential" note sent to the Secretary of State for War on May 16:

> I believe that the Kesselring trial and the sentence are beyond my competence, but perhaps you might be pleased to know my point of view. I am completely opposed to hanging or executing by firing squad yet another former enemy commander. I do not see any advantage in continuing with this sort of thing. We have now been at peace for two years. Personally I would not initiate any more trials: at this point, too much time has passed and no good can come of it for anyone.[24]

Neither the Secretary of State for War, Bellenger, nor the Attorney General, Hartley Shawcross, actually seemed inclined to change their minds about the sentence, but the Prime Minister, Attlee, pressed by Churchill and the military magistrates themselves, was by then fully aware not only of the contradictions that had characterized the trial, but also of the issue's political and moral significance.

The Presiding Judge of the Supreme Military Tribunal, Sir Foster MacGeagh, instead saw no reason for commuting the death sentence, contrary to the views of General Harding, the confirming officer who—as has been seen—was in favor of commutation. In order to save Kesselring it was necessary "to contextualize," namely, to relativize his actions: it was thus concluded that the system of orders had been dictated by the extraordinary imperatives of the summer of 1944 and imposed by Hitler. Harding willingly gave expression to the political pressure and the views widespread in diplomatic circles.

The ciphered text of his proposal is worth quoting almost in its entirety:

> One: I have decided to confirm the proof of guilt for both the indictments in the case of Kesselring, and for the first and only indictment in the cases of Mackensen and Mältzer.
>
> Two: In relation to the sentence in the Kesselring case, I have reached the conclusion that there were the following extenuating circumstances which deserve to be taken into consideration:
>
> (A). In his general behaviour during the Italian Campaign, Kesselring fought with impartiality and fairness, excepting the instances which are the subject of the charge against him in relation to the civilian population and Italian culture; furthermore he has always demonstrated a sense of human responsibility, as is evident from the testimony of Field Marshal Alexander and my own personal knowledge and experience of the facts.
>
> (B). If Kesselring had opposed Hitler's orders, regarding immediate and drastic reprisals for the incident of Via Rasella, he would have left himself open to the charge of not wanting to take immediate adequate measures for the safety of his troops, at a time when they found themselves in a critical situation, an accusation which any commander would have been reluctant to face.
>
> (C). The relative uncertainty about the limitations imposed on reprisals by the law and judicial usage, in the light of an increased and intimate link between the civilian population and Partisan fighters [. . .].
>
> (D). The period, during which the orders constituting the basis of the second indictment were in force, was limited and comparatively brief.
>
> Three: The extenuating circumstances mentioned in paragraph 2 (B) also apply to the cases of Mackensen and Mältzer. The latter, being less directly involved than Kesselring and Mackensen in conducting the military operations, but directly responsible for all the military activities in Rome, could, to a certain extent, be considered as having exercised a personal supervision over the methods of conducting the reprisal. In any case, I think it would be unfair to impose, on Mackensen and Mältzer, a heavier sentence than Kesselring's.

> Four: Apart from the above-mentioned extenuating circumstances, there is some doubt regarding the inhuman method with which the reprisal for Via Rasella was conducted. I would not be at peace with my conscience if I were to confirm the death sentence on Kesselring, Mackensen and Mältzer, while there remained even a remote possibility of Kappler getting a lighter sentence. I am convinced that such a possibility does exist.
>
> Five: I also maintain that it would be contrary to the dictates of humanity, even if legally possible, to defer a decision regarding Kesselring, Mackensen and Mältzer until Kappler has been tried and his case finally decided.
>
> Six: After exhaustive and careful reflection on these cases [. . .] I have decided, for the reasons given in paragraphs 2 to 5, to commute the sentences on Kesselring, Mackensen and Mältzer to life imprisonment.
>
> Seven: I would be happy to know if I can proceed with the promulgation of my decision. I have given preventive dispositions so that on 3 July I can pass my command on to others and leave Italy on 4 July. I would appreciate knowing as soon as possible, and not later than 3 July, whether, having put on record my decision regarding the three cases mentioned, I can proceed with such dispositions or not.
>
> Eight: Upon further reflection, as to what should be said when my decision is to be communicated, I would prefer the announcement to be limited to an outline statement. I would appreciate knowing whether this is approved by the Secretary of State. In case he felt that I should provide some reasons or offer some explanations for my decision, I would propose that a statement should be released along the following lines: "General Harding in his capacity [. . .] has confirmed the proof of guilt in the cases of Kesselring, Mackensen and Mältzer. Nevertheless, in view of the circumstances in which the war crimes in question were committed, bearing in mind the individually correct wartime conduct and, above all, the fact that the fate of those directly and personally responsible for the massacre of the Ardeatine Caves is still pending and uncertain, General Harding has decided to commute the sentence in the three cases to life imprisonment." I would be grateful for the most prompt instructions regarding the public announcement.[25]

In 1947 the political climate in which the Nuremberg Trials had been held had changed radically, and the Allies themselves tended to draw a veil of oblivion over the events of the war in order to avoid further embittering German public opinion. The legal framework within which the trials had been held, the differences in the interpretation of the rules of war, and the use that was being made of the Nuremberg Trials themselves in order to mold a politically correct public memory contributed to this outcome. The principles and procedures that had governed Kesselring's trial led back, in fact, to the legal framework of the Nuremberg Trials, whose judicial definition had proved to be extremely complex and whose outcome had not resolved all the doubts about being able to identify and punish the responsibilities at the various command levels of the political-military system.

In more general terms, the hypothesis of the legal prosecution of the political, military and economic leaders of the Third Reich can be traced back to the formalization in 1942 of the UN War Crimes Commission, with the adherence of eighteen Allied nations, as well as the subsequent declaration of Moscow, signed by the Four Powers in October 1943.[26] The Commission translated into investigative practice the plan, above all American, of indicting the leaders of the Axis for the aggression of World War II, codified "as a crime against peace," committed in violation of international law and conventions (the 1924 Geneva Protocol, the 1927 resolution of the League of Nations, the 1928 Franco-German Briand-Kellogg Treaty, and the 1929 Geneva Convention).

Subsequently, the charge of war crimes—drawn up on the basis of the principles codified by the "Convention of the Second Peace Conference of The Hague" of 1907[27]—was included in the International Military Tribunal for the Prosecution and the Punishment of Major War Criminals of the European Axis, the Nuremberg Charter, signed on August 8, 1945. After an intense political and juridical confrontation that lasted a further year, the crimes against "the laws of civilized humanity" were also included among the charges.[28] The crime of conspiracy against peace was defined as

> the direction, preparation, unleashing and prosecution of a war of aggression or violation of treaties, conventions and international agreements, through participation in a concerted plan or conspiracy to realize any of the preceding actions. [. . .] All the accused, in concert with other individuals, in the course of a certain number of years prior to 8 May 1945, have participated in the capacity of leaders, organizers or accomplices in the conception or execution of a concerted plan, or conspiracy, which had as its object the intention of committing crimes against peace, war crimes and crimes against humanity. [. . .] such a concerted plan, or conspiracy, has led to the perpetration of crimes against peace by reason of the conception, preparation, unleashing and conduct of a war of aggression [. . .]; of war crimes by reason of waging unrelenting wars against countries and civilian populations, conducted in violation of the rules and customs of war [. . .], including, without limiting itself to the following, the crimes of the assassination, maltreatment, deportation for forced labour or for other ends of the civilian populations of occupied countries, the assassination or maltreatment of prisoners of war [. . .], the execution of hostages, pillaging and looting of public and private property, the destruction and devastation of cities and villages not justified by military requirements [. . .]; of crimes against humanity, namely, the assassination, extermination, reduction to slavery, deportation and any inhuman action committed against any civilian

> population before and during the war for political, racial and religious motives, when these actions or persecutions—whether or not they have constituted a violation of the internal law of the country in which they were committed—have been committed following or in connection with any crime within the scope of this tribunal.[29]

The final clause had therefore very clearly bound persecution and extermination to conspiracy to commit a war of aggression, thus revealing all the reticence of the Anglo-Saxon members of the Tribunal to include the criminal acts connected with the pre-1939 persecution of the Jews. In particular, the massacre of the Jews had presented considerable juridical difficulties, and for this reason genocide came to be considered a variable of the military measures of the war of aggression. Thus the conspiracy against peace was codified as "a project which had involved the elimination of the European Jews," reducing the latter to a "general treatment, which has shown itself to be part of a general plan of aggression," as was maintained by Sir David Maxwell Fyfe, the Head of the British Delegation.[30]

That the Kesselring trial had also been closely bound to such a legal framework is attested to by the presence, among the trial records, of a report by Major Isham drawn up in June 1945, which recalled how "the criminal policies of the Nazi State" had been subdivided "for the purposes of the trial" into three main sections: "criminal aggression, the violation of the rules of war and the criminal organization of the Nazi State." Within the second category, the following, also applicable to the Italian situation, were to be included: "the seizure and execution of hostages [which] was part of an organized campaign of terrorism" and the implementation of "a plan for the elimination of elements considered undesirable."[31]

War crimes included thirty-three types of offenses already codified in 1919 by the Commission of Responsibilities set up by the preliminary Paris Peace Conference, which had identified and selected them on the basis of the text of the Hague Conference with the aim of indicting the sovereigns and military leaders of the Central Empires for the crimes committed against the civilian populations of the occupied countries and against the populations of their own States, for example, the deportations and massacres of the Armenians by the Ottoman Empire and of the Slavs by the Hapsburg Empire. However, in the period following the Great War, the legal procedures had proved to be ineffective, based on the idea of "une reglémentation accidentelle et dont la portée n'est pas claire."[32]

In the period following World War II, jurists once again encountered very uncertain rules, indicated in articles 46, 47, and 50 of the Convention, regarding the definition of an occupying authority's powers over the population of a foreign, enemy country. During the 1920s and 1930s, the disagreement over these powers had grown.

In the course of time, the attitude of the Western Allies had been neither consistent nor linear: for example, the United States, which in 1945 had proved to be the most resolute supporter of the need to try the leaders of Nazi-Fascism, had, instead, in 1919, expressed very strong reservations about the definition of "crimes against humanity," objecting that "principles of humanity are not a certain standard."[33]

The Charter of the International Military Tribunal at Nuremberg had, therefore, to a certain extent followed the principles stated by the Hague (1907) and Geneva (1929) Conventions, placing under the protection of the law all the countries that had taken part in the war and also promoting an important juridical innovation. Genocide, defined for the first time by the American jurist Richard Lemkin in 1944,[34] came to be included among the crimes against humanity, but this innovation, extremely positive on the juridical plane, nevertheless produced a further problem. If, on the one hand, it made it possible to prosecute those responsible for the genocide of European Jews, on the other hand it led to a clear violation of the principle of the non-retroactivity of the law. And it was also in order to avoid this serious infringement of legal principles that the judges decided on that occasion that genocide would fall under the jurisdiction of the International Military Tribunal, inasmuch as it had been committed in connection with the conspiracy against peace and the planning of the war by the Axis Powers.

It certainly cannot be maintained that that attempt was completely successful. However, one wonders whether the reason for the decision should only be attributed to a legal concern. The close link between genocide and a crime against peace served, in fact, to preclude—since the charge of conspiracy against peace had only been made against the Axis Powers—attention in the course of the trial turning to the possible crimes against humanity perpetrated by the Allied States.

In other words, Nuremberg served to introduce, however indirectly, a form of judicial and statistical selectivity that excluded any State that had been an enemy of the Axis from being implicated in war crimes and crimes against humanity,[35] sanctioning the principle that the behavior of the powers of the anti-Fascist coalition could not have been judged with the same legal standards as those applied to their enemies. The decision definitively exempted the massacre of the Polish officers at Katyn in Poland (certainly committed by the Soviets, but for a long time attributed to the Germans), the carpet bombing of European cities by the Allies, and the dropping of the atom bombs on Japanese cities from prosecution.[36]

The selective and partial law applied by the UN had the aim of sanctioning, through legal proceedings, the "definitive" historical judgment on National Socialism, but that decision produced a chain reaction that contributed to concealing the nature of total war and crimes against humanity.[37] The first effects were felt during the Nuremberg Trials themselves, when the officers of the High Command of the German armed forces appeared before the court and their condemnation reverberated as far as the trials held in Italy. Keitel and Jodl were charged with being responsible for the war of annihilation in Russia and the massacres of civilians in Western Europe, but they were only convicted with extreme difficulty.[38] The judges' uncertainties with regard to the accused emerged clearly, starting from the judicial definition itself of the crimes for which they had been indicted, which the contradictions of international law had not helped to resolve: it was a question of the same problems that would have reappeared in various European countries during the trials of the commanders of the German occupation and in Italy in the course of the Kesselring trial. The ambiguous effects of the judicial decisions of Nuremberg were beginning to build up.

The situation was also aggravated by the hopes the Allies had pinned on the Nuremberg Trials, from which they were expecting an essential contribution to the formation of a new European identity on the basis of the representation of the past and the continent's history sanctioned by the trials themselves. Some incontrovertible "truths" about the war were asserted by exclusively attributing the historical and judicial responsibility to Nazi Germany, with the resulting exoneration of every other country and its ruling class from any suspicion of having yielded to Nazi demands prior to 1939 and having collaborated with the new Hitlerian order after 1941. The fundamental reasons for the preparations for the international Nuremberg Trials thus proved to be undoubtedly the aim to condemn National Socialism and Fascism judicially as systems that had led, by reason of their intrinsic political logic, to the elimination of the Jews, crimes against humanity, and the war against civilian populations; but that judicial context itself was also conditioned by the politically motivated decisions aiming at the legitimization of the new Europe born from the anti-Fascist coalition.

It was not by chance, as has been seen, that the judicial definition itself of the charges proved to be anything but linear. In purely judicial terms, the classification of crimes against peace had never been a subject of controversy; however, the distinction between the other two categories, whose elements tended to a certain extent to overlap,[39] turned out to be more complex. There was, for example, great confusion between war crimes and crimes against humanity. Colonel M. C. Bernays, who in 1944 had been head of the special planning office of the U.S. Defense Ministry, had, at that time, presented a memorandum to the UN War Crimes Commission in which he had shown all the limits inherent in the category of war crimes. It would not have been possible to include in this category, for example, the persecution of German Jews; those living in territories annexed to the Reich, such as Austria after the *Anschluss*; or the Sudeten Czechoslovaks. With the agreement of London, an attempt was then made to overcome these difficulties through the drafting of the two new categories included in article 6, crimes against peace and crimes against humanity, in the charter signed on August 8, 1945. The charter stated that also those who—like the German military commanders—had maintained that they were acting legally according to the juridical canons in force in their own countries, as well as according to the previous (even if inadequate) international law, would have been punishable for having committed crimes against peace and humanity.

The fundamental rule—*nullum crimen sine lege*—had been very clearly infringed, and the violation of the judicial principle of the non-retroactivity of the law raised misgivings. An attempt was made to overcome them by showing how the new norms were only an extension of some old laws that could be traced back to The Hague (1907) and Geneva (1929) Conventions, but this produced a whole range of new interpretative controversies and a maze of contradictions that were never resolved. And yet the violation of non-retroactivity would have been amply justified, because the principle *nullum crimen sine lege* had, in some way, to yield to the superiority of another principle of a moral nature; it was necessary not to leave unpunished very serious crimes, like the elimination of the European Jews. Following a kind of heterogenesis of aims, that violation acted in a positive way on the law itself, because it made it possible for the first time to pass judgment on crimes that until then had remained unpunished. However, the atrocities not included in the category of war crimes according to the military codes of some countries, or defined in an uncertain way by international law (such as reprisals and the massacre of civilian populations), avoided legal redefinition and came to be judged by means of the old laws. Thus, during the trials of Kesselring and the military commanders of the German occupation system in Italy, the judicial basis remained the British Code, supplemented by international law based on The Hague and Geneva Conventions. The contradictions opened the way to a discussion of the divergences between the military codes of the different countries. The most important achievement of the Nuremberg Trials, the concept of "injury to the human condition and dignity," therefore had no effect at all on the way in which the trials of war criminals were conducted in the postwar period. The equalization and judicial equivalence of war crimes and crimes against humanity was arrived at much later, with the trials, held in France in the 1980s, of those in charge of the Vichy police, such as Maurice Papon and Paul Touvier, and the trial of Klaus Barbie. In Italy, it would have been necessary to wait for the second trial of Erich Priebke at the end of the 1990s in order to reopen the discussion about the inclusion of the notion of crimes against humanity in Italian legal codes.[40]

Chapter 5

A Brutal Peace and the Nuremberg Consensus

The trials of the Axis "war criminals" held by the Allies came to be justified by its twofold aim: on the one hand, to punish the war of aggression, the infraction of the rules of war, and the violation of the principles of human civilization; on the other hand, the democratic re-education of the vanquished. The trials were a combination of jurisprudence and politics and, inasmuch as they were decisive aspects of the Allied occupation policy in the territories of the Axis regimes, also ways of presenting the victors' moral virtue, as well as the condemnation without appeal of the defeated. They contributed to building between 1945 and 1948 the "orthodox" historical-political conception of Europe's recent past.

The juridical principles and the judicial proceedings molded the "substance of the trial" itself by selecting and deconstructing the historical events to be remembered and the forms of their codification through the perspective of the categories of crimes against peace, war crimes, and crimes against humanity; but, to a certain extent, they made National Socialist criminality a category removed from the context in which it had arisen. From this point of view, an example was the case of the elimination of the Eastern European Jews, of which macroscopic aspects—such as the massacres by mass shooting—linked to the dispositions issued by the Army Supreme Command for "Operation Barbarossa" and aimed at the elimination of "special categories" such as the members of the Resistance and the political commissars of the Soviet Army, were ignored in judicial terms and forgotten in time.

Furthermore, from the time of the Nuremberg Trials, it was difficult to set the Wehrmacht in the context of the Nazi terror apparatus. The Wehrmacht was too easily reduced to being considered only an imperialistic aggressor aiming at European domination. The idea of Marrus and others that the Nuremberg Trials have therefore been a historical "turning point"[1] needs to be reassessed: the boundless mass of documents accumulated for the trials can certainly be considered an important, or rather decisive, source for historical study, provided that the researcher does not allow himself to be influenced by the judicial categories of trials that did not succeed in satisfactorily conceptualizing "Nazi criminality." The aspects taken into consideration and correctly set in their context often led back to others that were decontextualized or even eliminated, resulting in a partial and selective historical reconstruction.[2] The judicial action against "Nazi criminality" did not, however, end with the trials for the war crimes committed against certain categories of victims, such as Allied prisoners or the civilian populations of the occupied countries. The thirteen Nuremberg Trials (the International Military Tribunal and the other twelve trials supported by Control Council Law no. 10, which was based on the IMT's charter itself) concerned themselves solely with the so-called "major war criminals,"[3] while in other European countries the Allied judicial authorities dealt with the "minor war criminals." Among the latter should be included the Kesselring trial itself. The Nuremberg IMT's judicial program was, in other words, the result of mediation between American government departments, in which Stimson and Roosevelt's line prevailed. It was based on interpreting Nazi criminality as the result of the conspiracy of the powers of the Third Reich to achieve European domination by means of war. All the trials that followed the IMT—the twelve linked to it and those held in the zones of occupied Germany, as well as in Italy—followed the same approach as the committal proceedings of Nuremberg, according to which the indictments necessarily stemmed from the Nazi conspiracy to dominate Europe through a war of aggression. Naturally, the charges also included the violation of treaties and international agreements, the criminal conduct of the war, and crimes against humanity.[4]

By applying a substantially positivist conception of the law, it thus became possible to document and substantiate the conspiracy plan because the IMT investigators ascertained the actions that could be attributed to the party organizations, the military structures, and the industrial apparatus and identified the individuals in charge of them. Identification of those in the "polycratic" structure, as it has been defined by Broszat, of the power apparatus involved in the formation and implementation of Nazi policy was reduced to an arbitrarily selecting its leading exponents, like the selection that led to the Nuremberg Trials, while it would have imposed a modification of the judicial organization.

The English Public Prosecutor had assured the Allies, in particular the French and the Soviets—the most determined to carry out the judicial operation—that the British Government would have participated in this series of new trials; the Foreign Office, however, showed itself to be reluctant to strike the most important entrepreneurs and financiers of the major German industries and banks, starting from Krupp and IG-Farben, with a second set of Nuremberg trials. It was not by chance that in the first of the Nuremberg Trials—that of Göring and the leading figures of the Third Reich—the banker Schacht had been acquitted.[5]

The same difficulties arose in the case of the indictment of the thirteen high-ranking officers of the Wehrmacht, the Luftwaffe, and the Navy, who were selected by Taylor for the crime of conspiracy against peace, among whom the most famous were the Commander in Chief of the Wehrmacht from 1938 to 1941, von Brauchitsch; the commander of the army that invaded Poland, von Rundstet; and General Manstein, the commander of the XI Army in the Soviet Union. They were all deeply involved in the planning and organization of "Operation Barbarossa."

Eventually, the great unease felt by public opinion in different European countries transformed itself in Great Britain into strong hostility against charges being brought once again against the military; the English officials in Germany, meanwhile, showed themselves more willing to try the members of the police forces, the SS, and the National Socialist apparatus. The cases of Kesselring and Manstein thus became the paradigm of British reluctance to tackle the central problem of the relationship between the German Army and the National Socialist totalitarian system.[6]

The strength of the interventions opposed both to the holding of Field Marshal Kesselring's trial and to his conviction—Headlan, Churchill, General Alexander, Lord de l'Isle, Lord Hankley, Stokes of the Labour Party, Archbishop G. Bell, and the writer T. S. Eliot—bears out how widely held, by then, was the intention of distinguishing clearly between the actions of the army and the responsibilities of the SS. Of course, all this demonstrates the complete lack of understanding of the nature of the total war put into practice by the Third Reich in Central-Eastern Europe and of the war waged against Italian civilians. The framework of principles, rules, and categories within which the trials were held and interpreted, therefore, constituted a form of selective justice; moreover, this selectivity was influenced by political criteria that were adopted after the trials themselves began both in order to stop any further judicial developments and to bring to a close the entire issue of trials in the climate of the incipient cold war.[7] The British attitude to the Wehrmacht in general and Kesselring in particular came to be "justified" by the necessity, deeply rooted in conservative political circles, in military nationalists like Alexander, and in Catholic and conservative writers like Eliot, of believing in the myth of the survival of a European and Christian culture common to the Germans and the English (rather than to the Germans and the Americans). The British advocates of Christian and conservative liberalism thus demonstrated all their difficulties in understanding how Fascism and Nazism had also been a consequence of that culture and that same tradition; that is, they had difficulty understanding that, after all, the Fascists and Nazis had done nothing other than utilize ideas, systems, and mechanisms that had been present for a long time in European society and its political rationality.[8]

Liberal conservatism and Prussianism shared at least two axioms of this rationality: first, the principle that respect for the law and the laws of war should be based on mutually-accepted codes of honor, as in the wars of the 1700s; second, the distinction—based precisely on the principle that has just been described—between a sphere of civilization characterized by the ethics of reciprocity and a world of barbarism alien to it. The Angles and the Saxons had always been linked to Christianity and Europe, namely, to civilization. The Wehrmacht itself, in fact, had tried, in propaganda terms, to present its own system of occupation in Western Europe—in particular in Denmark, Holland, France and Flemish Belgium—as being modeled on the code of the European tradition. Naturally, the world of the East, of the Poles, the Russians, and the Jews of Central-Eastern Europe, had to be considered in different terms.

After all, the Nazis had expected the barbarism of the *Partisanenkrieg* in the East. It was not by chance that for that area they had adopted in advance, at the beginning of "Operation Barbarossa," the countermeasures that would have unleashed terror. The outbreak of guerrilla warfare on the Western Front, after the Allied landings in Italy in 1943 and in France in 1944, had modified their mental outlook, and they had violated (as had the Resistance fighters, for that matter) the taboo of the illegality and dishonorable nature of the attacks on uniformed troops by civilians operating surreptitiously. The new forms of total war and the end of the distinction between the military and civilians were not, however, so easily accepted, not even by the Allies, who had, nevertheless, benefited from partisan warfare. This reluctance was only the other side of a culture of military honor common to all the traditional European elites, steadfast in their belief in the illegal and treacherous nature of guerrilla warfare. That Kesselring's ideas were not, after all, very different from Montgomery's would have emerged when, in 1948, at the Stockholm Conference, the British proposed some extremely significant criteria to define the legal character of a partisan liberation movement as an alliance with a belligerent in an international conflict, a formal declaration of war, the existence of a joint command, and so on. The political intention of denying the legitimacy of the colonial liberation movements of European empires was evident.[9]

It is not, therefore, by chance that, precisely from this perspective, the legacy of Nuremberg, which generations of defenders of human rights have identified as the milestone of the long journey towards the International Court with universal jurisdiction,[10] has always been extremely controversial. On the one hand, the verdicts formulated by the International Military Tribunal appeared to be based on a conservative vision, since all the death sentences were only imposed for violations of the traditional laws of war and not for crimes against humanity. On the other hand, at the end of the other twelve Nuremberg Trials, the Allies (starting with the Americans) were compelled to adopt a new judicial policy based on criteria of greater clemency and, between 1952 and 1953, forced to defend themselves from a campaign, not immune from Nazi sympathizers who were determined not to recognize the legal validity of the trials held at Nuremberg. Many years later, the American Prosecutor of the International Military Tribunal, Telford Taylor, commented that "Nuremberg consists of what actually happened there, but also of what people think happened—and the second aspect is perhaps more important than the first."[11]

Between 1950 and 1958, the Allies' new judicial policy therefore tried to respond to the pressure of German public opinion without challenging the legality of the proceedings, but bearing in mind the new and decisive element at stake in the European political agenda: the re-establishment of a German Army necessary for the equilibrium of the cold war. The Federal Republic's new parliament thus succeeded both in avoiding an official admission of responsibility for Nazi Germany's war crimes and in expressing sympathy towards the requests made by veterans' movements for the release of the military still held in custody.[12]

Freed in 1951, Field Marshal Kesselring became one of the most eminent spokesmen of the German veterans' movement, with the explicit aim "of finally freeing the question of the cases of war crimes from the intrusion of political issues."[13]

The peculiarity of National Socialism, in a historical context, therefore resides, above all, in its epilogue. The war afforded the victors not only victory but also the trial of the vanquished through the figures of some of the leading exponents of the Third Reich. The Nuremberg Trials were in fact an extraordinary novelty and a success that the Allies' predecessors, in 1918, had failed to achieve, but it was also a bad exercise of justice to the exclusive advantage of the victors, who did not grant the accused the guarantees they could have had if there had also been judges from neutral countries as well as German magistrates.

Joseph Rovan, who had been deported to Dachau and later became an expert in German history, denounced the unforgivable errors[14] and Bronislaw Baczko also stated that he was of the same opinion:

> The great merit of the procedure followed at Nuremberg resides in the definition itself of crimes against humanity. Having said that, its great fault was that of having limited the responsibility for such crimes, attributing them solely to the Germans. It was the trial in which the victors judged the defeated Nazi regime. At a single stroke and thanks to a tacit agreement between the Allies, the crimes committed, for example, by the Soviets were forgotten. Katyn is the most striking example. Nevertheless, if today it is possible to define the elimination of fifteen thousand Polish officers as a crime against humanity, then let us recognise that we owe it to the jurisprudence of Nuremberg.[15]

Starting from Nuremberg, the course of justice bifurcated. On the lopped branch were the Nazis responsible for shooting Ukrainian children, while on the branch that was intact those responsible for the bombing of Dresden managed to save themselves. As Léon Poliakov has written:

> Starting from that moment, there have been two distinct kinds of international law, one for the Germans, the other for the rest of the world.[16] The world of the victors also remained divided. If in the Soviet Union, in the press, the acquittals and light sentences given by the German courts were denounced, and if in Italy the left-wing newspapers conducted a press campaign against the release of Kesselring, Mackensen, Mältzer and the others, in the Anglo-Saxon countries there was, instead, another aspect subjected to intense criticism: the principle of the "collective guilt of a people," which, after the Nuremberg Trials, had been codified more in the European public memory than in the court sentences.[17]

In the postwar period in Germany the Allies tried another 5,006 people, of whom 794 were condemned to death (486 of them were killed). In the American Occupied Zone further trials consequent upon the Nuremberg assizes were held. At the time, the German press defined them on the basis of the social and professional status of the accused: there was thus a trial of doctors, one of generals, one of jurists, and one of the bureaucrats of the concentration camps. From 1947–48 the German legal system itself would have proceeded, even if with obvious reluctance and very insignificant results, with the preparation of several thousand further cases for trial, while in other European countries tribunals were set up: standard ones (as in Norway, Denmark, and Yugoslavia), special ones (as in Czechoslovakia and Poland), and military tribunals (as in Italy and Greece).

Everywhere, in other words, the trials presented, apart from the court verdicts, an attempt to overcome through the verdicts and the sentences the moral crisis that had assailed every European country and of which so-called "collaborationism" was only an epiphenomenon. All the countries of Western Europe recognised that their own legislation on treason was totally inadequate to deal with the unprecedented phenomenon of the long occupation and the widespread collaboration with the Nazis, but they all had to overcome this deficiency with one form or another of retroactive justice.[18] Thus, the purges and the course of justice appeared radically different from country to country: they were, for example, very harsh in Belgium and Holland, more uncertain in France and Italy, while it was obvious everywhere that such objectives lacked a solid legal and cultural basis.

In Belgium, the High Commissioner for State Security dealt with more than 150,000 cases of collaborationism (a very high percentage for the size of the country) but acted inconsistently, sometimes yielding to left-wing pressure that aimed at punishing the associations close to the Catholic Church, while in other cases protecting the financial and entrepreneurial elites necessary for the country's postwar economic reconstruction.[19] In the kingdom of the Netherlands it proved difficult to judge the conduct of the mayors—in that country, the public administrators were not elected, but appointed by the Crown—who had remained in office during the Nazi occupation at the government's (secret) direction. It was difficult in many cases to establish whether they had acted in the interests of the population or had exceeded those limits by collaborating politically with the regime of Arthur Seyss-Inquart.[20]

The justice system, nevertheless, played an authentically political part in the war-to-reconstruction transitional crises, while the political authorities played an often ambiguous public and civil role, arbitrarily selecting, through ritual, ceremonies, and commemorations, what should be remembered and what to consign to oblivion for the sake of the new identity conceived for their own country.[21] A great deal has been written about the purges in Italy.[22]

In this context the Italian situation appears significant because of the depth of the crisis that had led to the change in the unified-monarchical constitutional system and to the system that presented itself as a new State, not without strong elements of ambiguity and wishful thinking.[23] The Italian crisis could not, in fact, be traced back only to the collapse of the ruling class on September 8, 1943, but rather to a weakness linked to the genesis itself of the unified State,[24] even if, as Rosario Romeo has pointed out, the crisis of the nation and of patriotism had not been a solely Italian phenomenon but was, on the contrary, a transitional occurrence in progress throughout European society.[25] For Italy, the period 1943–47 was exceptionally important for the confused revision of the recent past by the institutions, above all by the government that, from July 25, 1943, had taken on both the legislative and executive powers and that combined all State and non-State powers—the law, the army, the National Liberation Committee—that claimed the right to direct the transition. While there was a gradual slowdown in the impetus of the Resistance, which had been, as Claudio Pavone has written, "an attempt to deal with the past,"[26] in Italian society the interpretative paradigms and celebratory styles of a selective and partial memory, which were destined to a long life in Republican society, were taking shape. That period witnessed the failure of the plan for a consistent national perspective based on a shared vision of the nation's past and therefore the idea itself of a new secular anti-Fascist religion. The cause of this failure did not lie in a weak intention, but rather in structural fragility, namely, in the break-up of the institutions and the crisis of legitimacy into which the State—which for over twenty years had monopolized the totalitarian political religion and its patriotic nationalist liturgies directed at the regime—had plunged.[27]

Thus, in Italy, in the postwar period, there was the striking failure of the celebration of public holidays (the Day of the Soldier and the Partisan soon ended, while April 25 remained a celebration directed by the Italian National Association of Partisans in an atmosphere of conflict); a cult of the fallen that could be traced back to the patriotic code that had survived up to the Great War did not emerge; the monuments and the memorial plaques did not have a uniform stylistic character in the lettering; decorations and medals were conferred on the basis of pressure from groups or communities and without any consistent national planning; the paradigm of Romantic heroism and of the myth of the ethical nature of war collapsed in the literature that only entrusted the possibility of re-establishing the nation's moral sense to its collective sufferings, interpreted as a necessary expiation.[28]

What happened then appears to have been marked, above all, by a crisis of legitimacy on the part of the State and the old ruling class that the lie of the anti-Fascist government, led by Bonomi, barely succeeded in masking, while it unrealistically tried to justify *a posteriori* the tortuous course of a country that had entered the war in 1940 allied to the Axis and had ended up on the opposite side.

> The Council of Ministers, in its first meeting, notes that, because of its political origins, it represents that great majority of the country which, as early as 1940, had been opposed to Fascist rule and Italy's entry into the war on the side of Hitler's Germany. Hence, as its first act, the Council states that Fascism alone is responsible for Italy's adherence to the Tripartite Pact and its entry into the war, and that therefore Italy's detachment from those who were not its allies, but the allies of Fascism, is nothing other than the legitimate consequence of the political change which has occurred.[29]

Thus the national identity was entrusted, above all, to the Italian people's shared feelings about the war, the defeat, the German occupation, and the resulting suffering.[30] Franco Calamandrei was able to write that the nation's adversities had laid the new foundations of the national attitude.[31]

Chapter 6

The "Mirror" of Vichy

One of the most important consequences of the selective memory constructed through the Nuremberg Trials and the trials held in various European countries was the introduction of a hiatus between the pre- and postwar periods: as if the end of the war in 1945 and the collapse of the new Hitlerian order and the different forms of Fascism had represented a kind of year zero for the European States. If the causes and reasons of many peoples' and governments' assent to totalitarianism had to be sought in the lack of confidence in parliamentary systems and the Liberal ruling classes that had become widespread throughout Europe in the 1930s, then, precisely for this reason, to underrate or, even worse, to ignore the historical link between the war of the 1940s and the two preceding decades would not fail to have negative consequences for public memory and historiographic understanding.

It is not mere chance that still today the nature of the Second World War, the significance of the opposing alliances in the conflict, and its epilogue are extremely controversial questions in the international debate, of which, though, almost the only aspect known in Italy is the translation of the most recent German discussion. And it should be noted that even that discussion is well known not for its important analysis of far-distant times (Meinecke and later the *Fischerkontroverse* of 1961) but for the recent and most ideologically inclined discussions, from the *Historikerstreit* of 1986–87 to the Nolte case of 1990, up to the 1995 debate on the role of May 8 and to the issue of the Hamburg Exhibition about the Wehrmacht.[1] As regards the not-so-well-known history of the French debate—to which I have already referred in connection with the Klaus Barbie trial—I now propose a digression that lays no claims to being systematic or complete, but that can be useful in shedding light on the interwoven links, which also occurred in Italy as early as 1946–47, between the political use of the history of the war of the Resistance and of Republican Fascism, the political and institutional history of the Republic, and the contradictions of Italy's national identity.

Considering the events in France can be useful because also in that country the interwoven links between the paths of historiographic research, judicial practice and political conflicts have always been very close, particularly concerning the memory of Vichy and its role in French consciousness.

The historiography of Vichy can be briefly divided into three periods: the years from 1954 to 1968, which constitute the period dominated by the cultural mood of the Liberation; those from 1968 to 1972, which correspond to the sudden appearance of the new international historiographic research, which was freer from the dogmas of the postwar period; and finally the period that began in the 1970s of the development of a French historiography capable of no longer considering Vichy as a static and monolithic historical subject.

The first period was dominated by the work of Robert Aron, published in 1954, a classic example of a retrospective interpretation influenced by the too-recent memory of the Liberation, the obscuring of the political complexity of the first phase of the regime (from 1940 to 1942), and the pre-eminence accorded to the judicial sources of the purge trials.[2] Aron's analysis rested on four main pillars, which have for a long time been the mainstay of historiographic common sense: the existence of the National Socialists' irrevocable *Diktat*; Vichy as a "shielding" regime, opposed to the *Diktat*; the secret double-dealing between Vichy and the Allies, and finally, French public opinion, essentially *attentiste*, that would have trusted Pétain but was ready to espouse the cause of the Allies, De Gaulle, and the French Communist Party.

Twenty-five years later, partial access to French archives, and above all to wartime German sources confiscated at the time by the Americans,[3] enabled historians, especially the non-French, to undermine Aron's paradigm, demonstrating that the regime, particularly in the first two years of its existence, had actively sought to go well beyond the limits of the 1940 Armistice and had established a voluntary collaboration—even though neutral—with the new Hitlerian European order. The very use that Vichy had made of its neutrality—for example, in Syria in 1941 and in North Africa in 1942—demonstrated the existence of an anti-Allied approach and the conviction of being able to pursue a national regeneration within the compass of a diplomatic compromise with a German victory, which then appeared irreversible. After all, as late as the mid-1970s, French public opinion maintained that those faced with the new Hitlerian order had only collaboration and resistance as alternatives. It is, above all, the merit of the American historian, Robert Paxton, to have shown that Vichy's central objective had, instead, been to find a third independent way for a neutral country in Hitler's Europe and, after 1942 (the occupation of the South Zone), to act as an arbitrator between the two camps.[4]

The success of Paxton's book eclipsed the merits of other historians who had, to a certain extent, anticipated some of his theses: the German Eberhard Jäckel, the Briton Geoffrey Warner, and the Frenchmen Yves Durand and Henri Michel.[5] Paxton's work itself enjoyed great popularity above all among the intellectuals of 1968, who were already inclined to criticize the Gaullist and Communist values of the previous generation,[6] but it was rejected by middle-class public opinion, which was still convinced that Pétain's gamble had been legitimate (and that Vichy had actually helped De Gaulle and the Allies).[7] The works that appeared between 1966 and 1972 have, therefore, demolished the four pillars of Robert Aron's paradigm. The main credit goes, however, to Robert Paxton: it was the Virginian historian who demonstrated that the supposed Nazi *Diktat* was in fact a bland compromise and that until the end of 1941 France had been left free to govern itself autonomously outside the zone of direct occupation; it was Paxton who documented how the Führer had been prepared to order the simple neutralization of the French State and military system and how such a solution had continued until the beginning of "Operation Barbarossa" in the Soviet Union, when, instead, the intensive exploitation of French resources and manpower was enforced. It was this turning point of 1941–42 that was at the root of the collaboration between the Milice and the German police and therefore of a more intense repression of the Resistance at the "service of forced labour"; but the German occupation in France remained nevertheless milder than in other parts of Western Europe (suffice it to say that until 1942 Germany managed to control French territory with barely forty thousand men of the *Landesschütz* battalions). It was the decision, taken spontaneously by the Vichy Government, to offer the Germans the widest concessions in the hope of obtaining in exchange the status of voluntary collaborator (and therefore greater political freedom to maneuver) that determined the conditions of a closer alliance and later of a harsher occupation:[8] the desire to attain (by granting it to the Germans) sovereignty over the two zones into which the nation was divided produced a closer integration of the national and German administrations. Finally, it should be remembered that Paxton and, more generally, the historiography of the 1970s also had the merit of exploding the myth of the "double-dealing" that Vichy would have practiced with the Germans and the Anglo-Americans.[9]

In the 1980s and 1990s, a national historiography (Azema, Rousso, Burrin, Bedarida, Peschanski, etc.) was taking shape in France, and PhD and master's theses were proliferating.[10] Questions about the continuity of the State, assent, and collaborationism naturally sprang to the forefront, and studies tended to underline the regime's originality compared to other types of Fascist totalitarian States (for example, the absence of a single party), revealing the role played by the prefects and the administration in running the regime and highlighting the bureaucratic and State centralization—a long-standing reality in the history of the State and of institutions—which would have continued after Liberation.[11] And, as regards assent, the research by Paul Laborie and John Sweets on postal and telephone surveillance succeeded in demonstrating the existence of a less-widespread conformism than had generally been supposed and a process of erosion of confidence in Pétain and the elites that had occurred prior to November 1942 and the occupation of the South Zone.[12]

It remains an open question, however, as to how much that assent, perhaps insignificant in society as a whole, could modify the decisions of the élites—the politicians, entrepreneurs, civil servants, prefects, military, trade unionists,[13] and intellectuals—who, instead, appear to have been decidedly inclined to collaborate, through a widely diversified gamut of behavior that, as Stanley Hoffmann has shown, ranged from cooperation for opportunistic self-interest and collaboration in the name of a misguided national interest to authentic ideological collaborationism.[14] Marc Bloch, in concluding his intellectual testament, *L'étrange défaite*, had, not by chance, singled out the ruling class, high-ranking officials and the intellectuals in order to identify the protagonists of a cultural and moral rejection of republican democracy that, he felt, could be traced back to the Dreyfus affair. And, half a century later, Burrin, the French-Swiss historian, documented the contribution to collaborationism from the nonconformist intelligentsia, the technocratically inspired radical and Socialist culture, and even from critical Communism and personalistically inspired Catholic social spirituality, demonstrating how Vichy mirrored the drifting of the French conscience.[15]

It is precisely in dealing with these problems—the assent of society, the *collaboration d'état* of the élites, and the non-parenthetic nature of the regime in the context of nineteenth- and twentieth-century French history—that the path of research has intersected those that the journalist Eric Conan and the historian Henry Rousso have defined, as "the wanderings of memory."[16] The public memory of Vichy has, in fact, experienced since 1944 numerous rifts and breaks in the course of a process of drafting that has been at the centre of media, press, and show business operations, as well as political conflicts and judicial battles.

As in the case of historiography, one can also consider the history of memory. The first period of public memory has in fact been defined as the "unrealized working-through of a bereavement" and coincides, in large measure, with the history of the Fourth Republic: a time marked by the summary liquidation of the past through excessive purges (11,000 summary executions, 58,000 criminal trials, 69 civil lawsuits, 30,000 sanctions against public officials, 800 death sentences carried out) and, subsequently, the creation of the Gaullist myth ("les valeurs de la France éternelles incarnées dans la Resistance"). Inevitably, this unrealized working-through of bereavement had to be followed by a phase of repression in the 1960s and 1970s. The myths of the postwar period would only have crumbled between the second half of the 1970s and the 1980s, above all with the discovery of French joint responsibility for the elimination of European Jews.

In 1993, Susan Zuccotti revealed the role of Vichy officials in the deportations;[17] a year earlier Anne Grynberg had discovered that it had been the Third Republic, in 1939, which had interned in concentration camps Spanish Republicans and the foreigners in exile from Fascist regimes, among whom there were many Jews.[18] Consequent to the historiographic revelations, between the 1980s and the 1990s, the lawyers Serge and Beate Klarsfeld thus began to seek out those who had been in charge of the Vichy Milice, such as Maurice Papon, who was responsible for the deportation of the Jews of Bordeaux, and judges and historians began to cross each others' paths and invade their respective fields. (Robert Paxton, for example, was called to give evidence in the Papon trial in 1993.) The persecution of the Jews very quickly became the parameter by which to formulate a judgement, no longer historical but ethical, on Vichy, when the autonomy of the regime's initiative for a census, the marking and exclusion of French Jews, and its insistence in cooperating with the Germans in the deportation of foreign Jews to the East were definitively proved by Asher Cohen.[19]

It was, however, the press and television reporters who distorted the collective perception of those important historiographic discoveries, even inventing false taboos, such as the presence of shameful State secrets concealed in the national archives or the presumed "conspiracy of silence" attributable to the "recurring Pétainism" of the French political class. Between the 1980s and the 1990s, a great deal was written about Jean Moulin, who was supposed to have been a crypto-Communist agent and eliminated because of rivalries within the Resistance. On February 3, 1993, a decree of the Balladur Government instituted the "National Day commemorating the racist and anti-Semitic persecutions committed between

1940 and 1944 under the *de facto* authority called the 'Government of the French State.'" What appears to be a right and proper act to the memory of the elimination of the Jews contains, in the specious formula designating Vichy as a "*de facto* authority," an insidious tendency to delegitimize a regime with full powers that had been acknowledged in 1940 by the vote, as totally legal as it was ignominious, in the National Assembly. By delegitimizing Vichy, Balladur was, in effect, aiming at making people forget the indisputable fact that it had been the French Parliament of the Third Republic that had consecrated its birth. The development of research and the wanderings of memory were, by then, openly intersecting the paths of politics and the judicial proceedings.

In 1994, the President of the Representative Council of Jewish Institutions, Jean Kahn, demanded a formal condemnation by the National Assembly of the regime's crimes, on the basis of the irrefutable fact of the responsibilities of the Assembly itself in its decision to confer full powers on Pétain in June 1940; at the same time, the National Front refused to participate in the ceremony commemorating the rounding up of the 13,000 Parisian Jews, who were arrested on July 16–17, 1942, by the French police ("la rafle du Vel'd'Hiv"), setting against this horror the "much more bloody" record of the revolutionary terror of 1793 and of the Commune, which would have produced—according to Le Pen—more victims than Klaus Barbie.[20]

In other words, in the 1990s, a new power struggle over the public memory was beginning to be waged; what was at stake concerned historical knowledge and its presumed power of legitimization. Inevitably, coming on top of this struggle was a clash between judicial and historical judgements, through which scientific and judicial powers and functions were reassigned.

In its turn, the oblique course of the trials and punishment of the war criminals and those responsible for crimes against humanity disrupted the traditional scenario through a series of reciprocal exchanges between the public agenda, the evolution of the law, and the construction of the historical memory. Three examples from different periods of France's long postwar period can shed light on this web of interrelationships: I am referring to the violent political battle in the 1950s that surrounded the trial of the massacre of Oradour-sur-Glane, the irruption of international law into French legislation and the opportunistic maneuvers connected with the Barbie trial in 1987, and the Touvier trial and the emergence of the political contradictions accumulated by the Fifth Republic regarding Vichy during the 1990s.

In considering the first case, we thus return to the immediate postwar period. Following the end of the phase of the purges, all the early Presidents of the Fourth Republic—De Gaulle, Gouin, Bidault, Auriol—had striven to rebuild the unity of the country, using their presidential powers themselves to suspend sentences and release those who were imprisoned. A first major amnesty, in 1951, had halved the number of those imprisoned for collaboration, and a second, on July 24, 1953, had reduced the imprisoned collaborators to less than 1,500. But in the same year, the trial for the massacre of the population of Oradour, a small village in the Limousin, had come to disturb this march towards judiciary oblivion, unleashing a clash, not only of opinions but also of procedures, between the political Right and Left and between different regions of the country, in particular between Limoges and Alsace. The massacre of Oradour had, in fact, been perpetrated by a platoon of soldiers of French nationality, incorporated with Nazi troops, like 160,000 other Alsatians "forcibly incorporated" after the annexation of the region to the Reich in 1940. In Parliament, the extremists and the moderates of this episode fought each other by means of legal measures in order to set off or defuse the explosive impact of a war-crime trial of French compatriots. First, a law was passed that accepted the collective responsibility of those who had belonged to the German military units guilty of war crimes, but a subsequent second law exempted the French (and therefore the Alsatians of Oradour). The Alsatians, in whose favor the National Assembly's incredible decision had discriminated, were, however, convicted in court because of proven individual responsibilities. In the final act of the drama, the stubborn will to achieve judiciary oblivion nevertheless won out, and an amnesty, exclusively reserved for them, was granted to those responsible for the Oradour massacre.[21]

The trial of Klaus Barbie, however, took place in a new legal context. Since 1964, in fact, Parliament had declared that crimes against humanity were not subject to the statute of limitations. Barbie, who in 1944 was head of the Einsatz Kommando of Lyons, was held to be responsible for the persecution of hundreds of French Jews, the elimination of many *maquisards*, and, above all, the death of Jean Moulin, the head of the Resistance and De Gaulle's emissary in the South Zone. Having escaped punishment after his arrest in Germany in 1945 thanks to collaboration with the American secret services, since 1951 he had been living in Bolivia (where Regis Debray had tried to apprehend him in 1973). In 1983 he was finally captured due to pressure from the French authorities and the Minister of Justice, Badinter. (At that time, the government included many former Resistance fighters such as Mitterand, Mauroy, and Cheysson.)

Klaus Barbie's trial was an event of multi-faceted significance, but in the first place, it represented the left-wing government's response to a poisoned cultural climate. Since 1978, theses denying the massacre of the Jews, maintained by figures such as Faurisson, Rassinier and Thion, had had a certain following in the country. The war against negationism, insistently waged at that time by Raymond Aron, Jacques Juillard and Pierre Vidal-Naquet, influenced the trial considerably. However, that sacrosanct intellectual reaction produced an effect as adverse as it was unwelcome: the trial, in fact, was held not to punish the war crimes committed by Barbie—including the killing of Jean Moulin—which, by then, twenty years later, were barred by the statute of limitations, according to French law, but rather for the crimes against humanity that were not statute barred. However, care was taken to ensure that the trial avoid laying bare the mortal sins of the French conscience and also, to a certain extent, the link between the "culture of the Left" and Vichy. In this episode, the symptoms of the "unmentioned"—which, as will be seen, would, though only later, have been strikingly revealed—had, however, already emerged clearly.[22]

During the trial, the clash between the judicial authorities concerned, above all, the interpretation of the concept of crimes against humanity. The investigating magistrate, Riss, concluded that Barbie's actions against the members of the Resistance had been war crimes and that therefore Barbie could only be tried for the crimes committed against Jews not involved in Partisan actions. The Court of Cassation and the "Chambre d'accusation" of the Paris Court of Appeal instead extended the category of crimes against humanity to include the persecution of Partisans and Resistance fighters, Jewish and non-Jewish, on the basis of the necessity of defining the torture and assassination of Resistance fighters, or the deportation of civilians to an enemy country, as *also* being a crime against humanity. The clause of article 6 of the 1945 Treaty of London, on the basis of which the International Military Tribunal of Nuremberg had been set up, thus found its first concrete application in a European country's legislation.[23]

Finally, in 1994, an important judicial battle took place concerning Paul Touvier, formerly in charge of the Information Service of the Milice, guilty of the 1944 deportation and elimination of hundreds of Jews and of the killing of Resistance fighters and Jews, such as the octogenarian Victor Basch, President of the League of the Rights of Man and a past supporter of Dreyfus. The Touvier trial closed this judicial and political chapter. The episode had incredible features; Touvier had already been arrested and convicted in 1946, then in 1947 he had escaped with ministerial complicity and had lived undisturbed for decades in his native Chambéry under the protection of the local church, from whose ranks he had come as a fundamentalist and militant Catholic of the Cross of Fire of the 1930s. Yet again, the path of the judicial authorities had intersected that of the historians, and the complicity of the traditionalist Catholic Church was brought to light thanks to a dossier published by the historian René Remond, courageously encouraged by Cardinal Albert Decourtray. The old anti-republican idiosyncrasies of transalpine Catholicism, the spread of anti-Semitism in society, and Catholic support for Vichy became the object of political debate, and the Gaullist ruling class itself became involved in the scandal of the protection accorded to the former Vichy commissioner; it had, in fact, been the President in office in 1971, Georges Pompidou, who had pardoned Touvier's crimes, which were not yet statute barred.[24]

We have thus reviewed the course of history. We have followed the uneven path of the law, which ranged from judiciary oblivion to unexpected initiatives on the part of justice. We have identified, above all between the end of the 1980s and the 1990s, the intersection of the paths of judges and historians, where criminal lawsuits became power clashes waged on legislative ground and that of memory.

We now have to ask ourselves why, in the 1990s (and not only in France), the paths of historiography, memory, and public opinion intersected each other and gave Vichy's "past" a contemporary relevance. Why did the question imperiously return to the agenda of the day, precisely when the generation of the protagonists was inexorably disappearing? There was no reason why this should happen. In the 1990s, the generation of the Resistance, of the wait-and-see policy, and of collaboration was, by then, no longer setting the pace, and the conflicting standpoints of the Resistance fighters and the parasites of the occupation no longer gave rise to any political rifts. The bonds of pride or shame, forged underground or in the collaboration regime, no longer played a part in any political alliance or connivance, and the survivors could be counted on the fingers of one hand: François Mitterand, Simone Veil, Charles Pasqua, and a few others. The new generations of the elected and electors, on the other hand, could not have any direct knowledge of those distant events. Rather than a better historical knowledge, it was, above all, the judicial events and the crisis of hegemony of Gaullism and Communism that gave the perception of Vichy's past a contemporary relevance and actually enabled it to be better understood than in the immediate postwar period, demonstrating a weak and fragmented historical knowledge, but free of the taboos and the mythical reworking of previous years.

But what enabled the judges and historians to "free" the recollection of Vichy? Until the end of the 1970s, Gaullism and French Communism, to their mutual advantage, had fostered the legend of an uncontaminated France, the former anchoring De Gaulle's 1958 authoritarian appeal to the improbable legacy of the national independence speech directed against Vichy on June 18, 1940, the latter concealing, behind the aura of the "party of the executed," the troublesome umbilical cord that tied the apparatus of the cadres to the Stalinist power structure. In other words, the two most important political parties had had a strong and convergent interest in painting épinal's holy picture of a France not compromised by the Nazi occupation (apart from the odd traitor). The politicians of the postwar period had thus received a double inaugural blessing: the forced sharing of the political legacy of the Liberation (economic nationalization, social security, the civil service statute, the role of trade unions, a mixed economy, and non-denominational schools) and the free erasure of the compromises of the past, which, in 1940, had gone so far as to touch even the radical center-left and the SFIO, the French Socialist Party.

For its part, 1968 had only been partially able to shatter the monuments of the two official memories. At the head of these two parties, at this point, were men who were scarcely distinguished, like Pompidou, who, during the period of the German occupation and Vichy, had not made any choices, or like Marchais, who had never offered any resistance whatsoever to forced labor in Germany. Pompidou, in fact, had declared that he wanted to "draw a veil" over the years of Vichy and the Resistance, and in 1971, as has been seen, he had pardoned Touvier. At that very time, the veil that had covered the black years of Vichy until then was rent. A new variable had, in fact, appeared on the scene of the reworking of memory. The films of Marcel Ophuls, *Le Chagrin et la Pitié* (1971); André Harris and Alain de Sédouy, *Français, si vous saviez* (1972); Louis Malle, *Lacombe Lucien* (1974); François Truffaut, *Le dernier Métro* (1978); and Claude Lanzmann, *Shoah* (1985–86) had a collective psychological impact that neither historical research nor the criminal lawsuits had ever dreamed of being able to exercise. It was, in fact, most probably show business and media events such as films that prepared the ground for the impact of the judicial proceedings of the 1980s and 1990s and created a public mood that was extremely sensitive to the problem of Vichy. All this tended to trace a new boundary that was no longer the dividing line between Resistance fighters and collaborationists but rather between those who persisted in preserving a memory and giving importance to the difference between the choices that had been made in 1940–44 (to resist or to collaborate) and those who by now tended to regard them as purely circumstantial alternatives.

In those same years, Giscard d'Estaing's presidency proposed a plan for the "secularization of institutions" that, in fact, favored the trivialization of the historical events of the 1940s, symbolized by the suppression of the commemoration of the anniversary of the victory over Nazism (May 8, 1945). A very significant, strong reaction ensued, above all on the part of the neo-Gaullists of the Rassemblement pour la République, who in 1979 even accused d'Estaing and his second head of the ministerial staff, Raymond Barre, of "vichysme."[25] The beginning of the long season of governments of the Left in the 1980s once again displaced the blocks of the political memory, while Mitterand went back to commemorating the victory over Berlin precisely when he was paying the greatest attention to the Franco-German dialogue and to the interests of the two national States as the authentic driving force of European integration.[26]

"People do not talk so much about memory because there no longer is one," as Pierre Nora then acutely observed in presenting the publication of *Lieux de la Mémoire*. It was only in the 1990s, in fact, that the awareness of the complete break with the past finally merged with the feeling of a collective memory, which was by then radically divided, while someone proposed removing the most controversial pages of the French history of the 1940s (the clashes between the Resistance fighters, the forms of collaboration, the role of the Soviet Union) from the agenda of public commemoration. But it was in that same period that French and international historiography—as has been seen—arrived at the most significant results.

In other words, in the 1990s, what was at stake in the legacy of the Liberation, at one time firmly held by the Gaullists and the Communists, was once again, through the impact of media, show business, and judicial events, an important element in a political context. The Mayor of Paris, Chirac, running against Mitterand in the presidential elections, found himself faced with the dilemma of his relationship with the National Front that explicitly claimed its direct descent from Vichy. In the face of the political ambiguity of the Center-Right, Mitterand on the Left took up the foundations of the Gaullist memory of the Resistance: he uninhibitedly paid tribute to Pétain as a soldier of the First World War, but, as De Gaulle would have done, he denied that Vichy's crimes towards its own Jewish fellow countrymen had been crimes of the French State for which the Republic could be held accountable. The controversy erupted violently in 1992, on the occasion of the already-remembered rounding up of the 13,000 Parisian Jews at the Winter Velodrome. Jacques Derrida, Pierre Boulez, Patrick Modiano, and Jean-Pierre Vidal-Naquet challenged Mitterand precisely on the point that the Vichy regime had been—as the President thought—a State that was "French only in name," since the civil servants and police who had deported the Jews had, on the contrary, been appointed by the Republican State. "For everything that has been done in the name of France, the French State is today responsible," the historians proclaimed.[27]

Once again, the paths of memory, politics, and justice intersected each other, because if two of the many people responsible for that tragic rounding up, Darquier de Pellepoix (commissioner "for Jewish matters") and Jean Leguay (the Vichy police representative in the occupied zone) were dead, a third, René Bousquet, was still alive. And he was certainly free thanks to François Mitterand, his friend since the days of Vichy.

Since 1949 Mitterand, at the time Secretary of State, had in fact done his best for an amnesty for René Bousquet, previously head of the Vichy police. (Bousquet, however, had only been sentenced to five years' imprisonment for *indegnité nationale*, even though his crimes were much more serious.) But Mitterand's links with Bousquet had continued in subsequent years thanks to Jean-Paul Martin, the former head of staff of the Director General of the Vichy police and, from 1947 to 1954, a member of Mitterand's cabinet in different ministries of the Fourth Republic. In the 1960s, Mitterand had even endorsed Bousquet's appointment as manager of the Bank of Indochina and the latter, in return, had financed Mitterand's election campaigns, his journeys abroad, and some of his political projects. Finally, in 1990, after Serge Klarsfeld's persistence had led to the discovery of Bousquet's role in the deportation of the Parisian Jews and therefore to the possibility that he could be tried again, this time for crimes against humanity, it was President Mitterand himself who forced the Minister of Justice, Georges Kiejman, to stop the judicial machinery. Obviously, the subject of Vichy was, for Mitterand, not only a political and penal question if he persisted in protecting an indefensible figure like Bousquet.[28]

The question of Mitterand's personal relationship with the institutions of the Vichy regime would, in fact, have erupted shortly afterwards, around the mid-1990s, a few months before the president's death. The "untold" aspect of the culture of the Left would thus have re-emerged in the most sensational way.

This time Mitterand counterattacked directly in historiographic terms, through his biography: *François Mitterand, une jeunesse française*, by Pierre Péan, published in 1994.[29] Since his public actions as president tended by then to utilize the archetypes of the official Gaullist memory, the eruption of the Bousquet case forced him to a certain extent to present his own "historiographic" truth about Vichy: Mitterand acted by exploiting in his own way both the French relationship with the memory of Vichy and the widespread consensus enjoyed by the hostility towards the representative democracy—ineffectual, bureaucratic, and antiquated—of the Third Republic, above all among the intellectual elite of the 1930s and 1940s.

Mitterand is presented in his biography as an authentic paradigm of the young French intellectual between the 1930s and 1940s: a volunteer in 1934–35 in the youth section of the Croix de Feu (an important nationalist and Catholic veterans' movement, led by a hero of the Great War, Colonel de La Rocque), a contributor to the *Echo de Paris*, a newspaper very close to the PSF (a pro-Fascist organization led by the former head of the Young Socialists, Marcel Déat), called up during the war, wounded and taken prisoner, from 1940 Mitterand had joined the Vichy administration, using his position to begin, almost immediately, his activities in the anti-German Resistance at the head of a movement of escaped prisoners. In other words, he presented himself as a "vichyste" and, at the same time, a Resistance fighter, the re-founder of French Socialism, following the Second World War, thus putting forward the theme of the relationship between the regime's politics and some sectors of the Resistance, which had enabled a fraction of the latter to enter into institutional and ideological relations with Vichy.

Daniel Peschanski, one of the most important historians of the last generation, has, in this regard, coined the term "vichyste" Resistance fighters, in order to define a range of very different choices, united by the need to use positions in the regime's institutions as a cover for conspiratorial activities in the army and the administration and above all by the illusion that Pétain could create a shield against the occupation.[30]

This is certainly an important aspect, even though it does not constitute the most original conclusion that could be drawn from a consideration of Mitterand's biography. Rather than merely giving us an indication, it tells us, in fact, of the existence of a deeper link between the young Mitterand's anti-liberal, anti-parliamentary and Catholic-Social attitudes in the 1930s, his collaboration with Vichy, and his subsequent support for Socialism.

In other words, Mitterand's biography is not reminiscent of the usual intellectual journey from Right to Left, even if he himself had on several occasions compared his own path with that of Lamartine or Hugo.[31] However, the issue appears more important than a personal biography and reveals the path followed by a generation of young writers, sociologists, journalists, and academics who, in the 1930s, had assumed "nonconformist" positions, as they were then defined. Intellectuals, fascinated by the modern and efficient decision-making approach of the authoritarian and fascist regimes, who had not tolerated the decaying Third Republic, preferring the corporative and nationalist movements and associations: they would have found in Vichy, a model of social cohesion to set against the disintegration of an individualistic society; many would have passed from Vichy to the Resistance and finally, after 1944, to the militancy of the anticapitalist and anti-individualistic Left.

It is not a question of insignificant names. Suffice it to recall Emmanuel Mounier, Maurice Merleau-Ponty, Jean-Marie Domenach, and Denis de Rougemont, not to mention the case—different, however, in some ways—of Jean-Paul Sartre. In the 1990s, the publication of Jean Paulhan's letters, Julien Green's diary, and Pierre Drieu La Rochelle's notebook brought back to public attention the memory of the roots of that intellectual fascination for Vichy[32] and for an anti-parliamentary social and national political culture that had passed, through Vichy and the Resistance, towards the anticapitalist opposition to the Fourth and Fifth Republics.

Mitterand's biography once again presents that intellectual journey and leads one to reflect on the unjust nature of many of the postwar trials and the purges of the "collaboration" intellectuals, with their most upsetting outcomes, such as the execution by firing squad of Brasillach and the pardon for Béraud, Celine's conviction and Drieu La Rochelle's suicide.[33] In 1944, François Mauriac had maintained that, ultimately, it would have been impossible to distinguish, among the intellectuals, between "les hommes de la Résistance" and "les hommes de la trahison," a comment for which Camus had censured him. A year later, the latter had to admit that Mauriac had been right and that the purges had been more of a settling of accounts in the universities, editorial offices of periodicals, and publishing houses than an act of justice.[34]

In more general terms, the whole history of the French public memory of the last sixty years, with its legal proceedings, purges, and lessons of history, seems, above all, to convey the ambiguities, the secretiveness, and the shadows of the postwar period and the years of the Fourth and Fifth Republics, with their left-wing and Gaullist mythologies, leading us to consider the memory of Vichy as mirroring the dark side of postwar democracy, as well as the nature of the that democracy's descent from the experiences of Vichy and from its most distant political and intellectual roots.

Chapter 7

Epilogue Without an End

After the end of World War II and up to the 1989 revolutions in Central-Eastern Europe, the European frontiers and the forms of collective identity associated with them were influenced not only by the model of Europe's political division drawn up at Yalta and subsequently frozen by the cold war but also by the wish, common to both sides of a divided Europe since 1946–48, to forget the recent past and build a new continental identity. In Western Europe, this impetus manifested itself as the movement for supranational unification linked to economic reconstruction and modernization. In Eastern Europe, there was a movement for unity imposed by the progress of a presumed social revolution, obsessed by the ethic of industrial productivity and the statist creation of society and the new man. On both sides of what Churchill defined as the "Iron Curtain" there were many good reasons for forgetting the experiences of the war and the occupation, totally embracing the rhetoric of the future and material progress. Both the nature of the wartime experience and the ways in which its memory came to be distorted and sublimated served to give the postwar era an identity model that was substantially falsified and based upon an artificial distinction between the present and the public memory of the recent past, which would, at least until 1989, have accumulated a number of insoluble and unresolved contradictions.

For many Europeans the war had been a new experience, horrible and destructive, above all in its final phase, particularly in areas like the Balkans, but also in western countries. France ended up by losing almost 75 percent of its ports and railway lines and Great Britain 25 percent of its prewar wealth. The war had been, in Central and Eastern Europe, but not only there, a combination of terrorism, destructive efficiency and technological violence, which could not be compared to any other event in living memory—excepting the analogous, but different, elimination of the Armenians. In Eastern Europe itself, however, that experience had not been equally tragic for all the countries and peoples and, in fact, some had even profited from it: the Bohemians and Moravians had seen their own natural and industrial resources increased by Nazism, at least until the final period; Slovaks and Croats had achieved independence; the Germans and Austrians had enjoyed the wealth and forced labor seized from occupied countries. Also, many among the French suffered deprivation, losses, and reprisals, but only after the Allied landings, in the final period of the conflict.

Through its ruling classes, bureaucratic structures, and governments, most of occupied Europe had learned to collaborate with the National Socialist system of occupation, or had resignedly accepted the presence and activities of the German forces. France and Norway had engendered actively collaborating regimes; the Baltic countries, Ukraine, Hungary, Croatia, Slovakia, and Flemish Belgium had seized the opportunity to gain territorial and ethnic advantages from the Germans' benevolent attitude, while active Resistance had, until the last few months of the war, been restricted to a few and selected opponents: Socialists, Communists, ultranationalists, and Jews (often opposed or even betrayed by the local population scared of reprisals). Thus, at the time of Liberation, most of the local populations were urged to find, hurriedly, any way to identify themselves arbitrarily with the victors, rushing to help the "just side" among the various factions in the many civil wars that had broken out in the final phase of the war and distancing themselves as much as possible from external and internal enemies in order to announce loudly the purges and punishments.[1]

Thus, the procedures and the measures of the judicial and political punishment[2] of the occupying Nazis and their collaborators became intertwined with the demands of material and political reconstruction, the international situation that led to the division of Europe, and the immediate creation of a memory of the recent past appropriate for different strategic projects. And among the factors that contributed, after 1948, to the construction of postwar Europe's official public memory there was, first of all, the unequivocal attribution to Germany, through the Nuremberg Trials, of the responsibility for the war.

This decision brought further advantages. Austria, for example, from being an accomplice, could become Germany's first victim and be absolved of all guilt, in line with the preconceptions of Churchill himself, who had always wanted to reduce Nazism to an offshoot of Prussian expansionism. The trials themselves, starting from those of Nuremberg, were almost exclusively reserved for the Germans, avoiding as far as possible any inquiry into the responsibilities of other countries: thus, above and beyond the undoubted legal function of the trials of the "major" or "minor war criminals," the discretionary criteria and the hypocrisy with which the Allies dealt with the issue of the trials contributed considerably to the restoration, in the postwar period, of an era of cynicism and false conscience, which reached its climax with the rapid winding-up of the phase of denazification. In Germany, as in Austria, the need to build a consensus around the new political systems, with an anti-Soviet aim, led to the outcome we know,[3] while at the same time, 15 million Germans were victims of expulsions, based on the criterion of ethnic cleansing, from Polish, Soviet, Czechoslovak, Yugoslav, and Hungarian territories.[4]

Postwar Europe, which soon got used to distinguishing between and separating the new forms of postwar violence and ethnic cleansing to which the Germans had been subjected and those perpetrated by the Nazis in the preceding years, thus prepared itself to live with two split memories—here, this trite expression does make sense—that of the crimes committed by the Nazis during the war and that of the retaliation against the "collectively guilty" Germans. These two memories were followed, with logical consistency, by two distinct moral codes, two diverse "languages," and two different historical versions of the past.

After having been exonerated of any compromise with the new European order of the National Socialist system, the European nations found themselves forced to confirm their virginal purity by inventing the myth of a Resistance representing the majority of the population; at the same time, many of the real Resistance fighters, but certainly not all, accepted this myth for political expediency in order to guarantee a minimum of social cohesion and to restore the authority of States delegitimized by the collapse of their ruling classes. Italian coalition governments, from Bonomi to De Gasperi, as well as De Gaulle in France, fell into line with this approach. Consequently, any claim to "revolutionary" renewal had to be hurriedly abandoned in favor of measures—starting from the Roman protocols of November 1944—that could guarantee the continuity of the State.[5] The Italian and French Communist Parties themselves were under the illusion that they could profit from the political capital of their contribution to the Resistance, claiming that they represented the interests and identity of the nation, with the hope of being able to assume the authority of speaking in its name.

The tangled web of aspirations, plans, interests and expediency on both sides of Europe's internal frontier is barely sufficient to explain the reasons why the trials, the punishments, and the purges of the war criminals followed, in the first instance—as has been seen—partial and selective criteria and finally collapsed in view of the impossibility of striking tens or hundreds of thousands of people who were necessarily involved *en masse* in totalitarian structures and even legitimized in this by their own governments in office at the time of the German occupation. This explains why the punishments and acts of vengeance were on a massive scale around the time of Liberation, and then fell away and stopped completely shortly afterwards.

The channeling of political violence merged with the ordinary dispensation of justice, and the latter, in turn, had to give way to a new (and at the same time old) symbolic function, that of a form of justice intent on legitimizing the new postwar institutions and the new democratic authority through symbolic acts of the nation's moral regeneration and the identification and execration of its enemies.[6] That same justice also produced outrageous acquittals, perpetuating—especially in Italy—the idea of two warring factions. In 1945, Hersch Lauterpacht, the eminent expert on international law, wrote,

> During the Second World War the exaltation of the rights of man has repeatedly been declared one of the main objectives of the war. The great challenge, on account of which civilization's spiritual legacy came to find itself in mortal danger, was imposed on the world by a power whose most fundamental characteristic was the denial of the rights of man in favour of the omnipotence of the State.[7]

Albert Camus, in one of his *Letters to a German Friend*, had expressed himself more soberly: "I continue to believe that this world does not have any ultimate purpose. But I know that something in it does have meaning, and that is man."[8]

The postwar trials, while an attempt to meet the demands of guaranteeing justice for the crimes committed and those of establishing peace "in accordance with the law" and in the interests of the victorious powers' political security, nevertheless influenced the collective memory. For a long time, all the experts on memory, as well as historians, would have utilized documents and recollections in a "politically correct" way, being afraid to damage the image of the great anti-Fascist alliance of the "Big Three."[9] The awareness of the legal and moral merits of the Nuremberg Trials and of all the proceedings against war criminals, including those conducted by the British in Italy—from which real advances resulted, such as the Convention for the Prevention and Repression of Genocide adopted by the U N in 1948, and the introduction of the category of crimes against humanity in the penal codes of many European countries—perhaps contributed to concealing the negative effects that they have had on Europe's public memory and collective identity.

Contrary to what Serge Fuster, who was at the time a member of the prosecution at Nuremberg, wrote, "the event of the trial" *did not* "lead to undeniable clarity regarding the event of the war,"[10] and, in fact, it can be maintained that the postwar justice towards the war criminals contributed to crystallizing a unilateral, distorted, and partial recollection of that tragedy.[11]

As a matter of fact, there is nothing extraordinary or pathological in this. In the international law relating to war criminals in 1946 and 1947 it is actually not difficult to spot traces of events and procedures that for centuries have surrounded the rites of justice. In the 1500s and 1700s, as in the 1900s, justice consisted more of emotion and summary enactments than of carefully documented analyses. But in the 1500s or 1700s emotions were stirred in the public squares by the display of torture—flogging, pillory, and capital punishment—while the reality and the symbolic image of the death penalty tended to fuse two aspects that are equally necessary for society.

The first of these functions was represented by outrage at the violation of the law, the expulsion of the criminal as a being foreign to the human species, and the exorcism of his monstrous and diabolical identity. In the part played by the press and the mass media in influencing public opinion and imagination at the time of the 1946–47 trials it is not difficult to spot the presence of that function, even if the outrage no longer expressed itself through the display of torture but by means of the transformation of the accused or convicted person into a "monster" by narrating his atrocities. Suffice it to mention the Venetian press reports of the Kesselring trial from February to April 1947.[12]

The second function consisted in the social practice by which the distinctiveness of the criminal and "monster" was reabsorbed, its characteristic feature neutralized, and the penitent was seen as cooperating in the survival and providential harmony of the social order, narrating the victory of the forces of good or, if possible, "the transformation of the delinquent into a repentant Christian, readmitted to the ranks of humanity."[13]

As Adriano Prosperi has observed, in this sense the confraternities and justice associations—charged with accepting the convicted person's repentance in order to transform the moment of the extreme rift between the individual and society into a recomposition of social cohesion—had overburdened themselves with the task of legitimizing political power.

Since the end of the 1700s—namely, from when visible and violent punishment had gradually been transformed into the most hidden aspect of the legal process in a system of constraints, deprivations, and suspended rights that aimed at influencing the mind and will of the convict—the function of the recomposition of social cohesion also began to be carried out following different procedures.[14] The new legal system, defined by the great codes of the 1700s and 1800s, imposed on trials other types of evaluation, modifying its rules of formulation and therefore transforming its role of political legitimization. The judgement of truth for a crime was no longer based on knowledge of the law, the identification of the guilty party, and the definition of the offense. This means that also in the major trials of those responsible for World War II and the violations of the law during that war there was already the problem of a very different truth, owing to this historical transformation of the functions of justice.

There was therefore, on the one hand, a historical course that "led judges to judge things other than crimes," introducing into the trial proceedings, between the 1800s and the 1900s, non-legal elements and partly transferring the power to judge to other contexts different from trials, such as public opinion.[15] There was, on the other hand—at Nuremberg, in the European trials of the war criminals and collaborationists, and in Kesselring's trial held in Italy by the Allies—a further transformation of the trial and penal process, which incorporated into trials the non-legal elements, not in order to define them in terms of the power to punish but to transform the straightforward nature of legal punishment into something different. The ways in which international justice was applied in 1946–47 can therefore be traced back to a change in its field of action and to the emergence of an unknown role in its operation. The punitive mechanism was no longer the purely sanctionary effect of legal and moral rules but also an act of knowing and, at the same time, a procedure having positive effects for political stabilization. In this sense, the trials initiated a presentation of the war and the responsibilities of totalitarianism based on a partial and selective memory and made a decisive contribution to the construction of the new European order and the formation of its identity.

After more than half a century, a balanced assessment of that operation is perhaps possible.

Notes

Introduction

1. See Yveline Pendaries, *Les Procès de Restatt* (Bern: Lang éditions, 1995), 49–55.
2. United Nations War Crimes Commission (Editor), *History of the Unites Nations War Crimes Commission and the Development of the Laws of War* (London: H. M. Stationery Office, 1948): 239–66; see also Shlomo Aronson, "Preparations for the Nuremberg Trial: The OSS Charles Dwork and the Holocaust," *Holocaust and Genocide Studies*, no. 12 (1998): 237–81.
3. F. Honing, "Kriegsverbrecher vor englischen Militärgerichten," *Schweizerische Zeitschrift für Strafrecht*, no. 62 (1947): 20–33.
4. Robert Sigel, *Im Interesse der Gerechtigkeit. Die Dachauer Kriegs Verbrecherprozesse 1945–1948* (Frankfurt: Campus, 1992).
5. See Robert Woetzel, *The Nuremberg Trials in International Law* (London: Stevens, 1960), 219–26; and Donald Bloxham, "The Trial That Never Was: Why There Was No Second International Trial of Major Criminals at Nuremberg," *History*, no. 285 (2002): 41–48.
6. See Donald Bloxham, *Genocide on Trial: War Crime Trials in the Formation of Holocaust History and Memory* (Oxford: Oxford University Press, 2001), 69–75.
7. Some of the most important books: Montgomery Belgion, *Epitaph on Nuremberg* (London: Falcon, 1946); Gallieni Gallus, *Nuremberg and After* (New Town: Montgomeryshire Printing and Stationery, 1946); H. A. Smith, *The Crisis in the Law of Nations* (London: Stevens and Sons, 1947); J. H. Morgan, *The Great Assize* (London: J. Murray, 1948); F. J. P. Veal, *Advance to Barbarism. How the Reversion to Barbarism in Warfare and War-Trials Menaces Our Future* (Appleton, WI: Nelson, 1948); Lord Hankey, *Politics, Trials and Errors* (Oxford: Pen-in-Hand, 1950); Reginald Paget, *Manstein: His Campaigns and Trial* (London: W. Collins, 1950).
8. *Jackson Papers*, Library of Congress, Container 191 (Justice Jackson Story), 1046–47, in D. Bloxham, *Genocide on Trial*, 51.
9. See Fritz Fischer, *Griff nach der Weltmacht* (Dusseldorf: Droste Verlag, 1961); on the "Fisher controversy," see H. W. Koch, *The Origins of the First World War* (New York: St. Martin's Press, 1991); and V. Berghaher, "Die Fischer Kontroverse 15 Jahre Danach," in *Geschichte und Gesellschaft* 6 (1980):

403–19. See H. R. Trevor-Roper, "Hitler's Kriegsziele," *Vierjahrshefte für Zeitgeschichte* 8 (1960): 127–33. Other contributions: Alan Bullock, "Hitler and the Origins of the Second World War," in *The Origins of the Second World War*, ed. E. M. Robertson, 189–224 (London: Macmillan, 1971); Andreas Hillgruber, *Hitler's Strategie. Politik und Kriegs führung 1940–1941* (Frankfurt: Bernard and Graefe Verlag, 1965); Klaus Hildebrand, *Vom Reich zum Weltreich. Hitler NSDAP und Koloniale Frage 1919–1945* (Munich: Fink, 1969), 279; Gunter Moltmann, *Weltherrschaftsideen Hitlers*, in *Europa und übersee Festschrift für Egmont Zechlin*, eds. O. Bruner and D. Gerhard, 197–240 (Hamburg: Verlag Hans Bredov Institut, 1962); Klaus Hildebrand, "Die Geschichte der deutschen Außenpolitik (1953–1945) im Urteil der neuren Forschung: Ergebnisse, Kontroversen, Perspektiven," in *Deutsche Außenpolitik 1933–1945. Kalkül oder Dogma*? (Stuttgart: Kolhammer, 1980), 188ff.; Gerhard Weinberg, *The Foreign Policy of Hitler's Germany. Starting World War II* (Chicago: University of Chicago Press, 1980), 657; Hans Mommsen, "National Socialism: Continuity, and Change," in *Fascism*, ed. Walter Lacqueur (Berkeley: University of California Press, 1976), 113.

10. The thesis on the Russian origin of *Protocols* has been upheld by Cesare G. de Michelis, *Il manoscritto inesistente. I 'Protocolli dei Savi di Sion'?: un apocrifo del XX secolo* (Venice: Marsilio, 1998), trans. Richard Newhouse as *The Non-Existent Manuscript. A Study of the Protocols of the Sages of Zion*(Lincoln: University of Nebraska Press, 2004). For a different point of view: Norman Cohn, *Warrant for Genocide. The Myth of the Jewish World Conspiracy and the Protocols of the Elders of Zion* (New York: Harper and Row, 1967); and Pierre Andre Taguieff, ed., *Les protocoles des Sages de Sion*, 2 vols. (Paris: Berg, 1992).
11. Carlo Ginzburg, *Storia notturna. Una decifrazione del Sabba* (Turin: Einaudi, 1989), 23–24; and Ginzburg, "Rappresentare il nemico. Sulla preistoria francese dei Protocolli," in *Il filo e le tracce*, ed. Ginzburg (Milan: Feltrinelli, 2006), 185.
12. It was only after 1977 that the UN revoked that rejection of the principle *nullum crimen et nulla poena sine lege*. See the *Protocol Additional to the Geneva Conventions of August 1949 and Relating to the Protection of Victims of Non-International Armed Conflicts*, June 8, 1977; this is now reprinted in W. M. Reisman and C. T. Antoniou, eds., *The Laws of War: a Comprehensive Collection of Primary Documents Governing Armed Conflicts* (New York: Vintage Books, 1994), 385–86.
13. Tony Judt, "The Past is Another Country: Myth and Memory in Post-War Europe," in *The Politics of Retribution in Europe. World War II and Its Aftermath*, eds. István Déak, Jan T. Gross, and Tony Judt, 293–324 (Princeton, NJ: Princeton University Press, 2000), 293.
14. Ibid., 297; see also Winfried Garscha, "War Crimes Trials in Austria: People's Courts 1945–1955," in *War against Civilians. Massacres and War Crimes in Europe and Italy during World War II*, by Garscha (paper for the International Colloquium at the University of Bologna, June 19–22, 2002).

15. Achille Battaglia, "Giustizia e politica nella giurisprudenza," in *Dieci anni dopo 1945–1955*, ed. Battaglia, et al. (Bari: Laterza, 1955), 335; Frank Buscher, *The U.S. War Crimes Trial Program in Germany, 1946–1955* (Westport, CT: Greenwood, 1989).
16. Roy Gutman and David Rieff, eds., *Crimini di guerra* (Milan: Contrasto, 2003); Roy Palmer Domenico, *Processo ai fascisti* (Milan: Mondadori, 1996); Marcello Flores, "L'epurazione," in *L'Italia dalla Liberazione alla Repubblica* (Milan: Mondadori, 1977); Mimmo Franzinelli, *I tentacoli dell'OVRA* (Turin: Bollati Boringhieri, 1998), 472ff.; Charles Gati, *Hungary and the Soviet Bloc* (Durham: University of North Carolina Press, 1986); Lamberto Mercuri, *L'epurazione in Italia 1943–1948* (Cuneo, Italy: L'Arciere, 1988); Peter Novick, *The Resistance Versus Vichy. The Purge of Collaborators in Liberated France* (New York: Columbia University Press, 1981); John Rawls, *Hiroshima, non dovevamo* (Milan: Reset, 1995).
17. Romano Canosa, *Storia dell'epurazione in Italia. Le sanzioni contro il fascismo 1943–1948* (Milan: Baldini e Castoldi, 1999); cf. Hans Woller, *I conti col fascismo* (Bologna: Il Mulino, 1997).
18. Lucio D'Angelo, *I socialisti e la defascistizzazione mancata* (Milan: Franco Angeli, 1997).
19. Adriano Sofri, *Altri Hotel. Il mondo visto da dentro 1997–2002* (Milan: Mondadori, 2002), 259.
20. Some parts of this text have been published in Michele Battini, "Sins of Memory: Reflections on the Lack of an Italian Nuremberg and the Administration of International Justice after 1945," *Journal of Modern Italian Studies* 9, no. 3 (Fall 2004): 349–62.

Prologue

1. Editor's note: In the fall of 1943, the Germans installed Mussolini as head of a puppet regime in Northern Italy, the Italian Social Republic (RSI), often called the Salò Republic. It was "Republican" in that it broke with the monarchy.
2. Mazowiecki's inaugural speech as prime minister, August 1989.

Chapter 1

1. Roberto Battaglia, *Storia della Resistenza italiana* (Turin: Einaudi, 1977), 351–55. Kesselring's words are taken from Alfred Kesselring, *Memorie di guerra* (Milan: Garzanti, 1954), 260.
2. Michele Battini and Paolo Pezzino, *Guerra ai civili. Occupazione tedesca e politica del massacro. Toscana 1944* (Venice: Marsilio, 1997); about which see L. Alessandrini, *L'Unità* (January 11, 1998); G. Gribaudi, "Guerra, violenza, responsabilità. Alcuni volumi sui massacri nazisti in Italia," *Quaderni Storici*, n.s., no. 100 (April 1999):135–50; Roberto Vivarelli, "Guerra ai civili e vuoti di

memoria," *Belfagor* (May 31, 1998); Mirco Dondi, "Memorie divise e anatomie di stragi," *Memoria e Ricerca* (June 1998): 1–7; Paolo Mieli, "Resistenza. Com'era rossa quella violenza," *La Stampa* (June 1998); republished as "Guerra partigiana: anche la sinistra rivede la storia," in *Le storie, la storia,* by Paolo Mieli, 301–10 (Milan: Rizzoli, 1999); Philip Cooke, "Recent Works on Nazi Massacres in Italy during the Second World War," *Modern Italy* 5, no. 2 (November 2000): 211–18. The international conference I am referring to is *Guerra ai civili. Stragi, violenza e crimini di guerra in Italia e in Europa durante la Seconda Guerra Mondiale: i fatti, le memorie, i processi,* organized by the Universities of Bari, Bologna, Naples, and Pisa with the collaboration of the Region of Emilia-Romagna and the Municipal District of Marzabotto, held in Bologna on June 19–22, 2002.

3. The Ardeatine Caves were the site of a notorious Nazi massacre of civilians. In retaliation for a partisan attack that killed 33 soldiers, German authorities in Rome, including Priebke, massacred 335 men and boys on March 24, 1944. See Robert Katz, *Death in Rome* (New York: Macmillan, 1967).
4. On the Priebke trial, see Michele Battini, Carlo Galante Garrone, Claudio Pavone, Alessandro Portelli, and Wladimiro Settimelli, *Priebke e il massacro delle Ardeatine* (Rome: Istituto Romano per la Storia d'Italia dal Fascismo alla Resistenza, 1996), 61–83. On the Priebke episode, see W. Lezl, *Anatomia di un processo* (Rome: Editori Riuniti, 1997). Naturally, the whole issue of Priebke's two trials is much more complex, just as the problem itself of the relationship between public opinion and justice cannot be examined only from this point of view (Paolo Mieli's reservations at the time should be borne in mind). Nor should these notes of mine be seen as being in agreement with the imprisonment of the very old defendant. See Paolo Mieli *Le storie, la storia,* 307.
5. On the question of the distorted memory of this episode, see Alessandro Portelli, *The Order Has Been Carried Out: History, Memory, and Meaning of a Nazi Massacre in Rome* (New York: Palgrave, 2003).
6. Michele Battini and Paolo Pezzino, *Guerra a civili. Occupazione tedesca e politiche del massacro Toscana 1944* (Venice: Marsilio, 1997).
7. Marc Bloch, *L'étrange défaite* (Paris: Folio, 1990).
8. See Diego Gambetta, *La mafia siciliana* (Turin: Einaudi, 1992): xv ff. Leonardo Sciascia's reservations about the decision regarding the maxi-trial should be borne in mind.
9. Raul Hilberg, *La distruzione degli Ebrei d'Europa* (Turin: Einaudi, 1995), 1:633 ff.; Kurt Pätzold and Erica Schwarz, *Ordine del giorno: sterminio degli ebrei. La conferenza del Wannsee del 20 gennaio 1942* (Turin: Bollati Boringhieri, 2000), 15–79. For a study of the historiography, cf. Ian Kershaw, *Che cos'è il nazismo? Problemi interpretativi e prospettive di ricerca* (Turin: Bollati Boringhieri, 1995), 121ff.

Chapter 2

1. It is Elena Aga Rossi's merit to have insisted on the historical significance the Armistice represented for Italy as a turning point that definitively averted the prospect of an unconditional surrender, overcoming a great deal of important opposition among the Allies. See E. Aga Rossi, *L'inganno reciproco. L'armistizio tra l'Italia e gli anglo americani del Settembre 1943* (Rome: Archival Heritage Central Office, 1993), 9–80; see also the later edition, *Una nazione allo sbando* (Bologna: Il Mulino, 1996); English edition: *A Nation Collapses*, trans. Harvey Fergusson, II (Cambridge: Cambridge University Press, 2000).
2. Federico Chabod, *L'Italia contemporanea 1918–1948* (Turin: Einaudi, 1961), 117–19; see also Dante Livio Bianco, *Guerra partigiana* (Turin: Einaudi, 1954); Giorgio Bocca, *Storia dell'Italia partigiana* (Bari: Laterza, 1966); *La guerriglia in Italia. Documenti della Resistenza militare italiana*, ed. Pietro Secchia (Milan: Feltrinelli, 1969); Pietro Secchia and Fillipo Frassati, *Storia della Resistenza* (Rome: Editori Riuniti, 1965); Gianni Oliva, *I vinti e i liberati, 8 Settembre 1943–1925 Aprile 1945. Storia di due anni* (Milan: Mondadori, 1994).
3. Claudio Pavone, "Tre governi e due occupazioni," *Italia Contemporanea*, no. 160 (1985): 57–79. But on the theme of the different wartime and postwar experiences of southern Italy, see A. degli Espinosa, *Il regime del Sud. 8 Settembre 1943–1944 Giugno 1944* (Rome: Migliaresi, 1946); and Nicola Gallerano, ed., *L'altro dopoguerra. Roma e il Sud 1943–1945* (Milan: Franco Angeli, 1985).
4. Benedetto Croce, *Quando l'Italia era tagliata in due. Estratto di un diario (luglio 1943–giugno 1944)* (Bari: Laterza, 1948), 84ff.
5. "They seem misfortunes and are opportunities," so wrote Vittorio Foa to his fellow-prisoner Bruno Corbi, in a dedication on the title page of Giovanbattista Vico's *Scienza Nuova*, when they were freed from the prison of Castelfranco Emilia on August 23, 1943. See Bruno Corbi, *Scusateci tanto (carceri e Resistenza)* (Milan: La Pietra, 1977).
6. See G. Sasso, "Ma l'8 settembre la patria era già morta," *Liberal* (May 1996): 18ff. It is an important reply to the book by Ernesto Galli della Loggia, *La morte della patria* (Rome-Bari: Laterza, 1996). And, for a more recent resumption of the debate, see M. Pirani, "Ciampi: Io, la Patria e l'antifascismo. A colloquio con il presidente della Repubblica dopo la commemorazione dell'eccidio di Cefalonia," *La Repubblica* (March 3, 2001): 8–9; but also Claudio Pavone, "In quell'isola ci fu un atto fondativo della Resistenza," in *La Repubblica* (March 3, 2001): 9. For in-depth studies of the Resistance of the Italian Armed Forces abroad, see the nine volumes of the historical series *Resistenza dei militari italiani all'estero*, ed. Selena Barba (Rome: Ministero

della difesa, 1995) with the contributions of M. F. Franzinelli, L. Mistico, L. Viazzi, P. Fuso, L. Taddia, S. Barba, G. Guidi, A. Bistarelli and M. Cantinori. See also the studies by M. Torsello, *Le operazioni delle unità italiane nel settembre-ottobre 1943* (Rome:Ufficio Storico Stato Maggiore Esercito, 1973); and A. Bartolini, *Per la Patria e la Libertà. I soldati italiani all'estero nella Resistenza* (Milan: Mursia, 1986).

7. Togliatti's so-called "svolta di Salerno" pledged the PCI's collaboration with Marshal Pietro Badoglio's new government and claimed that the first order of business was not a communist revolution but the expulsion of the Nazis from Italy.
8. See Guido Quazza, *La Resistenza italiana. Appunti e documenti* (Turin: Giappichelli, 1996), 158ff.; and G. Quazza, *Resistenza e storia d'Italia. Problemi e ipotesi di ricerca* (Milan: Feltrinelli, 1976); G. Quazza, L. Valiani, and E. Volterra, *Il governo dei CLN* (Turin: Giappichelli, 1996); Leo Valiani, G. Bianchi, and Ernesto Ragionieri, *Azionisti cattolici e comunisti nella Resistenza* (Milan: Rizzoli, 1971); Franco Catalano, *Storia del CLNAI* (Bari: Laterza, 1956).
9. See Enzo Collotti, *L'amministrazione tedesca dell'Italia occupata 1943–1945, Studi e documenti* (Milan: Lerici, 1963), 35ff.
10. N. Cospito and H. W. Neulen, *Salò-Berlino. L'alleanza difficile* (Milan: Mursia, 1992); but above all F. W. Deakin, *La brutale amicizia: Mussolini, Hitler e la caduta del fascismo italiano* (Turin: Einaudi, 1962), 113–249. See also L. Cafani and B. Mantelli, "Una Certa Europa. Il Collaborazionismo con le Potenze dell'Asse," *Annali della Fondazione Micheletti*, no. 6 (1994): 188ff.
11. Enzo Collotti, "L'occupazione tedesca in Italia," in *Dizionario della Resistenza*. Vol. 1, *Storia e geografia della Liberazione*, by E. Collotti, R. Sandri, and F. Sessi (Turin: Einaudi, 2000), 43–65; but see also Bruno Mantelli, "Deportazione dall'Italia," in ibid., 14ff.
12. Regarding the general collapse of the system of production and trade, as well as the failure of the technocratic vision of the RSI's Ministry of Corporative Economics, see Massimo Legnani, "Potere, società, economia nel territorio della RSI," *Italia Contemporanea*, no. 3 (1998): 178ff.
13. Deakin, *La brutale amicizia*, 592. See also Daniella Gagliani, *Le Brigate Nere* (Turin: Bollati Boringhieri, 1999), 165ff.; Deakin, "La Repubblica Sociale Italiana," *Annali della Fondazione Micheletti*, no. 2 (1986): 154ff.
14. The interpretation of Renzo De Felice in *Mussolini l'alleato*. Vol. 2, *La guerra civile 1943–1945* (Turin: Einaudi, 1997), is at odds with that of Pavone, from whom the quotation is taken; Pavone, *Una guerra civile. Saggio storico sulla moralità nella Resistenza* (Turin: Bollati Boringhieri, 1991), 235.
15. See Felix Gilbert, ed., *Hitler Directs His War* (New York: Oxford University Press, 1990), 37ff., as well as the work by Francis Harry Hinsley, *Hitler's Strategy* (Cambridge: Cambridge University Press, 1952). But see also the eyewitness accounts of Galeazzo Ciano, *Diario 1939–1943* (Milan: Rizzoli, 1946), 2:225; Leonardo Simoni, *Berlino. Ambasciata d'Italia 1939–1943* (Rome: Migliaresi, 1946), 299ff.; Deakin, *La brutale amicizia*, 221–44; as well as the

Atti del II Convegno di Storia del Movimento di Liberazione in Italia, Milano 5 dicembre 1954; La crisi italiana del 1943 e gli inizi della Resistenza, in *Il movimento di liberacione in Italia* (review), Special Issue, no. 35 (1955): 1–2. The German memoirs, on the other hand, require close scrutiny: Eugene Dollmann, *Roma nazista* (Milan: Longanesi, 1951); Enno von Rintelen, *Mussolini l'alleato* (Rome: Corso, 1952). Regarding the German intention of eliminating Italian institutions after September 8, see *The Goebbels Diary 1942–1943*, ed. and trans. L. Lochner (London: Doubleday, 1948), 572. As regards the question itself of the publication of the diaries—*Die Tagebücher von Joseph Goebbels. Sämtliche Fragmente, Herausgegeben von E. Frölich*, 4 vols. (Munich: Institut für Zeitgeschichte, 1992)—see Enzo Collotti, "La storia infinita. I Diari di Goebbels," *Passato e Presente*, no. 34 (January–April 1995): 165–70.

16. See Martin Broszat, *Der Staat Hitlers* (Munich: Deutscher Taschenbuch Verlag, 1969); Hans Mommsen, "Ausnahmezustand als Herrschafttechnik des NS-Regimens," in *Hitler, Deutschland und die Mächte*, ed. Manfred Funke, 30–45 (Düsseldorf: Droste, 1997). See also Peter Hüttenberg, "Nazionalsozialistische Polykratie," *Geschichte und Gesellschaft* 2 (1976): 417–42. For views opposed to the hypotheses of Broszat and Mommsen, see Klaus Hildebrandt, "Monokratie oder Polykratie? Hitlers Herrschaft und das Dritte Reich," in *Der Führerstaat. Mythos und Realität*, ed. G. Hirschfeld and L. Ketternacker (Stuttgart: Klett-Lotta, 1985), 95ff.; Enzo Collotti, *L'amministrazione tedesca*, 158ff.; Collotti, "Nazismo come Ordine-Disordine," *Parole-Chiave*, no. 7–8 (April 1995): 226ff.
17. Lutz Klinkhammer, *L'occupazione tedesca in Italia 1943–1945* (Turin: Bollati Boringhieri, 1993), 52.
18. Ibid., 61ff. (cf. Collotti, *L'amministrazione tedesca*, 153–61). See also Ivan Tognarini, *Kesselring e le stragi nazifasciste* (Rome: Carocci, 2002), xxxvii–xli.
19. Klinkhammer, *L'occupazione tedesca in Italia*, 360.
20. Kesselring, *Soldat bis zum Letzten Tag* (Bonn: Athenäum-Verlag, 1953), which would translate as "*A Soldier to the Last Day*," but it is published in English as *Kesselring: A Soldier's Record*, trans. Lynton Hudson (New York: Morrow, 1954).
21. Enzo Collotti, "Kesselring, Albert," in Collotti, Sandri, and Sessi, *Dizionario della Resistenza* 1:64–65.
22. Further (but not exhaustive) bibliographical references: Gallerano, ed., *L'altro dopoguerra*; F. Costantino, *Guerra, Resistenza, dopoguerra in Abruzzo* (Milan: Franco Angeli, 1993); L. Cortesi, G. Percopo, P. Salvetti et al., *La Campania dal fascismo alla Repubblica*, 2 vols. (Naples: Regione Campania, 1977); Gloria Chianese, ed., *Mezzogiorno 1943. La scelta, la lotta, la speranza* (Naples: Edizione Scientifiche Italiane, 1996); Chianese, ed., *Mezzogiorno: percorsi della memoria tra guerra e dopoguerra*, monographic issue of "Nord e Sud," no. 6 (1996).
23. Chabod, *L'Italia contemporanea*, 137.

24. See Giovanni De Luna, "L'insurrezione nella resistenza italiana," in *L'insurrezione in Piemonte* [Proceedings of the Turin Conference, April 18–20, 1985] (Piemonte: Instituto Storico della Resistenza, 1987).
25. See Guido Quazza, Introduction to *La Resistenza alle porte di Torino*, ed. G. Oliva, x–xvii (Milan: Franco Angeli, 1989); Quazza, "Aspetti della guerra partigiana in Italia," *Critica Storica*, no. 2 (September 30, 1963): 540–41; Quazza, *Resistenza e storia d'Italia*, (the theses of this work have also been reproposed in "Passato e presente nelle interpretazioni della Resistenza," in *Passato e presente della Resistenza. 50th anniversario della Resistenza e della Guerra di Liberazione* [Proceedings of the Rome Conference October 1–2, 1993], 44–56 (Rome: Prime Minister's Office, n.d.). For an assessment of Quazza's historiographic research, see G. Perona, "Guido Quazza. La storia come autobiografia," *Passato e Presente*, no. 41 (May–August 1997): 107–29.
26. Pavone, *Una guerra civile*, 413.
27. Ibid., 416.
28. Claudio Pavone, review of *La fine di una stagione. Memoria 1943–1945* by Roberto Vivarelli (Bologna: Il Mulino, 2000) in *L'Indice* (February 2001): 17–18.
29. E. P. Thompson, "Folklore, Anthropology and Social History," *The Indian Historical Review*, no. 2 (1978): 415.
30. Giaime Pintor, *Doppio Diario 1936–1943*, ed. Mirella Serri, intro. by Luigi Pintor (Turin: Einaudi, 1978).
31. Andrea Caffi, *Critica della violenza* (Milan: Edizioni Bompiani, 1966), 77–104.
32. Carlo Mazzantini, *A cercar la bella morte* (Milan: Mondadori, 1986), 52, 97.
33. See Claudio Pavone, review of *Death in Rome* by Robert Katz (New York: Macmillan, 1967) in *Il Movimento di Liberazione in Italia* 3, no. 8 (July–September 1967): 99–104.
34. Enzo Collotti and Tristano Matta, "Rappresaglie, stragi, eccidi," in Collotti, Sandri, and Sessi, *Dizionario della Resistenza*, 154ff. See also Tristano Matta, *Un percorso della memoria* (Milan: Electa, 1996), 152–55.
35. Matta, *Un percorso della memoria*, 156. See also Friedrich Andrae, *Auch gegen Frauen und Kinder* (Munich: R. Piper, 1995), Italian edition: *La Wehrmacht in Italia* (Rome: Editori Riuniti, 1997), 69ff.
36. This is the hypothesis put forward in Michele Battini and Paolo Pezzino, *Guerra ai civili. Occupazione tedesca e politica del massacro. Toscana 1944* (Venice: Marsilio, 1997), , 177–279. See also Lutz Klinkhammer, *Stragi naziste in Italia. La Guerra contro i civili 1943–1944* (Rome: Donzelli, 1997).
37. An anti-Partisan order.
38. Collotti and Matta, *Rappresaglie, stragi, eccidi*, 257.
39. Gerhard Schreiber, *Deutsche Kriegsverbrechen in Italien* (Munich: Beck'sche Verlagsbuchhandlung, 2000), trans. Marina Buttarelli as *La vendetta tedesca 1943–1945. Le rappresaglie naziste in Italia* (Milan: Mondadori, 2000), 4. Schreiber has estimated 6,800 soldiers massacred in September–October 1943

in the Balkans, Greece, and the Aegean; 22,720 Partisans "killed—often flouting international rules"; and 9,180 civilians wiped out (ibid., 8ff.).

40. *Hitlers Politisches Testament. Die Bormann Diktate von Februar und April 1945*, with an essay by H. R. Trevor-Roper and a postface by A. François-Poncet (Hamburg: Albert Knaus Verlag, 1981), 87; not to be confused with the "official political testament" written by Hitler on April 29, 1945, regarding which see instead H. R. Trevor-Roper, *Gli ultimi giorni di Hitler. Come muore una dittatura* (Milan: Rizzoli, 1967), 201–7.
41. Jens Petersen, "Die Organisation der deutschen Propaganda in Italien 1939–1943," *Quellen und Forschungen aus italienischen Archiven und Bibliotheken* no. 70 (1990): 515.
42. Schreiber, *Deutsche Kriegsverbrechen in Italien*, 42ff.
43. Ibid., 41. The author refers the reader to two fundamental documents: Bundesarchiv-Militärarchiv of Freiburg (henceforth BA-MA), RM 7/950, *Seekriegsleitung Mittelmeer Akte II, 16 "Alarich und Konstantin", "Achse" Op., Juli-Oktober 1943*, Ober Kommando Wehrmacht (henceforth OKW) WEST Nr. 005186/43 G, Kdos September 10, 1943; BA-MA, RW/4 v. 508a, OKW/Wehrmachtführungstab, *Grundsätzliche Richtlinien über die Behandlung der Soldaten der Italienischen Wehrmacht und Miliz*, Neuvereidigung, 1943–45.
44. As emerges from the records of the Nuremberg Trials, which Schreiber quotes from the German edition: *Der Prozess gegen die Hauptkriegsverbrecher vor den Internationalen Militärgerichtshof Nürnberg*. Vol. 41, *Urkunden und anderes Beweismaterial Nummer 1218-RF bis JN* (Munich: Delphin Verlag, 1989), 128ff.
45. BA-MA, RW 4/v. 689, OKW/WFSt/QU, *Op. Zonen Alpenvorland U. adriat. Küstenland la Nc. 1762/44 geh., 24.2.44.* See Enzo Collotti, "Occhio per occhio, dente per dente: un ordine di repressione tedesca sul litorale adriatico," *Il Movimento di Liberazione in Italia*, no. 86 (1963): 3–20.
46. BA-MA, RH 2/659, OKW, *Meldungen O. B. Südwest 1.-30.4.44*; here: *IC Nr 3677/44 Kdos., 6.4.44*; ibid., *1C Nr 3746/44 G. Kdos., 8.4.44.* Cf. Schreiber, *La vendetta tedesca*, 98; and Schreiber, *Kriegstagebuch OKW*. Vol. 4, *Januar 1944–2 Mai 1945*, ed. P. E. Schramm (Frankfurt: Bernard und Graefe, 1961), 486.
47. Zentrale Stelle der Landesjustiz verwaltungen zur Aufklärung von NS-Verbrechen (Ludwigsburg), JaG 260, *Strafverfahren Generalfeldmarschall A. Kesselring, Oberbefehlshaber Südwest und Oberkommando Heeresgruppe C in Italien*, Exhibit II, p. 5; Schreiber, *La vendetta tedesca*, 101.
48. Public Record Office-War Office (henceforth PRO-WO) 235/586. The translation of both texts is in Battini and Pezzino, *Guerra ai civili*, 422–27.
49. PRO-WO 235/586, *1st Parachutist Corps General Head Quarters. Operative Order n. 838 Secret*, July 20, 1944, *sig.ed von Hoffmann.*
50. PRO-WO 310/123.
51. PRO-WO 32/12206, *German Orders and Notices.*
52. Ibid., 15.

53. Ibid., 17.
54. Ibid., 18.
55. Schreiber, *La vendetta tedesca*, 106.
56. Bloch, *La strana disfatta. Testimonianza del 1940*, 119ff. That the problem is worthy of historiographic research has been denied by Roberto Vivarelli, *Guerra ai civili e vuoti di memoria*; see also Cooke, "Recent Works on Nazi Massacres," 211–18.
57. As an introduction, see G. Briglia, P. del Giudice and M. Michelacci, *Eserciti, popolazione e Resistenza sulle Alpi Apuane* [Proceedings of the International Conference of Historical Studies of the Western Sector of the Gothic Line, first part (*Aspetti geografici e militari*)] (Massa Carrara: Ceccotti, 1995); Richard Lamb, *War in Italy 1943–1945: A Brutal History* (London: Da Capo Press, 1993), 56–59. Cf. Chianese, "I massacri nazisti nel Mezzogiorno d'Italia," *Italia Contemporanea*, no. 208 (1998): 155–89; Chianese, "Rappresaglie naziste, saccheggi e violenze a morte nel Sud," *Italia Contemporanea*, no. 202 (1996): 71–84; Gribaudi, *Guerra, violenza, responsabilità. Alcuni volumi sui massacri nazisti in Italia*, 135–50; Giovanni Contini, *La memoria divisa* (Milan: Rizzoli, 1997); Paolo Pezzino, *Anatomia di un massacro. Controversia sopra una strage tedesca* (Bologna: Il Mulino, 1997). As regards Pavone, the reader must naturally be referred to Pavone, *Una guerra civile.*
58. This is the case with the widows of Guardistallo, a small village on the Tuscan coast, south of Leghorn, studied by Pezzino, *Anatomia di un massacro*, 9–10.
59. See Leonardo Paggi, "Storia di una memoria antipartigiana," in *Storia e memoria di un massacro ordinario*, ed. Paggi (Rome: Manifestolibri, 1996), 46; cf. also Contini, *La memoria divisa*, 9; Alessandro Portelli, "Lutto, senso comune, mito e politica nella memoria della strage di Civitella," in Paggi, ed., *Storia e memoria di un massacro ordinario*, 93. On the role of women in the events and in their cultural transformation see *Donne e uomini nelle guerre mondiali*, ed. Anna Bravo (Rome-Bari: Laterza, 1991); Anna Bravo and Anna Maria Bruzzone, *In guerra senz'armi. Storie di donne 1940–1945* (Rome-Bari, Laterza, 1995).
60. Pezzino, *Anatomia di un massacro*, 225, adopts the moral stance of Tsvetan Todorov, *Una tragedia vissuta. Scene di guerra civile* (Milan: Garzanti, 1995), 131–50.
61. Ibid., 143.
62. Various aspects of this theme have also been dealt with by Franco de Felice, "I massacri di civili nelle carte di polizia dell'Archivio Centrale dello Stato," in *Le memorie della Repubblica*, ed. Paggi (Florence: La Nuova Italia, 1999), 3–49, as well as in the studies of Claudio Silingardi, *Una provincia partigiana. Guerra e Resistenza a Modena 1940–1945* (Milan: Franco Angeli, 1998), 586ff.; and Massimo Storchi, *Combattere si può, vincere bisogna. La scelta della violenza fra Resistenza e dopoguerra. Reggio Emilia 1943–1946* (Venice: Marsilio, 1998), 38ff.
63. Klinkhammer, *L'occupazione tedesca in Italia*, 429–31.

64. Andrae, *Auch gegen Frauen und Kinder*, 197–98, 199. See also K. Mehner, ed., *Die Geheimen Tagesberichte der deutschen Wehrmachtführung im Zweiten WeltKrieg 1939–1945* (Osnabrück: Biblio Verlag, 1985): vol. 10 (*Berichtszeit 1.3 bis 31.8.1944)* and vol. 11 (*Berichtszeit 1.9 bis 31.12.1944*). See also G. Schreiber, "La linea Gotica nella strategia tedesca: obiettivi politici e compiti militari," in *Linea Gotica 1944. Eserciti, popolazioni, partigiani*, ed. Giorgio Rochat and Paolo Sorcinelli (Milan: Franco Angeli, 1986), 27ff.
65. PRO-WO 310/123, *Distribution for Action: Major War Criminals and Nazi State Organization*, July 9, 1945 (signed: V. A. R. Isham).
66. PRO-WO 310/123, Deputy Judge Advocate General, *London, War Crimes–German Generals*, January 13, 1946.
67. Ibid., 20.
68. PRO-WO 310/123, Office of Deputy Judge Advocate General, General Head Quarters Central Mediterranean Forces, *Subject: War Crimes–German Generals*; PRO-WO 32/14566, British War Crime Executive, *Subject: War Crimes in Italy; A Detailed Report on German Reprisals Based on Documentary Evidence Collected by the Section, Set Up for the Investigation of War Crimes*, September 6, 1945; PRO-WO 32/14566, Judge Advocate General Office London, *Loose Minute: Trial of German Generals for Illegal Reprisals Against Italian Civilians and Partisans*, April 29, 1946.
69. PRO-WO 235/586, Translation of the message of the Ober Kommando Wehrmacht Süd-West: *New Measures in Connection with Operations against Partisans*, May 10, 1944; PRO-WO 32/12206, *German Orders and Notices*; PRO-WO 32/12206, Allied Forces Head Quarters, British Section: *Report on German Reprisals for Partisan Activity*, July 9, 1945.
70. Lemelsen's order is in *Europa unter Hakenkreuz. Die Okkupationspolitik des deutschen Faschismus in Jugoslawien, Griechenland, Albanien, Italien und Ungarn 1943–1945*, Dok 293, pp. 944ff.: *14 Armee an Kommandieren General LXXV Armee Korps, 29.7.1944*. See also Andrae, *Auch gegen Frauen und Kinder*, 218. von Hoffmann's order is in PRO-WO 235/586, *1st Para Corps Quarters, Operations against Partisans*, July 9, 1944.
71. See AA. VV., *Resistenza in Toscana. La Resistenza e gli alleati in Toscana* (Florence: Instituto Storico della Resistenza, 1969); and AA. VV., *La Resistenza in Toscana* [Proceedings and Studies of the Historical Institute of the Resistance in Tuscany, Florence] (Florence: Olschki, 1970). Luigi Arbizzani, *Al di là e al di qua della linea Gotica 1944–1945. Aspetti sociali, politici e militari in Toscana ed Emilia Romagna* (Bologna-Florence: Regioni Emilia-Romagna e Toscana, 1993), 157ff.
72. Klinkhammer, *L'occupazione tedesca in Italia*, 358.
73. *Armee Abteilung von Zangen*, Ia Mr. 11115/44 g. Kdos, AA.H. Qu 29.6.1944, reproduced in Schreiber, *Il fronte occidentale della linea Gotica*, 35–36.
74. PRO-WO 311/359, *Voluntary Statement by Prisoner of War LD 1513, General Waffen SS Karl Wolff*, September 16, 1946; PRO-WO 311/359, *Voluntary Statement by Prisoner of War Major O. Beelitz, member of German Oberkommando in C. South West (Fieldmärshal A. Kesselring) from November*

1943 to September 1944; PRO-WO 311/359, *Voluntary Statement by Judge General Hans Keller*, November 1, 1946 (for the texts of the depositions, see Battini, Pezzino, *Guerra ai civili*, 459–64, 511–18).

75. Andreas Hillgruber, *La distruzione dell'Europa* (Bologna: Il Mulino, 1994), 55ff.
76. J. Friedrich, *Das Gesetz der Krieges, Das Deutsche Heer in Russland 1941–1945. Der Prozess gegen das Oberkommando der Wehrmacht* (München-Zürich: 1993), 15ff.; Omer Bartov, *The Eastern Front 1941–1945: German Troops and the Barbarisation of Warfare* (Oxford: Oxford University Press, 1985); G. R. überschar, W. Wette, *Der deutsche überfall auf die Sowjet-Union "Unternehmen Barbarossa" 1941* (Frankfurt: Fischer Taschenboch Verlag, 1991), 249ff.; C. Streit, *Keine Kameraden. Die Wehrmacht und die Sowjetischen Kriegsanfangenen 1941–1945* (Stuttgart: Klett-Lotta, 1978).
77. BA–MA LVI Armeekorps, 17956/a Kdr. Pz Crp4, 1a Nz. 20/4/g. Kdos, 2.5.1941, qtd. by J. Förster, "New Wine in Old Skin? The Wehrmacht and the War of 'Weltanschaungen,'" in *The German Military in the Age of Total War*, ed. Wilhelm Deist (Worcester: Deist, 1985), 310.
78. Enzo Collotti, "Obiettivi e metodi della guerra nazista. La responsabilità della Wehrmacht," in Paggi, ed., *Storia e memoria di un massacro ordinario*, 21–37.
79. PRO-WO 311/359, *Voluntary Statement by Prisoner of War Colonel D. Beelitz*, 2–3.
80. National Archives, Washington DC (henceforth NAW), RG 218/190/1/1/1 Box 1, Note of May 1, 1944: *Secretary of War to Secretary of State: Appendix: British Embassy Memorandum (Procedure for Dealing with German War Crimes against Italians)*, March 15, 1944, pp. 8–9.
81. The carabinieri were, and still are, Italian military police.
82. See the *Report from Captured Personnel and Material Branch Military Intelligence Division, U.S. War Department*, March 30–April 3, 1945, NAW, RG 153/270/211/4 Box 102, File 2.
83. See (only as instances among many examples) the two notes of November 8 and 11, 1946 (*Memorandum for the Allied Commission: Nazi War Criminals*, NAW, RG 6/3352/1307 and NAW, RG 6/3367/1311).
84. PRO-WO 32/15510, *Provisory Report on British Investigation on War Crimes in Italy*, August 18, 1944.
85. NAW, RG 492, Box 2047, *War Crimes Cases forwarded to Italian Government*, September 18, 1946.
86. PRO-WO 310/123, *Office of Deputy Judge Advocate General. GHQ. Central Mediterranean Forces. Subject: War Crimes-German Generals.*
87. PRO-WO 32/14566, British War Crime Executive, *Subject: War Crimes in Italy*. See also PRO-WO 32/14566, *Outward telegram. Particular Secrecy*, 27th July 1945. Regarding the UN War Crimes Commission, see PRO-WO 204/2190, *United Nations W.C. Commission. Secret-Progress Report Adopted by the Commission on 19th September 1944.*
88. PRO-WO 204/2190, UN War Crimes Commission, *Second Progress Report*, March 28, 1945.

89. PRO-WO 204/2190, UN War Crimes Commission, *Preparation and Presentation of Cases of War Crimes, Memorandum*, April 18, 1945.
90. PRO-WO 204/2190, Secret Annex II. *List of War Crimes drawn up by the Responsibility Commission of the Paris Peace Conference in 1919.*
91. PRO-WO 201/2190, *Memorandum for Files. War Crimes Against Italians*, May 26, 1945. Cf. also *Lettera del Ministro Scoccimarro al gen. Richmond, con allegati*, ISRT-Archivio dell'Instituto Storico della Resistenza in Toscana, Firenze, Fondo Medici-Tornaquinci, in *Storia e Memoria* [periodical of the Ligurian Institute for the Resistance], no. 1 (2001): 28–29. A copy of the Commission's institutive decree is in the Central State Archive, the Prime Minister's Office, Gab. 1944–47, busta 1.2.2./15626, and was found by Christian Vordemann, *Deutschland-Italien 1949–1961. Die diplomatischen Beziehungen* (Frankfurt: Peter Long, 1993); cf. F. Focardi, "La questione della punizione dei criminali di guerra in Italia dopo la fine del II conflitto mondiale," *Quellen und Forschungen aus Italianischen und Bibliotheken*, no. 80 (2000): 547.
92. PRO-WO 204/2190, *Allied Forces Headquarters, Central War Crimes*, June 19, 1945; the letter to the Honorable Scoccimarro, signed by Christenberry, is in PRO-WO 204/2190.
93. PRO-WO 32/12206, *War Crimes in Italy, Under Secretary of State*, August 11, 1945.
94. PRO-WO 32/14566, Under Secretary of State, the War Office London, October 6, 1945. *Trials against Minor War Criminals, German Reprisals against Italian Civilians for Partisan Activity*, March 15, 1946.
95. PRO-WO 32566, Under Secretary of State, The War Office London, *War Crimes*, April 9, 1946.
96. *Ibid.*
97. PRO-WO 32/14556, *German Reprisals against Italian Civilians*, Letter of Colonel J. E. M. Cunning, Deputy Judge Advocate General, to the Judge Advocate General, London, Cockspur Street, London S.W.1., April 15, 1946. For the background to the discussion about the preparation of the Italian trials of the "minor" war criminals and of those accused of local incidents, cf. PRO-WO/32 14566, *Record of the meeting held in Hobert House, London 10th August 1945, to discuss Trials of Minor War Criminals*; PRO-WO 32/14566, *Minor War Criminals Trials. Secretary of State, War Office*, London, October 6, 1945.
98. PRO-WO 32/14566, Under Secretary of State, the War Office, London, *War Crimes*, April 9, 1945.
99. PRO-WO 32/14566, Foreign Office, November 30, 1946. Writing to Colonel Breadshaw, Sir R. A. Beaumont conceded that "in principle, the German culprits could be handed over to the Italian Authorities."
100. PRO-WO 32/14566, *Foreign Office, Beaumont to Breadshaw*, December 16, 1945.
101. Ibid., *Loose Minute*, March 19, 1946.
102. PRO-WO 32/14566, *Judge Advocate General's Deputy to Supreme General Head Quarters*, March 21, 1946.

103. PRO-WO 32/14566, *Trial Against German Generals for Illegal Reprisals Against Italian Civilians and Partisans*, April 29, 1946.
104. PRO-WO 32/14566, *German Reprisals Against Civilians, Judge Advocate General to Supreme Head Quarters of Mediterranean Allied Forces* (signed Col. J. E. M. Cunning).
105. PRO-WO 32/12146, *(Foreign Office), War Office*, June 4, 1946 (signed Col. R. A. Beaumont); *Foreign Office to Viscount Hood, Head of British Representation to the Allies' Foreign Ministers Council in Paris*, June 14, 1946: *Hood to Beaumont*, June 10, 1946; "While it would clearly be much more satisfactory to set up an *ad hoc* Allied Committee, to select and weigh up the requests for both the categories of people mentioned in the treaty [war criminals and collaborators], it is now absolutely clear that the Russians will never agree to the establishment of any commission of this type." (see also PRO-WO 32/14566, UN War Crimes Commission, *Amendment suggested to articles on war criminals in draft Treaty of Peace with Italy and other countries*, September 4, 1946).
106. PRO-WO 32/12146, *Foreign Office to Lowe*, November 1946.
107. PRO-WO 310/123, *Major War Criminals and Nazi State Organisation.* On the contrary, Kesselring upheld, on various occasions during the interrogations and the trial, the thesis that reprisals were a procedure that any other military power would have justified. Cf. Kesselring, *Memorie di guerra.* Roscoe Drummond, in the *New York Herald Tribune* of September 1955, defined Kesselring's book as "the most pernicious, deliberate and massively distorting propaganda in favor of Nazi innocence during the war."
108. PRO-WO 310/123, *War Crimes. German Generals.* According to General Rodolfo Graziani, the units of the National Republican Guard and the X Mas, involved in the anti-Partisan operations in the North, had, in fact, been placed under the command of the SS General, Wolff, while the military units of Monte Rosa and San Marco had been employed in the North-Western Apennines by General Tensfeld. See PRO-WO 310/123, *Voluntary Deposition of Marshal R. Graziani.*
109. PRO-WO 310/123, *Major War Criminals*, 10.
110. Ibid., 8–9.
111. PRO-WO 309/1372, *War crimes. Atrocities against Italian civilians.*
112. PRO-WO 310/359, *Voluntary Statement by PW LD 1573, Gen. Field Marshal A. Kesselring on war against partisans in Italy from 1943 to 1945*, October 8, 1946.
113. Ibid., 2.
114. Ibid., 3–4.
115. Ibid., 5–7.
116. Ibid., 10.
117. PRO-WO 32/ 15488. This is the petition of Gen. Field Marshal A. Kesselring to his Britannic Majesty in favor of Generals von Mackensen (XIV Army Corps) and Mältzer (commandant of Rome) opposing the death sentence issued by the British Military Tribunal on 30 November 1946 in Rome (Rome, December 2, 1946).

118. PRO-WO 32/15490, *Judge Advocate General H. D. Forster Mac Geagh: Note on Kesselring's Trial* (Venice February 10–May 6, 1947), June 23, 1947.
119. PRO-WO 32/12206, which also contains a copy of Keitel's letter, filed with the abbreviation *Letter GI (BR), 15012/A-3 War Office*. See in particular pp. 1, 7, 8, 31.
120. Ibid., 14.
121. PRO-WO 311/359, *Voluntary Statement by PW LD 1573, Gen. Field Marshal A. Kesselring on atrocities occurred in operative areas of the Army Group C*, October 17, 1946, p. 2.
122. PRO-WO 310/123, *Voluntary Statement by General Joachin Lemelsen, former commander of 14 Army Group*, February 26, 1946.
123. PRO-WO 310/123, *Voluntary Statement by General Frido Von Sengerund Etterling, former commander of 14 Army Group*, March 5, 1946.
124. Ibid., 3.
125. PRO-WO 310/216.
126. 311/359, *Voluntary Statement by Prisoner of War LD 1670 General Judge Hans Keller*, November 1, 1946, pp. 3–7.
127. PRO-WO 235/586, *Voluntary Statement by Prisoner of War LD 1687 former SS Gruppenführer and General Leutenant des Waffen SS Max Simon. Report regarding the battles of Ib Panzergrenadier Division Reichsführer SS against Italian Partisans during the period 28 May–31 October 1944*, November 16, 1944, pp. 4–5. General Simon was tried for a series of massacres carried out between Molina di Quosa (Pisa), the Apuan Alps and the Tuscan-Emilian Apennines, including that of Sant'Anna di Stazzema. Although he was condemned to capital punishment on 5 November 1947, the death sentence was commuted to life imprisonment on 20 June 1948 and, subsequently, reduced to twenty-one years of incarceration. However, he was released twelve years later.
128. PRO-WO 311/359, *Voluntary Statement by PW LD 1482 General Leutenant Heinz Trettner. Short report on the employment of the 4th Paratroop Division in Italy with special reference to Partisan warfare*. Twenty years after the end of the war, the national council of the National Front of the German Democratic Republic published, in various languages—we only have the French edition at hand—a *Livre Blanc sur les crimes de guerre de l'inspecteur général de la Bundeswehr, le général Heinz Trettner* (Berlin 1964), on the occasion of Trettner's appointment to the post of the Inspector General of the Army of the German Federal Republic. The book reconstructed all Trettner's military ventures, from the role of the Condor Legion in the Spanish Civil War to the occupation of Czechoslovakia, from the invasion of Belgium and Holland to the Italian Campaign. See ibid., 33–35.
129. Geoffrey Best, "World War II and the Laws of War," *Review of International Studies*, no. 7 (1981): 73.

Chapter 3

1. NAW, RG 492/290/54/22/7, Box 2062, *War Crimes, Ardeatine Caves Massacre*, September 3, 1944.
2. PRO-WO 235/438, p. 72. The myth of the notices put up in Rome with the injunction to the members of the Italian Resistance movement, GAP, to hand themselves over to the German Authorities, on pain of a drastic punishment being inflicted on the population, has also been exploded by Alessandro Portelli, *L'ordine è stato eseguito* (Rome: Donzelli, 1998), 224ff.
3. Ibid., 198–227.
4. Ibid., 293.
5. The term in German was *Todeskandidaten.*
6. Ibid., 90–122.
7. Ibid., 87.
8. NAW, AP 0512, *Headquarters Mediterranean Theater of Operations Report and Records of War Crimes. Trial of Albert Kesselring.*
9. PRO-WO, *Proceedings of a Military Court for the Trial of War Criminals, held at Tribunale di Giustizia, Venice, upon the Trial of Albert Kesselring, German National, in charge of 317 Transit Camp, Pursuant to Regulation 4 of the Regulations for the Trial of War Criminals* (henceforth *Trial of Albert Kesselring*), Venice, February 10, 1947 (1st day).
10. The three *Voluntary Statements*, from which we have already quoted, were handed over and signed by the defendant on September 25, 1946 (PRO-WO 311/359, Report N. WCIU/LDC 1343, concerning the attack in Via Rasella in Rome on March23, 1944), on October 8, 1946 (PRO-WO 311/359, Report N. WGU/LDC 1344, concerning the events between 1943 and 1945), and on October 17, 1946 (PRO-WO 311/359, Report N. WCIU/LDC/1356/a, concerning the atrocities that occurred during the war against the Italian Partisans). The three documents have been published in full in Battini and Pezzino, *Guerra ai civili. Occupazione tedesca e politica del massacro. Toscana 1944* (Venice: Marsilio, 1997), 452.
11. *Trial of Albert Kesselring*, Venice, February 19, 1947 (3rd day).
12. Ibid.
13. Ibid.
14. *Trial of Albert Kesselring*, Venice, February 24, 1947 (8th day).
15. *Trial of Albert Kesselring*, Venice, February 25, 1947 (9th day).
16. *Trial of Albert Kesselring*, Venice, February 22, 1947 (6th day).
17. Ibid.
18. *Trial of Albert Kesselring*, Venice, March 1, 1947 (11th day).
19. *Trial of Albert Kesselring*, Venice, March 3, 1947 (12th day).
20. Ibid.
21. Ibid.
22. *Trial of Albert Kesselring*, Venice, March 5, 1947 (14th day).
23. *Trial of Albert Kesselring*, Venice, March 6, 1947 (15th day).
24. *Trial of Albert Kesselring*, Venice, March 10, 1947 (17th day).

25. *Trial of Albert Kesselring*, Venice, March 13, 1947 (20th day).
26. *Trial of Albert Kesselring*, Venice, March 11, 1947 (18th day). This is a reference to the order of February 8, 1945, issued by the OBK SW to the High Command of the SS and the police, the Commander of the XIV Army and the Commander of the Army of Liguria (General Graziani). The text can be found in NAW, KG. 4.153, Box 108, File 115/3, *Records of the Office of the Judge Advocate General.* In this same series, see also the translations of the orders of August 21, 1944, and September 24, 1944.
27. *Trial of Albert Kesselring*, Venice, March 14, 1947 (21st day). For the full text of the order of July 1, cf. NAW, R. 4.153, Box 108, File 115/3 (*Records of the Office of the Judge Advocate General*).
28. Ibid.
29. NAW, RG, 153, Box 108, File 115/3, *Records of the Office of the Judge Advocate General, The Führer to the Chief Command of the Wehrmacht, Top Secret,* Rome 1. 8. 1942 (*Useful information of other Commands*).
30. *Trial of Albert Kesselring*, Venice, March 15, 1947 (22nd day).
31. *Trial of Albert Kesselring*, Venice, March 17, 1947 (23rd day).
32. *Trial of Albert Kesselring*, Venice, March 18, 1947 (24th day).
33. The text referred to by Beelitz was *Rules of Land Warfare*, Washington, DC, 1940, paragraphs 358 and 359. Regarding the Judge Advocate General's criticisms, cf. *Trial of Albert Kesselring*, Venice, March 24, 1947 (29th day).
34. PRO-WO 32/12206, *German orders* (the translated text is in Battini, Pezzino, *Guerra ai civili*, 430–31).
35. PRO-WO 235/586, *1st Parachute Corps Headquarters, Operative Order n. 838, Secret*, July 20, 1944.
36. *Trial of Albert Kesselring*, Venice, March 22, 1947 (28th day).

Chapter 4

1. Editor's note: Although the UN Charter was not signed until 1945, FDR had issued a "Declaration of United Nations" on January 1, 1942, in which representatives of twenty-six nations pledged to fight the Axis.
2. On June 28, 1945, the eve of the Potsdam Conference, the Foreign Minister De Gasperi had sent a new memorandum with these requests to the Ambassadors of the United States, the Soviet Union, Great Britain, and France. The memorandum appears in *Documenti Diplomatici Italiani*, tenth series, vol. II (Rome: Istituto Poligrafico e Zecco dello Stato, 1992): 396–99.
3. The documents were found in the Historical Archives of the Foreign Ministry (DGAP, Germany 1952, envelope 174) by Filippo Focardi, who gave an account of it in Focardi, "La questione della punizione dei criminali di guerra in Italia dopo la fine del II conflitto mondiale," *Quellen und Forschungen aus Italianischen Archiven und Bibliotheken*, no. 80 (2000): 543ff.

4. Benedetto Croce, "Una proposta", in *Scritti e discorsi politici (1943–1947)*, vol. 2 (Bari: Laterza, 1963), 286–87, published by the newspapers on October 27, 1945.
5. This fear was expressed by the Italian Ambassador in Moscow in an express telegram addressed to the Ministry of Foreign Affairs on January 7, 1946 (Historical Archives of the Foreign Ministry, DGAP, Germany 1952, envelope 174, file 2, referred to by Focardi, "La questione della punizione," 552).
6. The two main defendants, charged with the massacre of Padule di Fucecchio (23 August 1944), were General P. E. Crasemann and Captain J. Strauch. The General was tried by the British Military Tribunal of Padua, May 13–22, 1947; Lieutenant-Colonel D. F. Yate-Lee was the Presiding Judge (cf. PRO-WO 235/335, *Trial General P. E. Crasemann*, Padua, May 13, 1947). Strauch's trial was one of the few insisted upon by the Allies and conducted by the Italian Military Authorities: cf. PRO-WO 310/105, *War Crimes Group. Request for the Indictment of J. Strauch addressed to the Chief Prosecutor of the Supreme Military Tribunal of Rome, 4 July 1947.* Strauch was tried by the Military Tribunal of Florence: cf. State Archives of Florence, Territorial Military Tribunal, *Procedimento contro Strauch Joseph di Joseph*, Paludi di Fucecchio, vol. I, II and II bis, *Raccolta Documenti 1948.* In the summer of 1994, both the documentation sent by the Allies to the Chief Military Prosecutor and that collected by the Italian Military Prosecutors were found by Dr. Antonio Intelisano in a cabinet in the Archives of the Chief Military Prosecutor's Office and it was ascertained that they had been deliberately concealed. See "Relazione approvata dal Consiglio della Magistratura Militare in data 23 marzo 1999," *Storia e Memoria* 7 (1998): 165–78.
7. See Paolo Pezzino, "Sui mancati processi in Italia ai criminali di guerra tedeschi," *Storia e Memoria* 10 (2001): 9–72. See also Mimmo Franzinelli, *Le stragi nascoste. L'armadio della vergogna: impunità e rimozione dei crimini di guerra nazifascisti 1943–2001* (Milan: Mondadori, 2002), 121–87.
8. Hans Woller, *I conti con il fascismo. L'epurazione in Italia 1943–1948* (Bologna: Il Mulino, 1997), 260–72; and Roy Palmer Domenico, *Processo ai fascisti 1943–1948* (Milan: Mondadori, 1996), 131–39.
9. Apart from the leading exponents of the PCI (the Italian Communist Party), one of the few prominent personalities to support the necessity of handing over the civil servants and the military to the authorities of the occupied countries was Gaetano Salvemini. See Gaetano Salvemini and Giorgio La Piana, *La sorte dell'Italia* (Rome-Florence-Milan: 1949), 223.
10. Focardi, "La questione della punizione," 60.
11. Claudio Pavone, "La continuità dello Stato. Istituzioni e uomini," in Enzo Piscitelli et al., *Italia 1945–1948. Le origini della Repubblica* (Turin: Giappichelli, 1974), 139–289; Claudio Pavone, *Alle origini della Repubblica* (Turin: Bollati Boringhieri, 1995), 70–169.
12. NAW, RG 153, Box 108, File 115/3, *Records of the Office of the Judge Advocate General, The Commanding General of the German Luftwaffe in Italy to the Commander in Chief,* October 21, 1944.

13. Ibid., *Commanding General of the German Luftwaffe in Italy*, December 9, 1944.
14. Ibid., *The German Ambassador and Plenipotentiary of the Greater German Reich in Italy to Kesselring*, Fasano, September 18, 1944.
15. *Trial of Albert Kesselring*, Venice, May 1, 1947.
16. *Trial of Albert Kesselring* (the Prosecution's concluding statement, Col. Halse), May 1, 1947, pp. 3–4. Cf. *Deuxième Conférence Internationale de la Paix, La Haye 15 Juin-18 Octobre 1907. Actes et documents*, 3 vols. (La Haye, 1908–1909); on the Conference, cf. J. Jarnez, *International Law and the World War*, vol. 1 (New York: Knopf, 1920), 282ff.). On reprisals in particular, cf. Yves De la Brière, "Evolution de la doctrine et de la pratique en matière de répresailles," in *Recueil des cours de Droit International de La Haye* 2 (1928): 269–77.
17. *Trial of Albert Kesselring*, May 1, 1947, p. 6. Cf. Pietro Cogliolo, *La legislazione di guerra* (Turin: Utet, 1916).
18. Ibid., 8.
19. Ibid., 9.
20. PRO-WO 310/129.
21. PRO-WO 310/129, Gen. Archibald, *Subject: Kesselring, Mackensen and Mältzer Trials*, May 1947. Alexander's telegram, addressed to 10 Downing Street, the British Prime Minister's residence, is in PRO-WO 32/15390.
22. PRO-WO 32/15490, *Winston Churchill to Prime Minister*, May 13, 1947. Churchill insisted that the execution should be the subject of a parliamentary debate (see PRO-WO 32/15490, *Letter of Leslie Rowan, Attlee's private secretary*, May 13, 1947). The Prime Minister, Clement Attlee, replied to Winston Churchill the same day, May 13, 1947, promising a parliamentary debate and a delay in the sentence (PRO-WO 32/15490, *Attlee to Churchill, 13th May 1947, 10 Downing Street*).
23. PRO-WO 32/15490, *Secretary of State. War Office: F. J. Bellenger to Prime Minister C. Attlee*, June 30, 1947.
24. PRO-WO 32/15490, *Secretary of State, Confidential*, May 16, 1947.
25. PRO-WO 32/15420, *Secret Cipher Telegram, from Gen. Harding to Foreign Office, Subject in the cases of Kesselring, Makensen and Mältzer [sic!]*, June 29, 1947.
26. Anette Wieviorka, *Le procès de Nuremberg* (Caen: Editions Ouest France, 1995), 16.
27. *History of the United Nations War Crimes Commission, Extension of the Commission's Competence to crimes not committed against United Nationals. (Draft prepared by the Chairman of the Commission, 4th May 1944)*, in *History of United Nations War Crimes Commission and the Development of the Laws of War* (London: H. M. Stationery Office, 1948), 123.
28. *Correspondence between the War Crimes Commission and H. M. Government in London, regarding the punishment of crimes committed on religious, racial or political grounds*, February 13, 1945, ibid., 176.

29. *Procès des grands criminels de guerre devant le Tribunal Militaire International* (Nuremberg: [s.n.], 1947), 169–70.
30. Raul Hilberg, *La distruzione degli ebrei d'Europa*, vol. 1 (Turin: Einaudi, 1995), 1148.
31. PRO-WO 310/123, *Main War Criminals and Nazi State Organisation*, July 9, 1945.
32. M. Huber, "Quelques considérations sur une revision éventuelle des Conventions de La Haye relatives à la guerre," *Révue Internationales de la Croix Rouge* (1955): 421. Huber is referring to the whole second section (Military over the territories of the hostile State, art. 43–50) of the *IV Convention concerning the Laws and the Customs of War and Land, II Peace Conference of the Hague 1907*, in *The Hague Peace Conference and other international Conferences concerning the Laws and Usages of War, Text of Convention with Commentaries* (Cambridge: Cambridge University Press, 1909). It is naturally the same text *Deuxième Conférence Internationale de la Paix*, referred to in note 15.
33. *Memorandum of Reservations, presented by the US representatives to the Report of the Majority of the Commission of Responsibilities, Annex II, Conference of Paris, 1919*, in *History of UNWC Commission and the Development of the Laws of War*, 33ff.
34. Raphael Lemkin, *Axis Rule in Occupied Europe* (Washington, DC: Carnegie Endowment for International Peace, 1944), 71–95. See Yves Ternon, *L'état criminel. Les Génocides au XX siècle* (Paris: Seuil, 1995), 17ff.
35. *The Charter of the IMT, annexed to the Agreement for the Prosecutions and Punishment of Major War Criminals of the European Axis*, August 8, 1945, in *History of the UNWC Commission*, 188. Regarding this point of view, see the perceptive observations of the Dutch representative of the war crimes research service, J. Deschumaeker, *Le Tribunal Militaire International des Grands Criminels de Guerre* (Paris: Librairie Armand Colin, 1947), 17.
36. Eugene Davidson, *The Nuremberg Fallacy* (Columbia: University of Missouri Press, 1998), 277–89.
37. John Nef, *La route de la guerre totale* (Paris: Librairie Armand Colin, 1949); Odile Debbasch, *L'occupation militaire* (Paris: Librairie Generale de Droit et de Justice, 1962); Debbasch, *Law and Civil War in the Modern War*, ed. J. Norton Moore (Baltimore: John Hopkins University Press, 1974), 499–518.
38. Telford Taylor, *The Anatomy of the Nuremberg Trials. A Personal Memory* (New York: Little Brown, 1992), 501; Raymond Cartier, *Les secrets de la Guerre dévoilés par Nuremberg* (Paris: Fayard, 1947), 7; *Procès des grands criminels de guerre devant le Tribunal Militaire International*, 5:372–77.
39. Ibid., 6:113–20.
40. Dossier, "Le Monde," *Le procès de Klaus Barbie*, July 1987, p. 40. On July 9, 1986, the Chambre d'Accusation of the Paris Court of Appeal rejected the decision of the Lyons Tribunal, which considered Barbie only indictable for crimes against humanity (not barred by the statute of limitations), but not for war crimes (statute-barred): thanks to the decision of the Parisian Chambre, the crimes committed by Barbie as "war crimes" (for example,

torturing Jewish members of the Resistance) were also equated with crimes against humanity (Paul Gauthier, ed., *Chronique du procès Barbie* (Paris: Les éditions du Cerf, 1988). For the extradition of Erich Priebke, I am quoting from the *Decision of the National Supreme Court of Justice. Buenos Aires 2. XI. 1995*, a typescript in my possession. For further considerations about the legacy of Nuremberg, see Robert E. Conot, *Justice at Nuremberg* (New York: Harper and Row, 1983); Bradley F. Smith, *The American Road to Nuremberg. The Documentary Record 1944–1945* (Stanford, CA: Hoover Institution Press, 1982).

Chapter 5

1. Michael R. Marrus, "The Holocaust at Nuremberg," *Yad Vashem Studies*, no. 26 (1998): 5–41; J. Wilke et al., *Holocaust NS-Prozesse* (Cologne: Bölhau, 1995). See also A. Rückerl, *NS-Verbrechen vor Gericht: Versuch einer Vergangenheitsbewältigung* (Heilelberg: C. F. Müller, 1982), 111–12; Dirk De Mildt, *In the Name of the People: Perpetrators of Genocide in the Reflection of their Post-War Prosecution in West Germany* (The Hague: Martinus Nijhoff, 1996); finally, see Mark Osiel, *Mass Atrocity, Collective Memory and the Law* (New Brunswick: Transaction, 1997).
2. See Donald Bloxham, *Genocide on Trial* (Oxford: Oxford University Press, 2001), 2.
3. See Bradley Smith, *The Road to Nuremberg* (London: Andre Deutsch, 1982); Anna Tusa, John Tusa, *The Nuremberg Trial* (London: Atheneum, 1983); Arieh J. Kochavi, *Prelude to Nuremberg* (Chapel Hill: University of North Carolina Press, 1998); G. Ginsburg and V. N. Kudriatsev, eds., *The Nuremberg Trial and International Law* (Dordrecht: Martinus Nijhoff, 1990); J. Heydesker and J. Leeb, *Der Nürnberger Prozess: Bilanz der Tausend Jahre* (Cologne: Kiepenheuer und Witsch, 1959); Peter Calvocoressi, *Nuremberg: The Facts, the Law and the Consequences* (London: Chatto and Windus, 1948).
4. Smith, *The Road to Nuremberg*, 35–43. Cf. also Tusa and Tusa, *The Nuremberg Trial*, 73.
5. Taylor, *The Anatomy*, 272–73.
6. There is still an echo of such an attitude toward the Marshal in British historiography: Kenneth Macksey, editor of the third edition (1988) in English (the first was in 1953) of Kesselring's *Memoirs*, and Shelford Bildwell, in 1989, have continued to foster the image of the first-class strategist and the soldier detached from the regime, conservative but liberally inclined. Kenneth Macksey, *Kesselring: German Master Strategist of the Second War* (London: Greuill Books, 2000), 203, originally published, *Kesselring. The Maker of the Luftwaffe*, 1978. See also S. Bildwell, "Kesselring. Field-Marshal Albert Kesselring," in *Hitler's Generals*, ed. Correlli Barnett (New York: Grove and Weidenfeld, 1989).
7. Bloxham, *Genocide on Trial*, 47ff.

8. Michel Foucault, *Dits et écrits 1954-1988*, vol. 4 (Paris: Gallimard, 1994), 306.
9. Pieter Lagrou, "Irregular Warfare and the Norms of Legitimate Violence in XXth Century Europe," paper presented at the International Study Conference, *Guerra ai civili. Stragi, violenza e crimini di guerra in Italia e in Europa durante la II guerra mondiale. I fatti, le memorie, i processi*, Bologna, June 19–22, 2002.
10. B. Pisik, "World Tribunal vs. Sovereignty," *The Washington Times*, October 26, 1998. The International Criminal Court was finally set up in July 2002. On the International Tribunal and Japanese war crimes, cf. Sabino Cassese, *I diritti umani nel mondo contemporaneo* (Rome-Bari: Laterza, 1988), 69ff.; and John Rawls, *Hiroshima, non dovevamo* (Milan: Reset, 1995).
11. Telford Taylor, *Nuremberg and Vietnam. An American Tragedy* (New York: Bantam Books, 2001) 130ff.
12. Frank Buscher, *The U.S. War Crimes Trial Program in Germany, 1946-1955* (Westport, CT: Greenwood, 1989), 284ff. See also Peter Maguire, *Law and War: An American Story* (New York: Columbia University Press, 2001), 130ff.
13. Maguire, *Law and War: An American Story*, 227.
14. See G. E. Gründler and A. von Manikoawsky, *Nuremberg ou la justice des vainqueurs* (Paris: Laffont, 1969), 38–52.
15. Qtd. in Annette Wieviorka, *Le procès de Nuremberg* (Paris: Editions Ouest-France, 1995), 180.
16. Leon Poliakov, *Le Bréviaire de la haine* (Paris: Calmann-Lévy, 1951), 274.
17. For a review of Italian press reports at the time of Kesselring's trial and the subsequent episode of the commutation of his sentence, see Ivan Tognarini, *Kesselring e le stragi nazifasciste* (Rome: Carocci, 2002), 67–207. Regarding the principle of collective guilt, see Anette Wieviorka, *Le procès de Nuremberg* (Caen: Editions Ouest France, 1995), 181.
18. Peter Novick, *The Resistance versus Vichy. The Purge of Collaborators in Liberated France* (New York: Columbia University Press, 1968), 269.
19. Lucien Huyse, "The Criminal Justice System as a Political Actor in Regime Transitions: The Case of Belgium 1944–1950," in *The Politics of Retribution in Europe*, ed. István Deák, Jan T. Gross, and Tony Judt, 157–72 (Princeton, NJ: Princeton University Press, 2000), 161.
20. Peter Romijn, *Snel, streng en rechtrvaardig. Politiek beleid inzake de bestraffing en reclassering van 'foute' Nederlanders 1944–1955* (Houten: De Haan, 1989).
21. Herbert Lottmann, *The People's Anger: Justice and Revenge in Post-Liberation France* (London: Hutchinson, 1986).
22. See, Roy Palmer Domenico, *Italian Fascists on Trial: 1943–1948* (Chapel Hill: University of North Carolina Press, 1991).
23. Nicola Gallerano, ed., *La Resistenza tra gloria e memoria* (Milan: Mursia, 1999), 298–329.
24. There is unanimous historiographical agreement on this aspect. See, at least, Paul Ginsborg, *Storia d'Italia dal dopoguerra a oggi. Società e politica 1943–1988* (Turin: Einaudi, 1989), 47ff.; Pietro Scoppola, *La repubblica dei partiti. Evoluzione e crisi di un sistema politico 1945–1996* (Bologna: Il Mulino,

1997), 35ff.; Silvio Lanaro, *Storia dell'Italia repubblicana* (Venice: Marsilio, 1992).

25. Rosario Romeo, *Italia mille anni. Dall'età feudale all'Italia moderna ed europea* (Florence: Le Monnier, 1981), 220–69; with regard to which, the following is useful: Gennaro Sasso, "Rosario Romeo e l'idea di nazione. Appunti e considerazioni," in *Il rinnovamento della storiografia politica. Studi in memoria di Rosario Romeo*, ed. Guido Pescosolido, 113–43 (Rome: Istituto dell'Enciclopedia Italiana, 1995).
26. Claudio Pavone, *Una guerra civile. Saggio storico sulla moralità nella Resistenza* (Turin: Bollati Boringhieri, 1993), 560.
27. Guri Schwarz, "Verso una religione civile antifascista. Memorie, simboli e liturgie. 1943–1984," postgraduate thesis in historical studies, Branch of Humanities and Philosophy, Scuola Normale Superiore of Pisa, Academic Year 2001–2002, p. 9.
28. See Giorgio Pullini, *Il romanzo italiano del dopoguerra 1940–1960* (Milan: Schwarz, 1965), 151–81; Raffaele Liucci, *La tentazione della casa in collina. Il disimpegno degli intellettuali nella guerra civile italiana 1943–1945* (Milan: Unicopli, 2002), 153ff.; which leads back, above all, to the work by Giuseppe Berto, *Il cielo è rosso* (Milan: Longanesi, 1947).
29. Official government document, June 1944. *Verbali del Consiglio dei Ministri.* Vol. 3, *Governo Bonomi 18 giugno 44–12 dicembre 44*, ed. A. G. Ricci (Rome: Presidenza del Consiglio dei Ministri, 1990), 3–11.
30. Giovanni Miccoli, "Cattolici e comunisti nel secondo dopoguerra: memoria storica, ideologica e lotta politica," in *La grande cesura. La memoria della guerra e della resistenza nella vita europea del dopoguerra*, ed. G. Miccoli, Guido Neppi Modana, and Paolo Pombeni, (Bologna: Il Mulino, 2001), 31–88.
31. See Franco Calamandrei, *La vita indivisibile. Diario 1941–1947* (Rome: Editori Riuniti, 1984), 215. See also Romeo, *Italia mille anni*, 215.

Chapter 6

1. The exhibition at the Hamburger Institut für Sozialforschung was seen by more than one million Germans and resulted in the publication of: Hannes Heer, ed., *Vernichtungskrieg. Verbrechen der Wehrmacht 1941 bis 1944* (Hamburg: Hamburger Verlag, 1995).
2. Robert Aron, *Histoire de Vichy* (Paris: Fayard, 1954), 215ff.
3. A wide range of German archive material that fell into Allied hands was microfilmed after the war by a joint commission of American, English and French historians. See *Documents on German Foreign Policy, Series A-D*, vols. 1–9 (Washington, DC: U.S. Government Printing Office, 1952–1956).
4. Robert O. Paxton, *Vichy France: Old Guard and New Order* (New York: Knopf, 1972). The book was translated into French in 1973. The American edition of 1997 was translated into Italian in 1999.

5. Eberhard Jäckel, *Frankreich in Hitlers Europa* (Stuttgart: Deutsche Verlags-Anstalt, 1966); Yves Durand, *Vichy 1940–1944* (Paris: Bordas, 1972); Henri Michel, *Vichy, année 1940* (Paris: Laffont, 1966); and Michel, *Pétain, Laval, Darlan, trois politiques?* (Paris: Flammarion, 1973); Geoffrey Warner, *Pierre Laval and the Eclipse of France 1931–1945* (London: Macmillan, 1968).
6. Henry Rousso, *La syndrome de Vichy de 1944 à nos jours* (Paris: Seuil, 1990), 270.
7. Some writers, sympathizers of Vichy, have continued, even in recent times, to support such ideas. See, for example, François-Georges Dreyfus, *Histoire de Vichy* (Paris: Perrin, 1990), 330ff.
8. For analogous issues, but in a completely different context, cf. Olivier Wieviorka, "Vichy a-t-il été liberal?" *Vingtième siècle*, no. 2 (July–September 1986): 64ff.
9. Jean-Baptiste Duroselle, *L'Abime* (Paris: Imprimerie Nationale, 1983), 119–29; and Marc Ferro, *Pétain* (Paris: Fayard, 1987), 637. See also Robert Franck, "Vichy et les britanniques 1940–1941: Double jeu ou double langage?" in *Vichy et les français*, ed. Jean-Pierre Azema and François Bedarida, 144–63 (Paris: Fayard, 1992); R. T. Thomas, *Britain and Vichy: The Dilemma of Anglo-French Relations* (London: Macmillan, 1979).
10. Jean-Pierre Azema and François Bedarida, "Vichy et ses historiens," *Esprit* (June 1994): 140ff.
11. Robert O. Paxton, "La Collaboration d'état," in *La France des années noires*, vol. 1, ed. Jean-Pierre Azema and François Bedarida, 333–61 (Paris: Seuil, 1993).
12. Pierre Laborie, *L'Opinion française sous Vichy* (Paris: Seuil, 1990), 289–92; John Sweets, *Clermont-Ferrand à l'heure allemande* (Paris: Plon, 1996).
13. On the *entrisme* of some trade union leaders, cf. Jean-Pierre Le Crom, *Syndicats nous voilà! Vichy et le corporatisme* (Paris: Editions de l'Atelier, 1995).
14. Stanley Hoffman, "Collaborationism in France during World War II," *Journal of Contemporary History*, no. 1 (1968): 374ff.
15. See Marc Bloch, *L'étrange défaite* (Paris: Folio, 1990), trans. Raffaella Comaschi as *La strana disfatta. Testimonianza del 1940* (Turin: Einardi, 1995), 140ff.; Pierre Burrin, *La dérive fasciste en France. Doriot Déat Bergery 1933–1945* (Paris: Seuil, 1986), 29–61.
16. Eric Conan and Henry Rousso, *Vichy ou les derives de la mémoire* (Paris: Fayard, 1994).
17. Susan Zuccotti, *The Holocaust, the French and the Jews* (New York: Basic Books, 1993).
18. Anne Grynberg, *Les camps de la honte. Les internés juifs des camps français 1939–1944* (Paris: La Découverte, 1994).
19. Asher Cohen, *Persécution et sauvetages. Juifs et Français sous l'occupation et sous Vichy* (Paris: Les éditions du Cerf, 1993); Robert O. Paxton and Michael Marrus, *Vichy et les Juifs* (Paris: Calmann-Lévy, 1981); Serge

Klarsfeld, *Vichy-Auschwitz. Le role de Vichy dans la solution finale de la question juive en France 1940–1944* (Paris: Fayard, 1993).

20. See *Le Monde*, July 22, 1993.
21. Sarah Farmer, "Post-War Justice in France: Bordeaux 1953," in Deák, Gross, and Judt, eds., *The Politics of Retribution in Europe*, 194–211.
22. See Lucie Aubrac, *Ils partiront dans l'ivresse. Lyon: mai 1943; Londres: fevrier 1944* (Paris: Seuil, 1984); Ladislas de Hoyes, *Barbie* (Paris: Laffont, 1984); Erna Paris, *L'affaire Barbie: analyse d'un mal français* (Paris: Ramsay, 1985); Lise Lesèvre, *Face à Barbie. Souvenirs-Cauchemars de Montluc à Ravensbrück* (Paris: Les Nouvelles Editions du Pavillon, 1987).
23. The best accounts of the Barbie trial are in *Le Monde*, May–June 1987, repr. *Le Monde* dossier: *Le procès de Klaus Barbie*, July 1987, pp. 40ff. See also Paul Gauthier, ed., *Chronique du procès Barbie* (Paris: Les éditions du Cerf, 1988).
24. Laurent Greilsamer, "Paul Touvier. Flic et dévot," *Le Monde*, March 17, 1994.
25. Patrick Jarreau, "Pour la V République, la page est tournée," *Le Monde*, March 17, 1994.
26. See *Le Monde*, May 7–8, 1995.
27. See Giampiero Martinotti, "Intellettuali contro Mitterand. Vichy fu un crimine francese," *La Repubblica*, July 16, 1992.
28. Edwy Plenel, Thomas Ferenczi, "Les révélations sur la jeunesse de F. Mitterand et ses relations avec l'ancian secrétaire générale de Vichy," *Le Monde*, September 9, 1994. Cf. also E. Faux, T. Legrand, and G. Perez, *La main droite de Dieu. Enquête sur F. Mitterand et l'extrème droite* (Paris: Seuil, 1994).
29. Pierre Péan, *Une jeunesse française: François Mitterand 1934–1947* (Paris: Fayard, 1994), 257ff.
30. Laurent Douzou, Denis Peschanski, "La Résistance française face à l'hypothèque Vichy," in *La France de Vichy*, Archives inédites d'Angelo Tasca (Milan: Annali della Fondazione Giangiacomo Feltrinelli, 1995), 3–42.
31. Marcel Ophuls, "Le prince et le professeur," *Le Monde*, September 22, 1994.
32. Jean Paulhan, *Choix des lettres 1937–1945* (Paris: Gallimard, 1992); Julien Green, *La fin d'un monde. Juin 1940* (Paris: Seuil, 1992).
33. Jean Marc Théolley, "L'exécution de Brasillach," *Le Monde*, February 5–6, 1995.
34. François Mauriac in *Le Figaro*, October 19, 1944; and A. Camus in *Combat*, October 20; 1944, qtd. by Tony Judt, *Un passé imparfait. Les Intellectuels en France 1944–1956* (Paris: Fayard, 1992), 86–88.

Chapter 7

1. Kenneth O. Morgan, *The People's Peace* (Oxford: Oxford University Press, 1990), 52.
2. See, at least regarding the French situation, Marcel Baudot, "L'épuration: bilan chiffré," *Bulletin d'Histoire de l'Institut du Temps Présent*, no. 25 (September 3, 1986): 37–53.

3. William B. Bader, *Austria between East and West 1945–1955* (Stanford, CA: Stanford University Press, 1966). Cf. Enzo Collotti, "Da Reder a Waldheim," *Belfagor* (1987): 89–96.
4. Radomir Luza, *The Transfer of the Sudeten Germans* (New York: New York University Press, 1964); Krystyna Kersten, *The Establishment of Communist Rule in Poland. 1943–1948* (Berkeley: University of California Press, 1991), 122ff.; Charles Gati, *Hungary and Soviet Block* (Durham, NC: Duke University Press, 1986), 28ff.
5. Paul Ginsborg, *Storia d'Italia dal dopoguerra a oggi* (Turin: Einaudi, 1988), 53ff.
6. On the concept of representative justice in modern Europe, see Adriano Prosperi, "Il condannato a morte: santo o criminale," in *Il delitto narrato al popolo*, ed. Roberto de Romanis and Rosamaria Loretelli (Palermo: Sellerio, 1999), 227ff.
7. Hersch Lauterpacht, *An International Bill of the Rights of Man* (New York: Columbia University Press, 1945), v–vi. In the following lines, the implicit reference is to Hans Kelsen, *Peace through Law* (Chapel Hill: University of North Carolina Press, 1944), 41–42.
8. The text is in Germaine Brée and George Bernauer, eds., *Defeat and Beyond. An Anthology of French Wartime Writings 1940–1945* (New York: Pantheon Books, 1970), 347.
9. Norman Davies, "The Misunderstood War," *The New York Review of Books*, June 9, 1994, (a review of Gerhard L. Weinberg, *A World at Arms. A Global History of World War II*, [Cambridge: Cambridge University Press, 1994]). See as well, also by Davies, "The Misunderstood Victory in Europe," *The New York Review of Books*, May 25, 1995, pp. 7ff.
10. Casamayor (Serge Fuster), *Nuremberg 1945, La guerre en procès* (Paris: Stock, 1985), 14. See also Telford Taylor, *The Anatomy of the Nuremberg Trials. A Personal Memory*.
11. Edgar Faure, *Memoires*. Vol. 2, *Si tel doit être mon destin* (Paris: Plon, 1984).
12. I will merely quote (in translation) some of the headlines from the main Italian national daily newspapers: "The War in Italy was called Kesselring," (*Corriere della Sera*, February 8, 1947); "Kesselring did not spend a single day in Italy without being guilty of an atrocious crime" (*L'Unità*, February 18, 1947); "Kappler, a scientific assassin, gives details of the massacre" (*L'Avanti!*, February 21, 1947); "The Germans did not even bother to count the number of victims" (*Il Nuovo Corriere*, February 21, 1947); "The trial of Marshal Kesselring. Pages dripping with blood" (*La Stampa*, February 25, 1947); "The defense invokes, for Kesselring, the humanity he never knew" (*L'Avanti!*, February 27, 1947); "Women and children routinely killed" (*Il Nuovo Corriere*, February 27, 1947); "Kesselring's ruthless orders: to destroy houses, refuges and human beings" (*Corriere della Sera*, February 27, 1947); "The destruction of everyone and everything ordered by one of Kesselring's generals" (*Corriere della Sera*, March 14, 1947); "German fury satiated itself with blood" (*La Stampa*, March 14, 1947). Naturally, one could continue at length.

13. Adriano Prosperi, *Il condannato a morte*, 225. See also Richard J. Evans, *Rituals of Retribution. Capital Punishment in Germany 1600–1987* (Oxford: Oxford University Press, 1996), 151ff.
14. "May the punishment, if I can put it like this, strike the soul, not the body," writes Mably. See Gabriel de Mably, *De la législation*. Vol. 9, *œuvres Complètes* (Paris: n.p., 1789), 326.
15. The obligatory work to be consulted is, naturally, Michel Foucault, *Sorvegliare e punire. Nascita della prigione*, trans. Alcesti Tarchetti (Turin: Einaudi, 1976), 25ff.

Index

Please note that page numbers in *italics* indicate endnotes.